Emerson and the Orphic Poet in America

The power of music, the power of poetry, to unfix
and as it were clap wings to solid nature, interprets
the riddle of Orpheus.
"History" (1841)

It seems, then, that Orpheus is no fable: you have
only to sing, and the rocks will crystallize; sing, and
the plant will organize; sing, & the animal will be
born.
Journals (1849)

Emerson
and the
Orphic Poet
in America

—

R. A. YODER

University
of California
Press
Berkeley
Los Angeles
London

University of California Press
Berkeley and Los Angeles, California

University of California Press, Ltd.
London, England

Copyright © 1978 by
The Regents of the
University of California

ISBN 0-520-03317-5
Library of Congress Catalog
Card Number: 76-24599

Printed in the United States of America
Designed by Wolfgang Lederer

1 2 3 4 5 6 7 8 9

Contents

Acknowledgments

I would like to acknowledge those who have permitted the use of various materials in this book. Lines from Emerson manuscripts on pages 112–113, 115, 160 are quoted by permission of the Houghton Library and the Ralph Waldo Emerson Memorial Association. The lines from Goethe and the translation on pages 50–51 are from *Goethe*, translated by David Luke (Penguin Poets, 1964: page 272), Copyright © David Luke, 1964; they are reprinted by permission of Penguin Books Ltd. Emily Dickinson's poem 985 (Copyright 1914, 1942 by Martha Dickinson Bianchi), poem 378, and lines from poem 419 (both under copyright 1935 by Martha Dickinson Bianchi, © 1963 by Mary L. Hampson) are reprinted from *The Complete Poems of Emily Dickinson*, ed. Thomas H. Johnson, by permission of Little, Brown & Company. Lines from poem 1545, from *The Life and Letters of Emily Dickinson*, ed. Martha Dickinson Bianchi, are reprinted by permission of Houghton Mifflin Company. The poetry of Stevens is quoted from *The Collected Poems of Wallace Stevens*, Copyright 1954 by Wallace Stevens, and the passages on pages 189–190, 193, 198–199 are reprinted by permission of Alfred A. Knopf, Inc. Similarly, lines of Frost on pages 185–187, 196 are quoted from *The Poetry of Robert Frost*, ed. Edward Connery Lathem. Copyright 1916, 1928, © 1969, by Holt, Rinehart and Winston. Copyright 1936, 1942, 1944, © 1956, by Robert Frost. Copyright © 1964, 1970, by Lesley Frost Ballantine. Reprinted by permission of Holt, Rinehart and Winston, Publishers. The lines from Ammons on pages 173, 189, 200–203 are from *Diversifications* Copyright © 1975 by A. R. Ammons, *Sphere: The Form of Motion* Copyright © 1974 by A. R. Ammons, and *Collected Poems 1951–1971* Copyright © 1972 by A. R. Ammons, all reprinted by permission of the publisher W. W. Norton & Company. Finally, permission to use material revised and quoted from my article "Toward the 'Titmouse Dimension': The Development of Emerson's Poetic Style," *PMLA* 87 (March 1972): 255–270 has been kindly granted by the Modern Language Association of America.

My own academic debts in this endeavor are chiefly to the writers indicated in my references. Were there others who contributed in a more direct way, this would be a better book than it is. It would probably not have been undertaken but for the encouragement given by several anonymous scholars who read its trying-out in essay form. Some former academic colleagues assured that as an author I would start "out of idleness, and not from out of toil." Giving such freedom, they probably didn't have Melville's harpooner in mind, but their kind of continuing service to things literary or political should not go unnoticed.

The writing of this book was supported indirectly and in part by payments from the Division of Employment Security, Commonwealth of Massachusetts, but primarily by my wife. It is being published with the aid of the Mellon Foundation. Its present, improved form is due largely to the work of readers and editors for the University of California Press, particularly Marilyn Schwartz, who did the copy editing. And I am indebted to Helene Tuchman for preparing the index.

R. A. Yoder

Abbreviations

——

The name "Ralph Waldo Emerson" is abbreviated in titles as "RWE." Major editions are also abbreviated in references as follows:

The Complete Works of RWE, ed. E. W. Emerson, Centenary Ed. (Boston, 1903–04)	volume & page, e.g., II, 318
The Journals and Miscellaneous Notebooks of RWE, ed. William H. Gilman, Alfred R. Ferguson, et al. (Cambridge, 1960–)	*JMN*
The Journals of RWE, ed. E. W. Emerson & Waldo E. Forbes (Boston, 1909–1914)	*J*
The Letters of RWE, ed. Ralph L. Rusk (New York, 1939)	*L*
The Early Lectures of RWE, ed. Stephen E. Whicher, Robert E. Spiller, Wallace E. Williams (Cambridge, 1959–1972)	*EL*
The Complete Poems of Emily Dickinson, ed. Thomas H. Johnson (Boston, 1960)	J with number of poem, e.g., J378

Introduction

▄▄▄

ACKNOWLEDGING EMERSON'S CENTRALITY in our literary history, I wish to ask where and wherein it lies. The answer I propose is that Emerson's conception of poetry and the poet belongs to a special Romantic tradition, one larger than American literature and encompassing much of it, and that in the actual practice of poetry Emerson changed his conception and so redirected this tradition in subsequent American art. Of all that is both American and Romantic, Emerson's work is the first to embody what William Blake might have called the Mental Life of contemporary Europe; and it is a little ironic that Emerson's remark about listening too long to the courtly muses of Europe has figured so largely in assessing his contribution to American thought. At the heart of *The American Scholar* is a giant imported myth, so widely assimilated by European muses from "an unknown antiquity" that any search for an ultimate source is probably beside the point. Emerson's "old fable" of the "One Man," the original whole as distinguished from subsequent fragments, is a version of the traditional "universal man," as Kathleen Raine summarizes it, "the Logos of the Platonists, the Adam Kadmon of the Cabala, the Divine Humanity of Swedenborg and Blake."[1] And this myth reaches out to the extremities of Emerson's own writing, from the early sermons on "The Genuine Man" and "The Miracle of Our Being" through the idea of the scholar to the conception of the poet as liberating god and the most complete or representative of men.

In Emerson's first and classic work *Nature* the figure of the Orphic poet embodies this conception. Invoking Orpheus in 1836 may have been a radical departure for America, but for Emerson it was an acknowledgment that the genius of this new country would speak the oldest truth. Like his most influential European contemporaries, Emerson thought of poetry as prophecy in the Renaissance sense of an unbroken tradition of revealed truth;[2] his assumptions and his method were syncretic—to go back to the beginning or "first day" and "recut the aged prints," and to winnow "the word unto the prophet spoken" that has remained in the world ever since. Emerson's traditionalism, in this sense, should remind us that as the American scholar he faced both ways, toward American independence but surely away from literary and critical insularity. That is why I try to place him in a larger Romantic tradition, as I think the best recent criticism has done in a more general way.[3]

It would be a mistake, however, to define Emerson's Romantic heritage primarily in terms of the esoterica filtering across the Atlantic, finally arriving in bulk when Bronson Alcott brought James Pierrepont Greaves' library back from England in 1842. At his most visionary peaks Emerson was still more directly engaged with the practical conduct of life than the writers of these assorted alchemical and hermetic tracts, and he always cared less than his Transcendentalist friends for fine distinctions or complex formulas. To Emerson it must have appeared, as it does to us, that the revival of Orphism was only a specialized aspect of the broader Romantic revival of poetic or imaginative man. The Romantics conceived of the poet as the "true center" (Emerson's phrase) of civilized life, and of poetry, insofar as it aimed to humanize the conditions of life, as the ideal vocation.

In the past we were encouraged to characterize Romantic literature as mystical, primitivist, vaguely idealistic, even revolutionary; these are misleading epithets, and M. H. Abrams has definitively righted this historical injustice in

Natural Supernaturalism. In his version Romanticism is far
from the "spilt religion" T. E. Hulme called it; indeed
Abrams' Romanticism might be better labelled "split religion," because its order always depends upon the felt con-
trarieties of existence. As art it took up the configurations
of Orphism and NeoPlatonism because it aimed at "the
reachievement of a unity which has been earned by un-
ceasing effort and which is, in Blake's term, an 'organized'
unity, an equilibrium of opponent forces which preserves
all the products and powers of intellection and culture."[4]
William Blake is named here, though in a way suggesting
what Abrams' book bears out, that Coleridge and Wordsworth and Carlyle are the major expositors of this Romanticism in England, and this is the Romanticism that chiefly
influenced Emerson.

Thus in *Nature* the Orphic poet is both seer and builder,
as the Orpheus-Christ invoked by Carlyle in *Sartor Resartus*
(III, viii) was a builder of cities and a civilizer of men. If
Emerson was not optimistic about the possibilities of life
in cities or even in communities, he nevertheless conceived
of the poetic imagination as a power that makes for culture.
Culture as an ideal or goal was possible in the nineteenth
century because the "key" to modern times, so Emerson
thought, was that "the mind had become aware of itself."
To the seminal minds of the age, as Elizabeth Sewell shows
in her study of the Orphic tradition, Orpheus represented
the reflexive or self-conscious activity of the imagination,
the power by which man distinguishes himself as the
single artificer of the world in which he sings.[5] What
proved to be the most important feature of the Orphic
myth for Emerson and his contemporaries was not the descent into the underworld or even the NeoPlatonic stress on
the continuity of truth, but the mythical fact of Orpheus
taming nature or the wilderness—when he sang, all the
rocks and trees and wild beasts arranged themselves in
order around this central man.

That is, in brief, Emerson's conception of the poet, well within the traditional Orphic and Romantic lines. Emerson's poet in practice is another matter. It is at the center of this book because, like any other artist, Emerson entered history essentially in his work, and there he reshaped the Orphic configurations in a way that has affected American voices ever since. The difference between the Orphic poet of *Nature* and the figure of the poet as developed and elaborated in Emerson's art makes this a study in the descent of Orpheus. Emerson turned to poetry in 1839 to express the indirect truths and powers that lie outside the prose domain of preachers and philosophers. In the poems of the next two decades the original Orphic figure lost first his direct supernatural connection, then his giant proportions and prophetic insight, so that he eventually descended, not to an underworld, but to a middle region where poetry is a limited power and the poet a man of common size or less. In this guise the Orphic poet descended in another sense, historically, to the American poets who have followed in Emerson's line.

I venture a judgment about Emerson's work as a whole, despite his reputation as an endless, deliberately inconsistent experimenter, because in the whole context of his art particular inconsistencies seem to be "rounded by the law of his being, as the inequalities of Andes and Himmaleh are insignificant in the curve of the sphere" (II, 58). Seeing Emerson's sphere curved back toward earth, I follow a line of informed judgment that can be traced to Stephen Whicher's biography of his inner life.[6] But the best source is still Emerson himself, who on several occasions gave the most telling criticism we have of his life as a poet:

> I am born a poet,—of a low class without doubt, yet a poet. That is my nature and vocation. My singing, be sure, is very husky, and is for the most part in prose. Still I am a poet in the sense of a perceiver and dear lover of the harmonies that are in the soul and in matter, and specially of the correspondence between these and those.
>
> (*L*, I, 435)

> I am a bard least of bards. I cannot, like them, make lofty
> arguments in stately, continuous verse, constraining the
> rocks, trees, animals, and periodic stars to say my
> thoughts,—for that is the gift of the great poets; but I am a
> bard because I stand near them, and apprehend all they
> utter, and with pure joy hear that which I also would say,
> and, moreover, I speak interruptedly words and half stan-
> zas which have the like scope and aim:—What I cannot
> declare, yet cannot all withhold.
>
> (*J*, IX, 472)

Quoting both these comments, one from 1835 and the
other from 1862, F. O. Matthiessen implied that Emerson's
idea of vocation had not changed in nearly thirty years.[7]
And yet a significant difference is told in these two passages: the youthful thinker is not a practitioner but a perceiver; he will sing—he has not yet sung—of certainties
directly perceived, the nearly self-evident harmonies of life
and the fundamental correspondence between nature and
the mind. The older poet looks back on verses sung and
glosses their Orphic aspiration, the humanizing or taming
of nature. Though he has failed to constrain nature—"the
slippery Proteus is not so easily caught"—and though he
realizes that his was not to be a "lofty" or "stately" strain,
still he loves the bards and takes satisfaction in their immortal melodies. In its wise, comfortable passiveness this
confession helps to explain the course of Emerson's art: the
practice of his poetic vocation, husky-voiced and in low
tones, was the highway toward "Experience" and the con-
sequent notion of an attainable, mid-world felicity that has
a secure place in the American literary tradition.

The plan of this book is relatively simple. The prelude is
a study of Emerson's Orphic aspirations as they relate to
his predecessors and as they are shaped in the development of his prose. My focus in the following section is on
the poetry, especially the poems growing out of Emerson's
heightened conviction, in 1839, that his thought demanded
a more dramatic form. Finally I try to assess the distin-
guishing features of Emerson's legacy in American poetry.

The Orphic poet has been fragmented and scattered in America in a way that often leaves him unrecognizable. Emerson's own modifications contributed to that process, but they also preserved patterns of Orphic inquiry and poetic aims in usable form for his successors.

PART ONE:

Prelude

———

And if with this
I mix more lowly matter; with the thing
Contemplated, describe the Mind and Man
Contemplating; and who, and what he was—
The transitory Being that beheld
This Vision; when and where, and how he lived;—
Be not this labour useless.
> —WORDSWORTH, Prospectus for "The Recluse"

Every form is a history of the thing.
> —EMERSON, "The Uses of Natural History"

I

The Growth of an Orphic Mind

———

The great obscurity and uncertainty in which the history of Orpheus is involved affords very little matter for our information; and even renders that little, inaccurate and precarious. . . . This alone may be depended on, from general assent, that there formerly lived a person named Orpheus, whose father was Oeagrus, who lived in Thrace, and who was the son of a king, who was the founder of theology among the Greeks, the institutor of their life and morals, the first of prophets, and the prince of poets; himself the offspring of a Muse; who taught the Greeks their sacred rites and mysteries, and from whose wisdom, as from a perpetual and abundant fountain, the divine muse of Homer, and the philosophy of Pythagoras and Plato flowed; and, lastly, who by the melody of his lyre, drew rocks, woods, and wild beasts, stopt rivers in their course, and even moved the inexorable king of hell; as every page, and all the writings of antiquity sufficiently evince.

—Thomas Taylor, *The Hymns of Orpheus*

ALL MYTHOLOGY IS PROTEAN, but Orpheus is one of the most elusive and amorphous of all mythic heroes. For some, indeed, he has come to mean the very power of transformation and metamorphosis that we observe, perhaps in its purest form, in the changes of language and music. Understandably Orpheus has been shaped anew by each of the Orphic poets who would be counted among his descendants. Perennially, however, every version of Orpheus evokes the questions embedded in the basic fable, about the relation between language and reality, and the ultimate harmony or unity that Orpheus through all his changes portends.

For most nineteenth-century Americans, and especially for those who knew of Alcott's "Orphic Sayings" in *The Dial*, anything "Orphic" was bound to be elusive, deep and mysterious. The word often shaded into irony, as it did for Miles Coverdale when he described his own Orphic wisdom in *The Blithedale Romance*. But for Emerson, who was of the party of Hope and not Hawthorne's kind of ironist, the lore of Orpheus portended the highest aspirations of his age. Orestes Brownson spoke for Emerson's party in 1836, announcing "our duty to bring out the ideal man," and "the great mission of our age . . . to unite the infinite and the finite." The man Brownson imagined was a high, rare, and perhaps impossible creature, but the method he proposed for attaining his goals was never exclusive: "We of the nineteenth century appear in the world as mediators . . . we are to conciliate hostile feelings, and harmonize conflicting principles and interests."[1] Brownson's mingling of hierophantic aims and democratic means is a clue to the symbolic appeal of Orpheus. Orpheus was, as Margaret Fuller later wrote, "a lawgiver by theocratic commission." Among men somewhat at sea with their freedoms, Orpheus held the authority to discriminate moral and aesthetic excellences. And yet "his Soul went forth toward all beings."[2] Besides authority, Orpheus stood for universality. His was a harmonizing capacity, and he imposed upon men by charming or winning their consent. Thus the work of Orpheus could be understood as achieving the "one vast system" Brownson desired, and the wisdom of Orpheus as an eclectic truth that would inspire general agreement.

The nineteenth century was indebted to the Renaissance for its image of Orpheus as synthesizer. Especially in the commentaries of the great Florentine Platonist Marsilio Ficino, and commonly among his successors, Orpheus was portrayed as a philosopher-priest who anticipated and confirmed the essential truth of Christianity, or as a magus able to invoke the powers of the spiritual world for man's benefit. This Orpheus held a significant place in the *prisca theologia,* the ancient wisdom represented by a supposed line of religious teachers usually including Zoroaster, Moses, Hermes Trismegistus, Orpheus himself, Pythagoras, Plato and the NeoPlatonists, all of whom were cited to demonstrate the basic similarity of Platonism and Christianity.[3] This syncretic view of the ancient world appealed tremendously to both American and English thinkers of Emerson's time. They lived—as Cassirer described Ficino and Pico della Mirandola living nearly four centuries earlier in Italy—on the brink of a new era of precise differentiation and articulation, and on that brink they liked to imagine all the varying intellectual systems of the past dissolved into a vague but fertile unity.[4] Emerson, Carlyle, Arnold, and most of the Coleridge latitudinarians, like Brownson, looked on history as an eclectic process: they saw differences rendered insignificant by the continual alternations of history; as philosophers or sages they aimed to counterbalance the extreme tendencies of every age and to achieve a synthesis, however blurry, that preserved the truth each era contributed. Thus if they believed in progress, it was progress toward the reestablishment of truth that had been available since the beginning of time.[5]

Apart from what he might have heard in Edward Everett's Harvard lectures (X, 332), Emerson's first lessons in Renaissance Orphism came from the modern Neo-Platonic revivalist Thomas Taylor, whose translations and commentaries began to appear in the last decade of the eighteenth century. Emerson read Taylor early, at Harvard and again before 1830, and later he would call Taylor "a better man of imagination . . . than any man between Milton and Wordsworth" (VIII, 50). Taylor depended heavily on Renaissance tradition for his view of Orphism, and he adopted the syncretic notion that Orphic truth was compatible with Christian doctrine. Taylor's version of the historical process was also cyclical or alternating, and he worried about the effects of opposing systems of truth upon the ancient wisdom he sought to preserve. In 1787 he could justifiably assert that the pursuit of particulars was ascendant, and he warned that with the triumph of empiricism general philosophical truth would be eclipsed. Long before Carlyle described the oscillations of Teufelsdröckh or Arnold made the tide a symbol of historical epochs in "Dover Beach," Taylor had stated similar general assumptions about the history of thought, and in terms that would have especially interested Emerson:

> There is doubtless a revolution in the literary, correspondent to that of the natural world. The face of things is continually changing; and the perfect, and perpetual harmony of the universe, subsists by the mutability of its parts. In consequence of this fluctuation, different arts and sciences have flourished at different periods of the world: but the complete circle of human knowledge has I believe, never subsisted at once, in any nation or age. Where accurate and profound researches, into the principles of things have advanced to perfection; there by a natural consequence, men have neglected the disquisition of particulars: and where sensible particulars have been the general object of pursuit, the science of universals has languished, or sunk into oblivion and contempt.[6]

Like his seventeenth-century English predecessor Ralph Cudworth, Taylor saw in Orpheus an ancient example of the subordination of particulars, or the multitude of pagan gods, to a single supreme idea or deity, and so he offered Orpheus to an era in which true religion would be harshly tested.[7]

This was Emerson's received Orpheus, and his view of history as well. Emerson reached intellectual maturity midway between Taylor's committed revival and the diffusion of Orphic matter into Victorian tropes, and as a young minister struggling to save faith through a more liberal Christianity, he must have welcomed Orpheus as the spirit of revealed, syncretic truth. "Revealed" and "syncretic" would have been conjunctive attributes in Emerson's conscious mind, I am sure, but for the moment consider them as distinct—"revealed" implying at least two worlds or realms of being, and a truth drawn from beyond; "syncretic," on the other hand, referring to a single, pluralistic world in which truth is a crossing of many differences. It is of crucial importance to my interpretation of Emerson that in the long run he did bend the poet's ascent back toward earth, thus curving the line of history, reducing two worlds to one, and making Orpheus serve primarily as a principle of synthesis or reconciliation of differences.

Emerson's first literary use of Orpheus, however, is the *locus classicus* in *Nature,* where the Orphic poet stands rather for truth revealed by supernatural commission and a literal influx of the divine, or at least for truth with the authority that Burke and Coleridge presumed in favor of ideas that have endured. Emerson introduces the song of the Orphic poet with these words:

> I shall therefore conclude this essay with some traditions of man and nature, which a certain poet sang to me; and which, as they have always been in the world, and perhaps reappear to every bard, may be both history and prophecy.
>
> (I, 70)

And as both nature and art reveal truth in "faint copies of an invisible archetype," so the Orphic poet comprehends the "cycle of the universal man, from whom the known individuals proceed" (I, 70). Orpheus, then, is a name for the Universal Man or Central Man of Emerson's own mythology, the one implied by every historical line of partial men, ancient or modern, and the one who would speak the complete "cyclus of Orphic words" that is now broken, like man himself, into fragments.

7

> In what I call the cyclus of Orphic words, which I find in
> Bacon, in Cudworth, in Plutarch, in Plato, in that which the
> New Church would indicate when it speaks of the truths
> possessed by the primeval church broken up into fragments
> & floating hither & thither in the corrupt Church, I perceive
> myself addressed thoroughly. They do teach the intellect &
> cause a gush of emotion; which we call the moral sublime;
> they pervade also the moral nature. Now the Universal
> Man when he comes, must so speak. He must recognize by
> addressing the whole nature.
>
> (*JMN*, V, 253–254)

Throughout Emerson's writings countless reiterations of
the catalogue of great thinkers testify to his vital belief in a
line of *prisci theologii*. In his first collection of essays (1841)
he looked backwards to "the high priesthood of the pure
reason, the *Trismegisti*, the expounders of the principles of
thought from age to age."

> This band of grandees, Hermes, Heraclitus, Empedocles,
> Plato, Plotinus, Olympiodorus, Proclus, Synesius and the
> rest, have somewhat so vast in their logic, so primary in
> their thinking, that it seems antecedent to all the ordinary
> distinctions of rhetoric and literature, and to be at once
> poetry and music and dancing and astronomy and
> mathematics. . . . The truth and grandeur of their thought
> is proved by its scope and applicability, for it commands the
> entire schedule and inventory of things for its illustration.
>
> (II, 346)

But Emerson concludes, wistfully and yet with amuse-
ment, that the "plainest argument" of these grandees is
neither understood nor heeded by the great majority of
men. Significantly, when the line appears again in *Essays:
Second Series* (1844), it is associated not with pure and clear
reason but with a dark, obscure meaning that paradoxically
men seem to comprehend better than the plain truth. Significantly, too, Orpheus heads this troop:

> But the highest minds of the world have never ceased to
> explore the double meaning, or shall I say the quadruple or
> the centuple or much more manifold meaning, of every

8

> sensuous fact; Orpheus, Empedocles, Heraclitus, Plato,
> Plutarch, Dante, Swedenborg, and the masters of
> sculpture, picture and poetry. . . . And this hidden truth,
> that the fountains whence all this river of Time and its
> creatures floweth are intrinsically ideal and beautiful,
> draws us to the consideration of the nature and functions of
> the Poet, or the man of Beauty.
>
> (III, 4)

This is indeed Emerson's own biography: for he was
drawn to poetry in the same manner, giving up the "didac-
tics" of "Intellect"—a word which he probably meant to
characterize the direct preaching in his early prose—and
adopting the poetic method of "indirections" in his later
essays and in his poetry. The poet, then, most nearly embodied the Universal Man, "for the poet is representative.
He stands among partial men for the complete man" (III,
5). Moreover, in "The Poet" Emerson defined the truth of
poetry as a process of metamorphosis rather than as a
purely descended revelation, and in his messianic call for
the poet who had not yet appeared he effectively reversed
the order of the *prisci theologii*, whose authority now depended on its end rather than on its beginnings, in a way
that obviously suited the intellectual temper of his times.

Along with this conception of a priesthood in service of
truth, the legacy of Orpheus for Emerson involved the relation between language and reality known traditionally as
the marriage of words and things. Through the power of
words and music Orpheus had tamed or civilized things.
Emerson's earliest conceptions of the Universal Man and of
the union between words and things seems to have followed the ethical tradition of the Renaissance which, on
the authority of Pythagoras, held that hearing is the most
moral of the senses, because sounds have the movement
characteristic of actions.[8] In a more practical vein, Emerson
saw words joined to things when they affect things and in
that way become involved in action, themselves actions.
This theme from the sermons, returning in *The American*

Scholar and "The Poet," is Emerson's first formulation of a theory of knowledge as reflexive, completed only by the participation of the knower.[9] Truth is that wholeness where there is no discrepancy between what is said and what is done; thus Emerson preached on "Words and Things" in November 1831, "In the best man there are no idle words, but his words are things."[10] Consonant with his myth of the Whole Man, for Emerson the aim of art was always to project the image of a man and to make real, exemplary men. By the canons of his time the work of art was judged inferior to the artist who creates himself through his work, and thus the real substance of poetry was the shape and character of men: "The supreme value of poetry is to educate us to a height beyond itself, or which it rarely reaches;—the subduing mankind to order and virtue. He is the true Orpheus who writes his ode, not with syllables, but men" (VIII, 65–66).

Beyond this ethical dimension, Emerson conceived of a power in words arising from their fitness or appropriateness to things. Language expresses the "radical correspondence between visible things and human thoughts" (I, 29), yet this crucial idea of correspondence is never expounded by Emerson in plainest argument. He did think that language was derived from nature, "borrowed from our experience in the material world" (*EL*, I, 24), but when he spoke in *Nature* of fastening words to things he did not mean to imply a conventional or nominalistic view of language; the attachment, as he wrote later, is "not art, but a second nature" (III, 22). The poet as namer or language-maker gives real names because he perceives mythically or symbolically, and because Emerson's assumed correspondence between the mind and nature means that the whole system of language will reflect the order of reality. Correspondence, in this sense, is a necessary, preexistent connection; the fact will not always be perceived, however, for

10

men must often pierce through "rotten diction" or re-
vitalize "fossil poetry" in order to see in a true light.

The doctrine of language in *Nature* rests upon· Neo-
Platonic assumptions: first, the concept of emanation by
which every "fact is the end or last issue of spirit" (I, 34),
implying the necessary connection or correspondence;
and, second, the allied view of history as degeneration or
distance from the spirit at the center. To exist is to have
emanated, and to emanate is to descend or fall from the
One. Emerson wrote later that "the discovery we have
made that we exist . . . is called the Fall of Man" (III, 75),
and in *Nature* "the corruption of man is followed by the
corruption of language" (I, 29). As present man is a "dwarf
of himself," so present language does not fulfill its promise; now the word falls short of the thing: "For language
itself is young and unformed. In heaven it will be, as
Sampson Reed said, 'one with things.' Now there are
many things that refuse to be recorded,—perhaps the
larger half. The unsaid part is the best of any discourse"
(*JMN*, V, 51: June 1835). To speak mythically, the world
has lost its Orpheus. Reed, Emerson's Swedenborgian
mentor, explained this dilemma as a reversal of the original
Orphic power in his influential essay *Observations on the
Growth of the Mind.*

> There was a time, when the human mind was in more
> perfect harmony with the Divine Mind, than the lower or-
> ders of creation; and the tale of the harp of Orpheus, to
> which the brutes, the vegetables and rocks listened, is not
> altogether unfounded in reality—but when the selfish and
> worldly passions usurped the place of love to our God and
> our neighbour, the mind of man began to be mute in its
> praise. The original order was reversed. The very stones cry
> out, and we do well to listen to them.[11]

Here, in Orphic terms, is the measure of man's Fall. The
regeneration of language is the beginning of the Orphic

work, as Emerson conceived it, and represents the Plotinian *epistrophe* or return of emanated things to their source. Reed's commentary also helps to clarify one of the central ambiguities of Emerson's theory of language: though language makes the world intelligible, as "the poet conforms things to his thoughts" (I, 52), the poet at the beginning of his long journey home must attend things or the appearances in nature as the first signs of his true direction. And Emerson as the outsetting bard heeded this advice, when he described himself as a "perceiver" of harmonies, or in the journals of 1834 as a "Watcher" with a "philosophy of waiting."[12]

Thus Emerson's Orpheus represents an expected reconciler or reconciliation, not merely ethical or linguistic, but apocalyptic in the sense that the looked-for reunion of words and things will be fulfilled only when earth becomes heaven or like heaven, when the spirit does "unfold its great proportions" and is actualized by a "correspondent revolution in things," as the Orphic poet of *Nature* prophesies (I, 76). And although, philosophically speaking, Emerson's doctrine of correspondence assured that "things are knowable" (IV, 62) and that the marriage "in actual life . . . not celebrated" (I, 74) is still possible, the present state of mankind gave Emerson considerable pause before he attempted even a literary consummation of his faith. Was he, after all, his own Orphic poet? Even *Nature*, which can properly be called Emerson's apocalypse, masks any answer to this question. What Emerson inherited, finally, from the tradition of Orpheus, was a sense of the gigantic proportions of the poetic task, and his personal response to this burden is best recorded in the inner life of his journals and notebooks. There he was Sisyphus, watching and waiting for the saviour Orpheus (*JMN*, III, 45). The trial of poetry left him more often than not a dissatisfied experimenter—"Why can not I write verses," he scribbled (and later cancelled) beneath the "Gnothi

Seauton" lines in his journal of 1831, and "could I translate into dull English the poem of my dream" is the enigmatic heading for verses drafted in 1842. That he at first resolved the problem of vocation by entering the ministry suggests that as a young man the great American antinomian of the nineteenth century needed some support like Dimmesdale's iron framework. And this choice undoubtedly conditioned his artistic form: a minister's mastery of oration led him in the 1830s to the most obvious role for "scholars out of the church," that of secular preacher, and both within and without the church the orator relied less on evidences and demonstration—Emerson's arguments, as Carlyle said of his own, lacked the "nerve of proof"—and more on a line of Christian or Orphic authority, and on the persuasive power of his own prose music. He could write, then, in 1841, perhaps taking justified pride in his own contribution, that "the very finest & sweetest closes & falls are not in our metres, but in the measures of eloquence, which have greater variety & richness than verse" (*JMN*, VIII, 97). But he still looked forward to great poetry as yet unwritten.

That Emerson's Orpheus sang first in prose is a cultural as well as a personal fact. There is no recognizable "age of sensibility" in the early republic, and what William Charvat called the "incubation of Romanticism" in America, between 1815 and 1830, is a period still dominated by Augustan attitudes and presided over by Scotch reviewers.[13] Even while he complained that poetry had been shackled by the past, young Emerson reflected the traditionalism of his milieu in the poetry he was willing to recite publicly and in many of his journal judgments. In undergraduate's verses (*JMN*, I, 237) he scorned literary self-reliance and elsewhere he echoed the Edinburgh critics on the "mania for originality" that had infected the new Romantic poets (*JMN*, I, 163). Most important, Emerson asserted the kind

13

of separation between poetry and religion that would pre-
clude an Orphic conception of art (*JMN*, II, 170). There
were a few influences against the tide, particularly in the
Dana–Channing circle that had already begun to inveigh
against Augustan elegance, and Emerson's youthful resentment against "the world" or what he later termed "the
Establishment" (X, 325) surfaces in some of his early
poems like "Good-Bye" (IX, 3; *JMN*, II, 223, 243). But this
is still Emerson as Sisyphus, not Orpheus, who speaks.

Emerson's first turn toward Orphic aspiration can be
dated clearly in 1826, and if there was a primary influence
it was not Edward Everett's rather dry commentary on
Orphic remains, but the mind of William Ellery Channing,
who contributed a unique sweetness and light to the reason of the Unitarian Church and Harvard Divinity School
during this decade. Channing had made a special point of
visiting both Wordsworth and Coleridge when he travelled
to England in 1823, and in the years after his return became
Emerson's teacher in theology. Channing's larger service,
however, was the inspirational power of his sermons and
the bond he uncovered between poetry and Christianity.
In January 1826 Channing published in the *Christian
Examiner* an article on Milton that Emerson later called one
of the most important of its time (X, 339; *JMN*, VIII, 283).
Appropriately on the foremost representative of prophetic
and religious poetry in the English language, this essay set
out a poetic ideal remarkable for its fusion of Miltonic
genius and Romantic principles:

> Of all God's gifts of intellect, [Milton] esteemed poetical
> genius the most transcendent. He esteemed it in himself as
> a kind of inspiration, and wrote his great works with some-
> thing of the conscious dignity of a prophet. We agree with
> Milton in his estimate of poetry. It seems to us the divinest
> of all arts; for it is the breathing or expression of that princi-
> ple or sentiment, which is deepest and sublimest in human
> nature; we mean, of that thirst or aspiration, to which no
> mind is wholly a stranger, for something purer and lovelier,

something more powerful, lofty, and thrilling, than ordinary and real life affords. No doctrine is more common among Christians than that of man's immortality; but it is not so generally understood that the germs or principles of his whole future being are *now* wrapped up in his soul, as the rudiments of the future plant in the seed. As a necessary result of this constitution, the soul, possessed and moved by these mighty though infant energies, is perpetually stretching beyond what is present and visible, struggling against the bounds of its earthly prison-house, and seeking relief and joy in imaginings of unseen and ideal being. . . . He who cannot interpret by his own consciousness what we now have said, wants the true key to works of genius. He has not penetrated those secret recesses of the soul, where poetry is born and nourished, and inhales immortal vigor, and wings herself fcr her heavenward flight. In an intellectual nature, framed for progress and for higher modes of being, there must be creative energies, powers of original and ever-growing thought; and poetry is the form in which these energies are chiefly manifested. It is the glorious prerogative of this art, that it "makes all things new" for the gratification of a divine instinct. It indeed finds its elements in what it actually sees and experiences, in the worlds of matter and mind; but it combines and blends these into new forms and according to new affinities; breaks down, if we may so say, the distinctions and bounds of nature; imparts to material objects life, and sentiment, and emotion, and invests the mind with the powers and splendors of the outward creation; describes the surrounding universe in the colors which the passions throw over it, and depicts the soul in those modes of repose or agitation, of tenderness or sublime emotion, which manifest its thirst for a more powerful and joyful existence.[14]

This passage in particular and the entire essay must have had a striking effect upon Emerson in 1826. In the first place, Channing was writing "On the Character and Writings of Milton," and he praised the man, in a word, for *"magnanimity,"* for an extraordinary devotion to virtue and to the great prophetic duty that Milton assumed. To Emerson, then, Milton not only justified watching and waiting until his powers were equal to a great task, but better than any other delineated the "heroic image of man" in both his life and his art. Milton made man whole again, and satisfied Emerson's Orphic ideal by writing his odes with men, that is, with his own experience; this is the theme of Emerson's 1835 lecture on Milton, and he quotes the man himself, who wrote that " ' he who would aspire to write well hereafter in laudable things, ought himself to be a true poem' " (*EL*, I, 149–150).

In the second place, Channing's account of the divine art of poetry, by paraphrasing Coleridge and Wordsworth, underscored the affinity between the Romantics and Milton that is most dramatically propounded in Wordsworth's Prospectus for "The Recluse" published with *The Excursion* in 1814. For Emerson personally, as indeed for America at large, Wordsworth is the most significant literary index of the 1820s. Emerson never placed Wordsworth at the summit of his Parnassus, but it was an increasingly appreciative study of Wordsworth that carried him, once and for all, beyond the confines of Augustan and Edinburgh taste. Reading *The Excursion* in 1826 he still complained of too much philosophy and too little joy (*JMN*, III, 39); at about the same time he reiterated his general disapproval for versified metaphysics and Romantic agonies, but added an important qualification:

> Mar. 14. I hate this vasty notion of poetry that is going the rounds nowadays thro' the whole circle of pulpits, criticism, & poets. This "aliquid immensum &c" is best left to each man's youthful & private meditations. This straining to say what is unutterable & vain retching, with the imbecile uses of great words is nauseous to sound sense & good taste. 'Tis a forgotten maxim that "accuracy is essential to beauty."
>
> I know something may be well said for what I impugn. There is a philosophy in expectation & wonder; & this account of mind, beneath which language sinks, is bottomed on the fine verse
>
> "Est deus in nobis, agitante calescimus illo."
>
> (*JMN*, III, 12)

Emerson's most proximate source for this Ovidian phrase would have been Hugh Blair's *Lectures on Rhetoric and Belles Lettres*, a set book at Harvard in 1820, where the Latin line is quoted to explain the poetic sublime. Before the year was out it would already have justified a new respect for "the Vast" and for Wordsworth in particular.[15] Perhaps the most telling evidence of Wordsworth's new status is that Emerson soon began to write plain and meditative blank verse. "The River," dated June 1827 in the Centenary Edition (IX, 385), and the following journal lines are unmistakably Wordsworthian in cadence and setting:

> He is a man who tho' he told it not
> Mourned in the hour of manhood, while he saw
> The rich imagination that had tinged
> Each earthly thing with hues from paradise
> Abandoning forever his instructed eye.
> . . . .
> But he was poor & proud & solitary
> He would walk forth at moonlight, for the moon
> And quick eyed stars do sympathize with all
> Who suffer. . . .
>
>   When thy soul
> Is filled with a just image fear not thou
> Lest halting rhymes or unharmonious verse
> Cripple the fair Conception. Leave the heart
> Alone to find its language. In all tongues
> It had a sovereign instinct that doth teach
> An eloquence which rules can never give.
> (JMN, III, 84–86)

Consonant with his earlier resentment of the *beau monde*, Emerson identifies here with Wordsworth's rural wanderer and with a homely, sincere language that comes spontaneously from the heart.

Although the idea of spontaneous meditation did affect Emerson's poetic voice when it finally matured, the more important impact of Wordsworth in 1826 can be gauged only in conjunction with another event. In August

Sampson Reed published the *Observations on the Growth of the Mind*: Emerson read it immediately, discussed it in letters with his Aunt Mary Moody Emerson (*L*, I, 173), and wrote in October that Dr. Channing had referred to it in a sermon and that the Swedenborgians found independent testimony to their founder's truth in Wordsworth (*J*, II, 124). For the last point Reed must have been Emerson's authority. One of the chief doctrines of his essay was the intimate connection of memory and the affections, and he thought of poetry as the "soul of science," a relationship Wordsworth had approached in his 1802 Preface to the *Lyrical Ballads*. For Reed naming was knowledge, and names corresponded to the reality or essence of things. And as to the form of poetry, he asserted that rhyme adds nothing, and "the poet should be free and unshackled as the sages."[16] All of this would represent an invitation to reconsider Wordsworth's "mania for originality," and Reed's passages on the harmony between mind and the objects it names point directly to the high argument of Wordsworth's Prospectus.

> How exquisitely the individual Mind
> (And the progressive powers perhaps no less
> Of the whole species) to the external World
> Is fitted:—and how exquisitely, too—
> Theme this but little heard of among men—
> The external World is fitted to the Mind;
> And the creation (by no lower name
> Can it be called) which they with blended might
> Accomplish:—this is our high argument.

This coincidence of Wordsworth and Swedenborgian doctrine in 1826 may have struck Emerson as evidence of a new poetic tradition similar to the ancient priesthood, lodged in a sequestered, sometimes abused line of prophetic poets through whom the great truth of correspondence was being passed. During the next decade he continued to associate Wordsworth and Swedenborg, and the prime testimony to the importance of this conjunction comes in "Poetry and Imagination":

> I have heard that there is a hope which precedes and must precede all science of the visible or the invisible world; and that science is the realization of that hope in either region. I count the genius of Swedenborg and Wordsworth as the agents of a reform in philosophy, the bringing poetry back to Nature,—to the marrying of Nature and mind, undoing the old divorce in which poetry had been famished and false, and Nature had been suspected and pagan.
>
> (VIII, 66)

One of the implications of Emerson's spousal metaphor is the essential unity of poetic and scientific method, and although the passage in "Poetry and Imagination" may have been written as late as the 1860s, Emerson drew that theme from his reconsideration of Wordsworth in 1826. Once again Reed had guided him with an epigraph from *The Excursion* on the title page of the *Observations*:

> So build we up the Being that we are;
> Thus deeply drinking-in the soul of things,
> We shall be wise perforce; and while inspired
> By choice, and conscious that the Will is free,
> Shall move unswerving, even as if impelled
> By strict necessity, along the path
> Of order and of good.
>
> (*The Excursion*, IV, 1264–1270)

The full passage (lines 1132–1274) is one of Wordsworth's touchstones for the Romantic imagination from Emerson to Wallace Stevens: nature ever speaks to man, even in its scrawniest cry, that echoes back from the abyss in choral rings of eternal harmony; but nature teaches by both imaginative shocks and milder gradations. The specific burden of the Wanderer's harangue is that we should attend, in proper balance, both the higher and the lower communications of nature, in effect, both the languages of imagination and of science; thus we develop those progressive powers exquisitely suited to the external world, and "whate'er we

see / Or feel, shall tend to quicken and refine."[17] Science,
then, is auxiliary to the imagination, and leads us to the
same occult recognitions that vitalize *Nature* in 1836. Emerson was not ready to recognize them in 1826 when he
wrote this illuminating criticism of Wordsworth:

> Mr. W. is a poet with the same error that wasted the genius
> of the alchemists & astrologers of the Middle Age. These
> attempted to extort by direct means the principle of life, the
> secret & substance of matter from material things; & those
> to extract intelligence from remoter nature, instead of ob-
> serving that science is ever approximating to truth by dint
> of application to present wants & not by the search after
> general & recondite Truth.
>
> > (*JMN*, III, 39)

But he soon joined the search for truth in stones. Lecturing on science in 1833 he counted among "The Uses of Natural History" the "salutary effect" of scientific method
upon the character of man, and Wordsworth, who named
the powers of observation and description first among
those requisite for poetry in his 1815 Preface, was one of
his authorities—

> Can the effect be other than most beneficent upon the
> faculties dedicated to such observations?—upon the man
> given
>
> > To reverend watching of each still report
> > That Nature utters from her rural shrine.
>
> Moreover, the state of mind which nature makes
> indispensable to all such as inquire of her secrets is the best
> discipline. For she yields no answers to petulance, or
> dogmatism, or affectation; only to patient, docile
> observation.
>
> > (*EL*, I, 20: the quoted lines are from Wordsworth's
> > "Written upon a Blank Leaf in 'The Complete
> > Angler' ")

What this observation reveals, Emerson enthusiastically
reported in 1834, is the extraordinary adjustment of species

to the environment and a perfect balance in the whole system. His conclusion to "The Relation of Man to the Globe" is a rehearsal for *Nature*:

> I conclude further, that the snail is not more accurately adjusted to his shell than man to the globe he inhabits; that not only a perfect symmetry is discoverable in his limbs and senses between the head and the foot, between the hand and the eye, the heart, and the lungs,—but an equal symmetry and proportion is discoverable between him and the air, the mountains, the tides, the moon, and the sun. I am not impressed by solitary marks of designing wisdom; I am thrilled with delight by the choral harmony of the whole. Design! It is all design. It is all beauty. It is all astonishment.
>
> (*EL*, I, 48–49)

Choral songs in *The Excursion* (IV, 1163) came in imaginative visitings because, as Wordsworth implied in the 1802 Preface, science had not yet created a revolution in our condition and our consciousness; he added that if it did, the poet would then follow the scientist. When Emerson reflected upon the science of his times in the 1830s, he decided that the revolution had been accomplished. At its best, science would make disagreeable appearances vanish, as the Orphic poet in *Nature* says they will, and restore the music of the spheres.

> We are to come into nature from a higher law & classify it anew. There is no mire, no dirt to chemistry: the ignorant, the foul know of dirt; the chemist sees all dissolved into a chain of immaterial, immortal, irresistible laws. Even so must we come into nature, that is, so walk & work & build & associate. We must not scold, we must not lay our hands on men but being inspired must awe their violence & lead them by our eye into harmonic choirs.
>
> (*JMN*, VII, 416: January 1841)

In this later journal comment the work of the scientist is clearly related to the Orphic work of subduing mankind to order and virtue.

21

Thus Channing and his evocation of the Miltonic heritage, Reed's version of Swedenborg, and Wordsworth combined to work Emerson's conversion to the new poetry in 1826, and among the major fruits of that awakening, ripened by his extensive reading in the next six years, was Emerson's recognition of design, the harmony and symmetry in the whole, and of a method, painstakingly architectonic, that serves both poetry and science. These are in a real sense the foundations for his earliest art, the poems of 1834 and *Nature*, which are both remarkable for the same qualities of elaborate and precise organization. But given these foundations, there remains the missing All—the spirit of Emerson's great essays: the driving force, or what Coleridge called more cumbrously the "mental initiative," has hardly been accounted for. Wordsworth, after all, looked backward in 1814, but Emerson himself was looking forward in 1826 to "the vision and the faculty divine." The unique power of *Nature* must be discovered elsewhere than in its foundations, in great passages cantilevered into the Vast, well beyond the substructure given by method and order.

> 'Build therefore your own world. As fast as you conform your life to the pure idea in your mind, that will unfold its great proportions. A correspondent revolution in things will attend the influx of the spirit. . . . The kingdom of man over nature, which cometh not with observation,—a dominion such as now is beyond his dream of God,—he shall enter without more wonder than the blind man feels who is gradually restored to perfect sight.'
>
> (I, 76–77)

There is a difference in kind between the power of observation in the rehearsal of 1834 and the visionary power of this performance in 1836. Behind the closing words of the Orphic poet, even behind such specifically relevant glosses as Luke 17:20–21 and Bacon's *Great Instauration*, is the whole history of millennial and apocalyptic vision that, in Emerson's view, each man knows by reliving.[18]

This full knowledge was precipitated for Emerson, even before his lectures or writing trials, by the death of his young wife Ellen Tucker in February of 1831. Out of the psychic turbulence of his grief came the shock of rec-ognition—*deus in nobis*, "God dwells in thee"—marked by Stephen Whicher as Emerson's intellectual dawn,[19] and first appearing in the extraordinary journal verses titled "Gnothi Seauton."

> If thou canst bear
> Strong meat of simple truth
> If thou durst my words compare
> With what thou thinkest in the soul's free youth
>
> Then take this fact unto thy soul—
> God dwells in thee.—
> It is no metaphor nor parable
> It is unknown to thousands & to thee
> Yet there is God.
>
> . . . .
>
> He is the mighty Heart
> From which life's varied pulses part
> Clouded & shrouded there doth sit
> The Infinite
> Embosomed in a man. . . .
>
> (*JMN*, III, 290–291)

The rough-hewn, ungainly form of this private poem is quite as revolutionary—compared, say, with Emerson's stylized poetry of 1834—as its central idea. Casual, unfin-ished repetitions, counterpointed couplets, rhyme intrud-ing or disappearing at will—these are devices that distin-guish later major poems like "Merlin" or the "Ode, In-scribed to W. H. Channing." "Gnothi Seauton" resembles no other poetry; in this first, perhaps unconscious, experi-ment a self-reliant poet does emerge. The loss of Ellen paradoxically unlocked Emerson's faith in human power, previously encumbered by his own hesitancy and by a Wordsworthian wise passiveness. It took form in the idea

23

of an immanent, indwelling God, and as self-reliance it poured forth with urgency, with the sense of unnecessary bondage and imminent liberation that dominates Emerson's most famous writings.

It is tempting to interpret even this personal history in the light of Orpheus, and not wholly unwarranted. Orpheus appealed to mediaeval Christians as a type of intercession with death, and for the year after 1831 Emerson's journal was something of a journey to Eurydice. Even then he was compelled to visit her tomb and open her coffin.[20] On a broader, symbolic scale, his grief demanded that the world a scientific lecturer could close into a single, perfect whole be split or enlarged to accommodate the one he had lost. His subsequent quest for the *matutina cognito*, the dawning knowledge of God and the Spirit, is a meditative acting out of his hope that he would meet Ellen again in "the firmament of thought"—"I know that in the deep / Of new power & the realms of truth / Thine affections do not sleep" (*JMN*, III, 230: June 1831). Neither the power of observation—on this the Orphic poet is explicit, the kingdom "cometh not with observation"—nor the idea of correspondence, that expressed Emerson's awakened admiration for the cosmic order, comprehended this sense of new power. What he felt, however, Emerson discovered that tradition had named, and of all writers in English Coleridge, in this respect, had named things most precisely after their essence.

Americans who took Coleridge seriously in 1830 regarded him first as a thinker and only secondarily as a poet and literary critic. Channing was already directing his friends and students to Coleridge in the 1820s,[21] but it was in the next decade, after James Marsh had published an edition of the *Aids to Reflection* at Burlington in 1829, that American Coleridgeans caught fire. Coleridge was especially valuable as a religious thinker because his analysis of mind and the grounds of religious knowledge fueled arguments against both the deterministic legacy of Jonathan Edwards and the later rationalism of the Unitarians. Noah Porter, who was a divinity student during the so-called Yale revival of the 1830s, along with Nathaniel Taylor and Horace Bushnell, later wrote of the clash between the Coleridgean spirit and the sterner traditions of New England: below the surface of logic and common sense, Coleridge had "deepened the channel of psychological inquiry," and he offered a "growth in grace by the magic influence of symbols, rather than by the manly diet of prayer and preaching."[22] Porter disapproved of the "magic"—that is, the rituals—of High Church Episcopalianism, which adopted Coleridge in New York, and so the liberal theologians left the "magic influence of symbols" to be explored in a poetic and Orphic sense by Transcendentalists like Emerson and Alcott. Thus Emerson, eulogizing Coleridge in 1835, affectionately welcomed him into the band of grandees:

> But death hath now set his seal upon him, and already his true character and greatness begin to be felt. Already he quits the throng of his contemporaries and takes his lofty station in that circle of sages whom he loved: Heraclitus, Hermes, Plato, Giordano Bruno, St. Augustine.
>
> (*EL*, I, 380)

This was natural enough, since all of Coleridge's work, and *The Friend* in particular, is a repository of Orphic interpreters, and Coleridge had honored Wordsworth upon the completion of his Miltonic task (*The Prelude*, "an Orphic song indeed") in similar terms:

> O great Bard!
> Ere yet that last strain dying awed the air,
> With stedfast eye I viewed thee in the choir
> Of ever-enduring men. The truly great
> Have all one age, and from one visible space
> Shed influence! They, both in power and act,
> Are permanent, and Time is not with them,
> Save as it worketh for them, they in it.

Nor less a sacred Roll, than those of old,
And to be placed, as they, with gradual fame
Among the archives of mankind, thy work
Makes audible a linkéd lay of Truth.

("To William Wordsworth")

Emerson's debt to Coleridge is immense and varied, but what he needed most in 1831 was the talisman of the Trismegisti for the "linkéd lay of Truth" inaudible to ordinary human ears. Coleridge named it "Reason" as distinct from the Understanding, and Emerson first used this distinction in February 1831, the month when Ellen had passed into the world of the spirit.[23] "'O Reason! Reason! art not thou He whom I seek'" (*L*, I, 413: Emerson, quoting Fenelon, in 1834).

Emerson never precisely defined this "key," as he called it, perhaps because he felt that the sages had, but the two passages that illuminate it best are his letter to his brother Edward, 31 May 1834 (*L*, I, 412–413), and the journal essay on the "First Philosophy" written in June 1835 (*JMN*, V, 270–275, with several related passages). Briefly we can say that Reason was to Emerson what Coleridge defined as "vision" and what we might ordinarily call the power of intuitive insight.[24] What it implied for him, apart from the crisis over Ellen's death, was, first of all, the primacy of poetic speech:

> Poetry preceded prose, as the form of sustained thought, as Reason, whose vehicle poetry is, precedes the Understanding. When you assume the rhythm of verse and the analogy of nature, it is making proclamation, "I am now freed from the trammels of the Apparent; I speak from the Mind."
>
> (*JMN*, V, 51)

His prose was always poetic in this sense, though later, as I have already suggested, he turned to poetry as a vehicle of darkling indirection rather than the *éclaircissement* that is implied in the language of 1834–1836. Occasionally, led by

Coleridge at his most methodical in *The Friend* and by Bacon's notion of an inductively established *prima philosophia*, Emerson tried to rationalize his own "First Philosophy," in which Reason was identified with the highest level of generalization.[25] But Emerson's Reason, like Plato's dialectic, always issued in mythopoesis; it was an imaginative force, irrationally inspired, Dionysian as well as Apollonian. It was, indeed, a name he discovered for the collective and common power of the *prisci theologii* whom Coleridge had lately joined. Thus in order to properly "strengthen the hearts of the waiting lovers of the primal philosophy" Emerson thought he should lecture not just on Aristotle, Plato, Bacon, and Coleridge, but on the half-fabulous line of the Trismegisti as well, from Heraclitus through Swedenborg (*JMN*, IV, 354–355).

He touched that line in explaining figuratively the effects that Reason might work in the world.

> The Mind is very wise could it be roused into action. But the life of most men is aptly signified by the poet's personification 'Death in life.' We walk about in a sleep. A few moments in the year or in our lifetime we truly live; we are at the top of our being; we are pervaded, yea, dissolved by the Mind: but we fall back again presently. Those who are styled 'Practical men' are not awake, for they do not exercise the reason. . . .
>
> What a benefit if a rule could be given whereby the mind dreaming amidst the gross fogs of matter, could at any moment east itself and find the Sun. But the common life is an endless succession of phantasms. And long after we have deemed ourselves recovered & sound, light breaks in upon us & we find we have yet had no sane hour. Another morn rises on mid-noon.
>
> (*JMN*, V, 274–276)

Reason calls us to the things of another world, in moments of ecstasy when we are dissolved by the god within us and brightened beyond the light of common day. The great exhortation of Emerson's early essays is that we should make these moments characterize our days.

27

The central metaphor for the work of purification that would restore man's original wholeness is the dissolving of all that the Understanding implies by the superior power of Reason. Thus Reason is poetic and Orphic because it can move or melt stones and the settled world. Similarly the imagination moves mountains in Shakespeare's stories of the night and is explicitly a dissolving force for Coleridge and Wordsworth. Devoting an entire lecture to "Water" in 1834, Emerson the naturalist stressed its disintegrating effects—

> Water everywhere "appears as the most active enemy of hard and solid bodies. . . . On the shores the fragments of rock once detached become instruments of further destruction and make a part of the powerful artillery with which the ocean assails the land; they are impelled against the rocks from which they break off other fragments and the whole are thus ground against one another. Whatever be their hardness, they are reduced to gravel," whose smooth surface and round figure is the best proof of the irresistible force of this ceaseless friction.

At the same time Emerson noted its abundant recompense:

> The same power that destroys in different circumstances is made to reproduce. And few phenomena in nature are more full of interest than the series of changes by which new strata are formed and consolidated and mineralized to be again decomposed.
>
> (*EL*, I, 53–55: Emerson quoting John Playfair,
> "Illustrations of the Huttonian Theory of the Earth")

The work of water is analogous to Coleridge's poetic power that dissolves in order to recreate. Thus poetry and science confirmed the Christian and NeoPlatonic idea of divine influx, especially as interpreted by the Swedenborgians whom Emerson then knew personally. After meeting with Reed and Thomas Worcester on January 26, 1832, he quoted in his journal Worcester's remark, "God not so much sees us as dissolves us" (*JMN*, III, 324). Originally, according to Swedenborg, the spirit poured into man, circulated through him, and overflowed into the natural world which in this way was quickened through the life of man. In the corruption since the first day, however, the waters gradually retired and man himself shrunk to a drop: the giant form is reduced to a dwarf of himself. This is the language of the Orphic poet in *Nature* and the basis for the great fable of *The American Scholar*. Emerson undoubtedly thought of this motif of dissolution as reaching beyond its varied sources to traditions, which, as he put it, have always been in the world. Eventually he accepted the ancient opinion of Thales and Pindar that water is first and best among the elements because, he said, it "can run out to infinity in any direction" (*JMN*, VII, 179; cf. *EL*, I, 50). Water is said to be primarily a symbol of chaos in the Bible, but in the hermetic and alchemical traditions it is often referred to as the universal solvent and simultaneously the substance of the philosopher's stone or the *prima materia*, which is the goal of the alchemical process.[26] The circulation of water, especially its seeking the lowest level and so focusing on a central point, also figures in the alchemical work (as the *circumambulatio*) and as an image of natural precision and organization from Emerson's lecture on "Water" (*EL*, I, 55) to Thoreau's rhapsody on a thawing hillside in *Walden*.[27] Water reorders or recreates what it dissolves, and thus the way back to primordial chaos is also the way to unity, the method of reintegration for the Orphic task.

Coleridge was Emerson's *"poeta che mi guidi"* to Reason, and Reason itself was a gift brought by the long file of Trismegisti. In 1835 Emerson's mind, fired by the God within and attuned to Orphic light, saw on the darker side of things only the present and not the paradoxical way that poets and pilgrims take in their long journey to the sun. Reason is the vital energy that made *Nature* possible, because Reason justified the idea of truth revealed as distinct from truth merely synthesized, and Reason assured men of the linear, progressive history necessary for an apocalypse whose end, or return to unity, is a higher, more refined state than the original. In terms of the traditional Romantic form of spiral ascension, then, it was the idea of Reason that lifted Emerson's spires of form off the ground. Armed with this force that unfixes the solid world, Emerson's Orphic poet of 1836 could prophesy a miracle of the spirit available to every man.

Writers on Emerson who have felt the need to chart the lines of his thinking (or what Stephen Whicher called the "controlling geography of Emerson's mind") have all acknowledged the vertical line, determined by the precedence Reason takes over the Understanding, as his major axis.[28] This is a sufficiently approximate map for Emerson's first high arguments, but in 1836 the powers of the Orphic poet had hardly been tested in either prose or verse, and it is Emerson's subsequent struggle for artistic form that shows the need of cartographic revision.

II

High Arguments in the Negative Way

━━━

The way up and the way down are one and the same.

There is a harmony in the bending back, as in the cases of the bow and the lyre.

The raving Sybil utters solemn, unadorned unlovely words, but she reaches out over a thousand years with her voice because of the god within her.

> —fragments of Heraclitus, copied in Emerson's commonplace book from Coleridge's translations in *The Friend* and *The Statesman's Manual*

*E*MERSON'S PROBLEM OF VOCATION and his continuous dissatisfaction with his own art are well known. He conceived of the Orphic task in Miltonic terms, as an illumination of eternal providence; but speaking unlovely words in a husky voice, he sometimes wondered if the god was truly within. For the idealist or Transcendentalist art inevitably falls short of vision, and there is "no perfect form" that binds the "eternal fugitive" (*IX*, 89).

That was certainly Emerson's mature view, and yet for a time his work resonated with consummation, with the sounds of triumph and joy that might be expected to accompany the new kingdom his poet announced. He worried, as he prepared his first book for publication, about a crack in *Nature*, but that work was solid enough for him to describe it to Carlyle as an "entering wedge," and for Carlyle to respond by identifying this brief book as not just a first chapter but "the Foundation" and "true Apocalypse."[1] One of the things that distinguishes apocalypse as a literary motif is a sense of breaking through and of ultimate victory. Apocalypse as prophecy or actual event extirpates the *status quo*, revealing it as a false, intermediate state, and rejoices in liberating the spirit from the restraint of present forms.

Nature is an apocalyptic release from the "sepulchres of the fathers," achieved in Emerson's annunciation of the powers of Reason to his American contemporaries.[2] The crack he complained of in *Nature* was never really soldered, but somehow transcended by the impelling energy of his discovery. Through the first five chapters of his book, the idea of correspondence holds Reason and Understanding in balance, but in "Idealism" a "noble doubt" prompts Emerson to distinguish Reason as a dissolving agent and thus as the antagonist of the Understanding or things as they are:

> To the senses and the unrenewed understanding, be-
> longs a sort of instinctive belief in the absolute existence of
> nature. In their view man and nature are indissolubly
> joined. Things are ultimates, and they never look beyond
> their sphere. The presence of Reason mars this faith. The
> first effort of thought tends to relax this despotism of the
> senses which binds us to nature as if we were a part of it,
> and shows us nature aloof, and, as it were, afloat. Until this
> higher agency intervened, the animal eye sees, with won-
> derful accuracy, sharp outlines and colored surfaces. When
> the eye of Reason opens, to outline and surface are at once
> added grace and expression. These proceed from imagina-
> tion and affection, and abate somewhat of the angular dis-
> tinctness of objects. If the Reason be stimulated to more
> earnest vision, outlines and surfaces become transparent,
> and are no longer seen; causes and spirits are seen through
> them.
>
> (I, 49–50)

Reason as visionary power sets nature afloat and, as Uriel prophesies, dissolves the fixed angles of objects. So poetry too dissolves things, and is above all the work of Orpheus, not merely to move but to tame into humane forms.

[The poet] unfixes the land and the sea, makes them re-
volve around the axis of his primary thought, and disposes
them anew. Possessed himself by a heroic passion, he uses
matter as symbols of it. The sensual man conforms
thoughts to things; the poet conforms things to his
thoughts. The one esteems nature as rooted and fast; the
other, as fluid, and impresses his being thereon. To him,
the refractory world is ductile and flexible; he invests dust
and stones with humanity, and makes them the words of
Reason. The Imagination may be defined to be the use
which the Reason makes of the material world.

(I, 51–52)

This is the Orphic message, foreshadowing the later passage in "Poetry and Imagination" (VIII, 65–66), and
Shakespeare is the exemplary Orpheus of *Nature*, in all his
poetry but most sublimely for Emerson in the magic of
Ariel and Prospero, whose storm and mysterious night
work beget a morning tide of Reason in Alonzo and his
companions. And the same visionary force pervades
philosophy, science, and religion, in Emerson's most extreme statement "degrading nature and suggesting its de-
pendence on spirit" (I, 57–58).

Reason, or in the words of the Orphic poet, that mo-
mentous influx of the spirit that "alters, molds, [and]
makes" nature what it is, animates Emerson's prose after
Nature, during his years of assertion and challenge. Ironically, the power said to dissolve fixities is often fixed itself
upon the iron framework of self-reliance; that is, the dialectical structure in many of the early essays is rigidly clear
and uncompromising, nowhere as elaborately balanced
and gradually sloped as in *Nature*. "Trust thyself" rever-
berates, the lyre's single string, and the imagination is en-
listed as "an arm or weapon of the higher energy."[3] If
Emerson was still a watcher and a listener after 1835, he
was no longer listening to nature or even to the great
bards—

33

> Familiar as the voice of the mind is to each, the highest
> merit we ascribe to Moses, Plato and Milton is that they set
> at naught books and traditions, and spoke not what men,
> but what *they* thought. A man should learn to detect and
> watch that gleam of light which flashes across his mind
> from within, more than the lustre of the firmament of bards
> and sages.
>
> (II, 45)

Emerson's martial cadenzas rose spontaneously, he maintained, from his own "unknown Center," and to express
this flash-of-lightning faith he summoned not argument or
proof, but the very shape of the energy he avowed: wave
upon wave of assertion, all striking from one direction, and
so building a tremendous cumulative force and finally
shattering the rock of opposition. There is Emerson's
primary Orphic metaphor, in martial dress, and a splendid
later quatrain epitomizes the strategy and effect of his early
prose:

> All day the waves assailed the rock,
> I heard no church-bell chime,
> The sea-beat scorns the minster clock
> And breaks the glass of Time.
>
> (IX, 345)

Scorning the clock-logic of the Understanding, Emerson
assails the ordinary with all the repeated power of a central, oceanic awareness, and nearly every paragraph of essays like "The Over-Soul" or "Spiritual Laws" works as an
analogy or variation of this assault.

In such art Emerson's high argument found its first meters and he was for a time a singer in prose, chanting an
exuberance that is rare in any literature. This is, as Bloom
has said, Emerson closest to Blake: Urizen is the god of
boundaries or the Understanding, and Ulro its rocky
prison; the supposition of "Idealism," that nature exists
only "in the apocalypse of the mind," opens the prospect
of *Nature*, which is an awakening of the giant Albion.

34

The ruin or the blank that we see when we look at nature, is in our own eye. The axis of vision is not coincident with the axis of things, and so they appear not transparent but opaque. The reason why the world lacks unity, and lies broken and in heaps, is because man is disunited with himself.

(I, 73–74)

Similarly, Emerson himself quoted Blake in his journal— "For the eye altering alters all" (*J*, IX, 557)—and more extensively in "Poetry and Imagination":

William Blake, whose abnormal genius, Wordsworth said, interested him more than the conversation of Scott or of Byron, writes thus: "He who does not imagine in stronger and better lineaments and in stronger and better light than his perishing mortal eye can see, does not imagine at all. The painter of this work asserts that all his imaginations appear to him infinitely more perfect and more minutely organized than anything seen by his mortal eye. . . . I assert for myself that I do not behold the outward creation, and that to me it would be a hindrance, and not action. I question not my corporeal eye any more than I would question a window concerning a sight. I look through it, not with it."

(VIII, 27–28)

This Emersonian lustre from "A Vision of the Last Judgment" was first published in 1863 among the selections that Dante Gabriel Rossetti made for Alexander Gilchrist's *Life of Blake*; there is no evidence that Emerson had read Blake (whom he referred to as "the painter") before that year.[4]

Thus it appears that Emerson even at his closest to Blake in 1836 did not know him, and he kept a distance we should carefully observe. The architectonics or minute organization of *Nature* that suggests Blake's "Organiz'd Innocence" is the legacy of correspondence that Emerson took most directly from Swedenborg, Wordsworth, and the book of natural history. Both Blake and Emerson eventually rejected Swedenborg, and for similar reasons—

impatience with the machinery of dogma, and in Blake's words, with the "confident insolence sprouting from systematic reasoning." Blake added another, significantly, that Swedenborg conversed only with angels and not with devils; he lacked the "Energy, called Evil" that is "Eternal Delight" and that Blake and other Romantics associated with Milton's grand creature Satan. Had he read *Nature* Blake might have pronounced the divine energy in the chapter on "Spirit" as of the body and Satanic. Indeed, Emerson's Orphic poet edges toward Orc or Prometheus, the classical Lucifer. The Orphic poet of *Nature* is certainly closer to Bacon's Prometheus, who exalted man above his common station in *The Wisdom of the Ancients*, than to Bacon's Orpheus, who civilized man under law. Bacon was Emerson's source for the version of Prometheus he gave in his lecture on "The Age of Fable" in 1835 (*EL*, I, 257–259), and Emerson later (*JMN*, VII, 506–507) called the myth a true history of the "invention of the mechanic Arts" and the *Prometheus Bound* of Aeschylus a "grand effort of Imagination" showing the power of the poet to construct a whole and take a place in the world. Like his hero, Aeschylus was, in Emerson's view, a constructivist of the imagination, a builder and a maker of things. Moreover, the power of Reason in *Nature* can be adequately re-mythologized as the spark of heaven, the original virtue linking man with a prior and essentially different order of being, to use the language of Milton in the *De Doctrina Christiana*, and of Coleridge, who used identical terms to decipher the myth of Prometheus in 1825.[5]

The Orphic poet undertakes a Promethean role as rebel and artificer of actual change when he boldly, if ambiguously, prophesies a "correspondent revolution in things"; so does the single man of *The American Scholar* who plants himself on his instincts waiting for the huge world to come round to him (I, 115), and the preacher who tells the Divinity School students, "Wherever a man comes, there comes revolution" (I, 144). If Emerson reins in this energy with softer modulations, as he did through much of *Nature*, there are no limits in "Self-Reliance":

> And truly it demands something godlike in him who has cast off the common motives of humanity and has ventured to trust himself for a task-master. High be his heart, faithful his will, clear his sight, that he may in good earnest be doctrine, society, law, to himself, that a simple purpose may be to him as strong as iron necessity is to others!
>
> (II, 74–75)

The ministerial Dimmesdale in Emerson is now left to others; this is the rare, authentic voice of Prometheus in America, to be heard again in *Moby-Dick* when Father Mapple calls out for the delight of an inexorable selfhood and awakens Captain Ahab, or when the declining Thoreau is inspired by the meteorite John Brown. For a moment Emerson placed himself centrally within the tradition interpreted by Blake:

> On my saying, "What have I to do with the sacredness of traditions, if I live wholly from within?" my friend suggested,—"But these impulses may be from below, not from above." I replied, "They do not seem to me to be such; but if I am the Devil's child, I will live then from the Devil."
>
> (II, 50)

But over time this Promethean voice turned out to be double-edged: if it pointed toward wildest freedom and the renewal of spirit promised by the Orphic poet of *Nature*, it also undercut the hierarchy of Reason.

In *Nature* the world Emerson envisioned was truly fluid, for the "angular distinctness" of objects, their outlines and surfaces, are said to disappear when we see imaginatively. At the same time, the world of *Nature* was ordered and knowable, because, as Emerson wrote later, "things correspond." Emerson's Reason did not operate within an unstructured universe, and in the essays it depends upon an implicit vertical and hierarchical order. As an artist

Emerson needed the assurance of that order, so that in denying the distinction between "above" and "below" he may have exalted the human imagination in general, but he also weakened the foundations of his established aesthetic form. In the end the great difference between Emerson and Blake is the difference between the man who wrote, "I have no System" (*J*, V, 326) and the one who makes Los say, "I must Create a System or be enslav'd by another Man's." It is Uriel's "unit and universe are round" and Emerson's dream of no circumferences opposed to Blake's golden rule of life and art set down in the "Descriptive Catalogue" for his 1809 exhibition—"the more distinct, sharp, and wirey the bounding line, the more perfect the work of art, and the less keen and sharp, the greater the evidence of weak imitation, plagiarism, and bungling." When Emerson pursued the full implications of his discovery that "everything is in flight" (VIII, 5), he veered away from Blake, who believed that for the imagination to follow nature in this way could lead only to "watr'y Shadows."

In this shifting intellectual stance is the beginning of Emerson's negative way. It is not a matter of personal crisis, though he certainly recognized the kind of experience dramatized in Romantic autobiographies and in 1839 spoke of "this crisis in the life of each earnest man, which comes in so forbidding and painful aspect" (*EL*, III, 102). In fact, for Emerson "negative" was at first an attribute of Reason, probably in the same sense that the *via negativa* has traditionally been the necessary means to knowledge of God.[6]

> I know nothing of the source of my being, but I will not soil my nest. I know much of it after a high negative way, but nothing after the understanding.
>
> (*J*, III, 517)

The "high negative way" of this journal entry in 1835 underlies the transcendence of *Nature*, yet it should be noted that the comparable passage in *Nature* (I, 59) is actu-

ally intended to restrain Emerson's idealism. The limits of
negative affirmation are even sharper in his fullest artistic
version of the negative theology, a poem which according
to the Centenary editor (IX, 510) must have been written
before 1840:

> In many forms we try
> To utter God's infinity,
> But the boundless hath no form,
> And the Universal Friend
> Doth as far transcend
> An angel as a worm.
>
> The great Idea baffles wit,
> Language falters under it,
> It leaves the learned in the lurch;
> Nor art, nor power, nor toil can find
> The measure of the eternal Mind,
> Nor hymn, nor prayer, nor church.
>
> (IX, 359)

"The Bohemian Hymn" acknowledged that revelation
must be, in Baconian terms, a dark or poetic way; it hinted,
too, of an ultimate and necessary failure, and at the very
point in Emerson's life when the energy generated in *Nature* began to falter under the great task of definition.

In 1836 Emerson had been positive and assured, speaking almost *ex cathedra* about our knowledge of the world.
"Philosophically considered, the universe is composed of
Nature and the Soul," and if nature or the NOT ME, taken as
a whole, was a problem to be solved, he expressed utter
confidence that the solution was at hand:

> Undoubtedly we have no questions to ask which are un-
> answerable. We must trust the perfection of creation so far
> as to believe that whatever curiosity the order of things has
> awakened in our minds, the order of things can satisfy.
> Every man's condition is a solution in hieroglyphic to those
> inquiries he would put. He acts it as life, before he ap-
> prehends it as truth. In like manner, nature is already, in its
> forms and tendencies, describing its own design.
>
> (I, 3–4)

The "order of things," foreshadowing the full doctrine of correspondence, justified this assurance. When Emerson wrote that Plato acknowledged the ineffable yet believed things were knowable, he added, "They are knowable because, being from one, things correspond. There is a scale; and the correspondence of heaven to earth, of matter to mind, of part to the whole, is our guide" (IV, 62). For the interpretation of hieroglyphics we were asked not to cipher or calculate but simply to depend upon "Reason" or spontaneous moments of inward revelation when answers come effortlessly and astonishingly clear. Thus the Orphic poet of 1836 pierced easily into central truth.

Three years later this native simile was distinctly jarred. The universe could be perceived differently, as "*two*," "Me and It," not as one, and with things unknowable because they are unrelated—so the poet confided (*JMN*, VII, 200). Still he reassured himself that the destiny of man was to advance continuously into "Chaos & the Dark" (*JMN*, VII, 12), and through this shadowy world he would have followed the first guides of the negative theology, Plato and Heraclitus.[7] Yet in the summer of 1841, lecturing at Waterville, Maine, he admitted that he was unable to pierce an inch (I, 196). "The method of nature: who could ever analyze it? That rushing stream will not stop to be observed" (I, 199). The old question, "To what end is Nature?" (I, 4), could no longer be posed—nature "does not exist to any one or any number of particular ends, but to numberless and endless benefit" (I, 203–204). Such multiplicity defies definition or reduction. The order of 1836 had been grounded in the belief that "every appearance in nature corresponds to some state of mind" and "there is nothing lucky or capricious in these analogies" (I, 26, 27). In contrast to this rather fixed, Swedenborgian correspondence, the flux of words as well as things is paramount in Emerson's journal of 1841:

> The Metamorphosis of nature shows itself in nothing
> more than this that there is no word in our language that
> cannot become typical to us of nature by giving it em-
> phasis. . . . Swifter than light the World converts itself into
> that thing you name & all things find their right place under
> this new & capricious classification.
>
> (*JMN*, VIII, 23)

The analogies that were in 1836 neither lucky nor capricious are now exactly that; the symbol held up earlier as
knowledge of a discrete world is now offered for its "shock
of pleasure," the surprising, kaleidoscopic insight it gives.
Symbolic knowledge is still a kind of knowledge—indeed,
perhaps the only kind of knowledge—but valuable now
because things are free rather than fixed, and because no
one set of correspondences is adequate to express nature—"the slippery Proteus is not so easily caught" (IV,
121).

The idea of metamorphosis liberated Emerson as a practicing poet, but it also washed away some of his foundation
for transcendence. Figuratively, after 1840, nature is no
longer transparent but opaque and impenetrable, so that
no man can pronounce confidently on its underlying form:

> I conceive a man as always spoken to from behind, and
> unable to turn his head and see the speaker. In all the
> millions who have heard the voice, none ever saw the
> face. . . . That well known voice speaks in all languages,
> governs all men, and none ever caught a glimpse of its
> form.
>
> (I, 209)

In Emerson's metaphor of the "rushing stream," the
power of Reason to dissolve the natural world is transferred to nature itself. "I grow" is nature's only response to
man's inquiries in "The Method of Nature," and there is
no hint of anything beyond or below this "perpetual in-
choation" to make transcendence even conceivable—
nature contains all.

Emerson maintained that metamorphosis was progressive, changing always in the direction of greatest benefit for the whole, but he could not free himself from the notion of mere process, of "equivalence and indifferency" (II, 317), that prompted darker questions: "Must we not suppose somewhere in the universe a slight treachery and derision?" (III, 193). As lecturer and essayist he labored to explain away his own supposition, but could not rest upon proofs. Sometimes he admitted that in the philosopher's long-run game of chance there were no winners:

> The whole game at which the philosopher busies himself every day, year in, year out, is to find the upper & the under side of every block in his way. Nothing so large & nothing so thin but it has two sides, and when he has seen the outside he turns it over to see the other face. We never tire of this game, because ever a slight shudder of astonishment pervades us at the exhibition of the other side of the button,—at the contrast of the two sides. The head & the tail are called in the language of philosophy *Finite & Infinite*, Visible & Spiritual, Relative & Absolute, Apparent & Eternal, & many more fine names.
>
> (*JMN*, VIII, 82)

In the essays written between 1841 and 1844 this continuous turning confounds the thrust of assertion based on Emerson's certain sense that Reason pointed "above" and the Understanding "below." The ascending, vertical axis of his earlier work is flattened, so that Reason cannot defeat or even complete the Understanding; instead, the two are set against each other in an equitable and horizontal polarity. After 1840 Emerson's writing moves by such balanced antitheses or counterstatements, and not in parallel waves of assertion. Victory seems indistinguishable from defeat (*JMN*, VIII, 228), and the essays themselves appear as stalemates, games of rhetoric played with mellowed detachment in place of imaginative zeal. They illustrate Emerson's recognition that "the play of the understanding & the use of the hands" can be as effective as "transcendent methods" (*JMN*, VIII, 343). If they rise to divine conclusions, they do so not with Plato's architecture of ascent but by Merlin's "staircase of surprise," a verbal magic that astonishes us if it does not always convince. This is the "anti-method" induced by metamorphosis, and through it Emerson became the man Margaret Fuller described, who "really seemed to believe there were two sides to every subject, and even to intimate higher ground from which each might be seen to have an infinite number of sides."[8]

Turning in this Heraclitean flux, Emerson drew closer to the dark ways of contemporaries like Hawthorne, Melville, Poe, and Dickinson.[9] Like Clifford and Hepzibah Pyncheon in *The House of the Seven Gables*, he learned that even his beautiful figure of an ascending spiral curve had its two sides: progress toward unity or the One is, on its other side, the restrained and retrospective return to origins which is the discipline of history. Thus the "seeker with no Past" at his back (II, 318) would also write that no god "can shake the Past / . . . Alter or mend eternal Fact" (IX, 258). Like Ishmael in *Moby-Dick*, too, when he has looked too long on one side of nature and so lost his bearings, Emerson sought a compensatory balance, rescuing himself with great metaphors of "Rest" and "Motion" or "Identity" and "Diversity."[10] Looking over the edge of the vortex or out beyond the dip of bell, Emerson pondered the true relation between center and circumference; in its adjustment to slippery surfaces and peripheries his art loses the logic and certainty of the negative theology.[11]

Whim, or the principle of succession by moods, is the existential counterpart of the antithesis in prose, and it dictated much of Emerson's inner process during these years so that his path is difficult to trace. But unquestionably he reached a philosophical abyss after the death of his five-year-old son Waldo in 1842. In a sense, intellect had prepared for this crisis, and perhaps it was Emerson's prior attention to appearances that made him write in 1843 that

grief taught him nothing of reality (III, 48–49). Nevertheless, it did crack his faith, assuring him that the "ugly
breaks" in experience were irreparable (*J*, VI, 488). This
loss of a child sent to repair faltering language (*JMN*, VIII,
164) was a "broken prophecy" (IX, 154) and proof that
words and things were irreconcilably separated.

> We learn with joy & wonder this new & flattering art of
> language deceived by the exhilaration that accompanies the
> attainment of each new word. We fancy we gain somewhat;
> we gain nothing. It seemed to men that words came nearer
> to the thing; described the fact; were the fact. They learn
> later that they only suggest it. It is an operose circuitous
> way of putting us in mind of the thing,—of flagellating our
> attention. But this was slowly discovered. With what good
> faith these old books of barbarous men record the genesis of
> the world. Their best attempts to narrate how it is that star
> & earth & man exist, run out into some gigantic mythology,
> which, when it is ended, leaves the beautiful simple facts
> where they were, & the stupid gazing fabulist just as far
> from them as at first. Garrulity is our religion & philosophy.
> They wonder and are angry that some persons slight their
> book, & prefer the thing itself. But with all progress this
> happens, that speech becomes less, & finally ceases in a
> nobler silence.
>
> (*JMN*, VIII, 286–287: October 1842)

The "nobler silence" of this passage is not the pure silence
of Keatsian melodies nor the golden silence of Carlyle; it is
rather a disillusioned and stoic denial of the apocalyptic
marriage and apparently a rejection of Emerson's once revered "band of grandees." The impotence of words, of
myth, and of the fabulist himself is an awesome subject for
the artist, begetting what is perhaps the final Romantic
irony, the language of silence and the inevitable dismem-
berment of Orpheus the poet. After 1842 Emerson's art is
never free from this ironic awareness that would deny his
own vital mythology, and the silence that stole into his
poetry overcame the man in his last years. As a Romantic
poet Emerson faced the spectre of correspondence—"this

discrepance," he definitively named it in the essay titled "Experience."

This lately recognized masterpiece is the true complement of *Nature. Nature* was, in a deeply personal sense, a sublime elegy, the recreation of a spiritual order in which Emerson might be reunited with his dead wife; "Experience," alluding to the death of his son, is a persevering refusal to mourn the destruction of that order. No bare conclusion or frame can do justice to the texture of this work. There is throughout a sense of the old architecture ruined, of Emerson adjusting his art when he cannot drive down pilings—the poetic strategy of "Experience" is suggested in his journal remarks about nature being "without depth, but with immeasurable lateral spaces" (*JMN,* IX, 68) and the sage's discovery that his "wedge turns out to be a rocket" (*JMN,* VII, 457). If *Nature* was a wedge into the center of things, "Experience" is an exploration of the surface lighted by a brief candle. It moves in a procession of the lords of life, but it is not orderly or clearly ascending;[12] rather, as the opening suggests, the staircase or ladder of the Romantic spiral appears like a demonic, Piranesian or Dickensian parody: "Where do we find ourselves? In a series of which we do not know the extreme, and believe that it has none. We wake and find ourselves on a stair; there are stairs above us, many a one, which go upward and out of sight" (III, 45). The labyrinth of the lords, true to Emerson's aggregate imagery of distorting glass and revolving barrels, is intentionally disorienting; Emerson's readers are spoken to from all angles and lost in the bewildering vicissitudes of life.

The lesson of "Experience" is the necessity of accommodation. Caught in this swirling motion, we must, as Emerson suggested more leisurely in the 1843 journal, use the faculty of the Understanding and its extension in our hands and feet. The high Romantic quest must assume the lower, more practical path of the Christian pilgrim, as

Michael Cowan has shown in his fine treatment of this essay.[13] Redemption is on the highway, but Emerson warns against misconception of the journey. Like Hawthorne, Emerson was suspicious of Celestial Railroads; Mr. Smooth-it-away could not simplify this tortuous and baffling route, nor would a Promethean like Ethan Brand find succor on this way. For Brand's quest, symbolized by a dog chasing its own tail, was doomed by subjectiveness, and he did not realize until too late that such a completed circuit, as Emerson writes of the kitten, is merely a "solitary performance" and a dark parody of any real human connection (III, 80).

The problem of "Experience," then, is how do we lose ourselves to find ourselves, and how is the way down also a way up. Emerson cannot rest in central truth or the paradoxes of the negative theology because "life is not dialectics," and because "subjectiveness," the backlash within reality or idealism, tells him that the abyss cannot be denied: "Marriage (in what is called the spiritual world) is impossible, because of the inequality between every subject and object" (III, 77). Flaxman's drawing of *The Eumenides* is an emblem of "this disparity," "the irreconcilableness of the two spheres" (III, 82). In the closing paragraph Emerson still does not know "the value and law of this discrepance," though he insists that someday he will. "We shall win at the last," he says, if we are not deceived by time, if we ask not for rash effects but patiently use a sufficient private fruit. This private fruit is consciousness without correspondent results, bolstered by the faith that God is "a native of these bleak rocks," and I take it to be the only paradise at the end of the circuitous journey of "Experience." In Christian and Miltonic history there is an end or apocalyptic juncture where the two spheres meet, and an explicit apocalyptic vision of that event, as in Revelation and in Book XII of *Paradise Lost*. In "Experience"

46

Emerson is true to his initial awareness that the spiral stairs go upward and out of sight, and the slumbering Eumenides dramatize the gap between man and god as well as the endlessness of that condition. Thus the end of the journey is never envisioned but can only be guessed at by observing the natural process, which, as Emerson wrote later in "Fate," pleases at "sufficient perspective" (VI, 36).

In a very literal sense, then, God inhabits these bleak rocks because providence is another word for natural history. Without the vision, the endless pilgrimage can be redeemed only by a revised understanding of walking, which is commended at every step of "Experience." The steps themselves are transvalued in what may be called the motif of the "wayside paradise"—this phrase, epitomizing the Indian summer atmosphere that often steals into New England literary pilgrimages, is taken from *The Marble Faun*:

> [Miriam and Donatello] had reached a wayside paradise, in their mysterious life-journey, where they both threw down the burden of the before and after, and . . . were happy in the flitting moment.
>
> (XLVII)

The burden of prophecy removed, they savor a brief moment along the way, not for its flash of visionary power but for some less exalted sense of satisfaction. Such moments are the goal of "Experience":

> To finish the moment, to find the journey's end in every step of the road, to live the greatest number of good hours, is wisdom.
>
> (III, 60)

These are not the brief experiences of "The Transcendentalist" (I, 352), which were cherished for the substance of their vision; under the reign of metamorphosis all tropes are convertible, and so moments are valued for the surprise or pleasurable shock they afford. Surprising, for example, is Emerson's interpolation of Luke 17:20 compared with its place in *Nature*: there it meant that the kingdom of man over nature is seen not with but through the eye; in "Experience" there is no kingdom over nature, and "the kingdom that cometh without observation" (III, 68) means only that nature is indirect and practical successes often occur without our really noticing them. These successes are exercises of talent or craftsmanship: "We live amid surfaces, and the true art of life is to skate well on them" (III, 59). Thus we are advised to acquiesce in the present fragmented state of man:

> A man is like a bit of Labrador spar, which has no lustre as you turn it in your hand until you come to a particular angle; then it shows deep and beautiful colors. There is no adaptation or universal applicability in men, but each has his special talent, and the mastery of successful men consists in adroitly keeping themselves where and when that turn shall be oftenest to be practiced. . . . Of course it needs the whole society to give the symmetry we seek. The party-colored wheel must revolve very fast to appear white.
> (III, 57)

This is a fairly explicit renunciation of the myth of the Whole Man, substituting a myth of the whole in which each man is a specialized part. Its implications carry over into *The Conduct of Life*, where the first step in the economy of power is "stopping off decisively our miscellaneous activity and concentrating our force on one or a few points," and even poetry is resolved as the right application of force, a product of necessity rather than inspiration (VI, 73–74). Nature, the whole, "is reckless of the individual," and we become truly "victims of adaptation" (VI, 138–139).

"Experience" is the spiritual nadir of Emerson's prose. It cannot be read as any kind of imaginative entrance into the Celestial City[14] because, although the way down may be also a way up, there is no end to this spiral journey, no connection between the two realms. Emerson seriously parodies the Romantic staircase by converting it to a maze of illusions. At the same time, "Experience" is not an un-mitigated nightmare, for the remedy of the "wayside paradise" is as serious a proposal as the parody.[15] The poet of "Experience" seeks his proper level and would walk the hairline of this present state; if he probes neither in deep nor out far, then

> everything good is on the highway. The middle region of our being is the temperate zone. We may climb into the thin and cold realm of pure geometry and lifeless science, or sink into that of sensation. Between these extremes is the equator of life, of thought, of spirit, of poetry—a narrow belt.
>
> (III, 62)

The reiterated compromises of "Experience," embracing the "mid-world" and a "strong present tense," suggest that the "true romance" of Emerson's conclusion is realized in the conversion of genius to talent and the adap-tation of the poet to the method of nature.

III

Orpheus in the Mid-World

———

Freudig war, vor vielen Jahren,
Eifrig so der Geist bestrebt,
Zu erforschen, zu erfahren,
Wie Natur im Schaffen lebt.
Und es ist das ewig Eine,
Das sich vielfach offenbart:
Klein das Grosse, gross das
    Kleine,
Alles nach der eignen Art;
Immer wechselnd, fest sich
    haltend,
Nah und fern und fern und nah,
So gestaltend, umgestaltend—
Zum Erstaunen bin ich da.
         —GOETHE, "Parabase"*

The two extremes are equally disowned
By reason: if with sharp recoil, from one
You have been driven far as its opposite,
Between them seek the point whereon to build
Sound expectations.
         —WORDSWORTH, *The Excursion*, IV

Unity or Identity, & Variety. The poles of philosophy.
It makes haste to develop these two. A too rapid
Unity or unification & a too exclusive devotion to
parts are the Scylla & Charybdis.

Nor mount, nor dive; all good things keep
The midway of the eternal deep.
         —EMERSON, Journals and "Saadi"

---

*Many years ago, as now, my mind strove with eager delight to
study and discover the creative life of Nature. It is eternal Unity in
manifold manifestation: the great is little, the little is great, and

GOD IN NATURE . . . weed by the wall,"—Emerson described his own psychic oscillations in "Circles" (II, 307). Out of these moody highs and lows that spot the essays and journals of the 1840s he seems to have concluded that the primary task of the artist is to create the mid-world that is best. From this dialectic emerges a new Orpheus, no longer the philosopher-priest who sees revealed truth and molds the world in its image, but Orpheus as the poet of metamorphoses who synthesizes or reconciles the manifold meanings of every dark, flowing fact.[1] This poet follows the method of nature, since nature is the perfect whole. As the myth of the Whole Man recedes in Emerson's attention, so does the name of Orpheus, who is not prominently mentioned in the later essays. But the Orphic lineaments are plain in Emerson's protagonists and idealized poet-figures; in poems and essays the Renaissance Orpheus is not so much abandoned as naturalized, often through the interpretations of Emerson's immediate Orphic predecessors.

Coleridge and Goethe are most important in this respect, for they both suggested theories of polarity as the essential method of nature, and both implied that this knowledge had been long preserved in the oldest philosophical traditions. Coleridge had inspired Emerson's lofty concept of Reason in the early 1830s, at a time when the *Aids to Reflection* might well have been the most important book in America for liberal theologians. Emerson's own assessment of Coleridge's works in 1836 is therefore especially instructive:

---

everything after its kind; ever changing and yet preserving itself, near and far and far and near, and so shaping and re-shaping itself—I am here to wonder at it.

His works are of very unequal interest; the Aids to Reflex-
ion, though a useful book I suppose, is the least valuable. In
his own judgment, half the Biography and the third volume
of the Friend from the beginning of the Essay on Method to
the end with a few of his poems were all that he would
preserve of his works. In this judgment, if you add the
invaluable little book called Church and State which was
written afterwards, I suppose all good judges would
concur.

(EL, I, 379)

Valuable as the distinction between Reason and Understanding was, Emerson seemed to be turning his interest
toward Coleridge's analysis of philosophical method. The
chapters of *The Friend* referred to are best known for the
attempt to reconcile Plato and Bacon who differ, according
to Coleridge, simply in approaching truth from opposite
poles, ideal and material respectively. Coleridge's "bi-
polar" or dynamic philosophy is the subject of several
chapters in the *Biographia Literaria*, where it is traced
through the Renaissance NeoPlatonists and Jacob Boehme
to F.W.C. Schelling and then sketched, in Chapter XII,
once again in terms of opposite poles, subjective and objective, which necessarily imply each other. Coleridge's most
complete exposition of polarity, *The Theory of Life*, was not
available until 1848, but the importance of this idea could
be gauged from one of his typically awesome footnotes in
The Friend:

> EVERY POWER IN NATURE AND IN SPIRIT *must evolve an opposite, as the
> sole means and condition of its manifestation*: AND ALL OPPOSITION IS
> A TENDENCY TO RE-UNION. This is the universal Law of Polarity
> or essential Dualism, first promulgated by Heraclitus, 2000
> years afterwards re-published, and made the foundation
> both of Logic, of Physics, and of Metaphysics by Giordano
> Bruno. The Principle may be thus expressed. The *Identity* of
> Thesis and Antithesis is the substance of all *Being*: their
> *Opposition* the condition of all *Existence*, or Being man-
> ifested; and every *Thing* or Phaenomenon is the Exponent

of a Synthesis as long as the opposite energies are retained
in that Synthesis.

(The Friend, I, xiii)

Actual or phenomenal life, Coleridge repeated in both *The
Statesman's Manual* and *The Theory of Life*, is the equilibrium, the balance or "indifference" of opposite energies.[2]

After 1836 Emerson went to Coleridge's own sources,
Heraclitus and Plato most intensively in 1840, but reading
also in Boehme and, as his German improved, in Schelling. Already in 1840, however, he told Carlyle that he had
read all fifty-five volumes of Goethe's *Werke* (1828) in German,[3] and he certainly knew Goethe in translation as well.
A profound and painstaking corroboration of Coleridge's
method was to be found in Goethe, who carried Emerson
furthest along the way to a reconciliation between poetry
and science. Wordsworth represented that role before
1835, a naturalist poet reinforcing Swedenborg from below. In *The Dial* for 1840 Emerson wrote that *The Excursion*
"was a great joy," nearer to nature than any predecessor,
but from Wordsworth he turned almost immediately to
Goethe who most fully represented the tendencies of the
age (XII, 320–322). Method for Emerson implied observation and "progressive arrangement" (*JMN*, VI, 222). The
epithet "Writer," given to Goethe in *Representative Men*,
means primarily recording observer (Emerson uses the
word "secretary"), and this characterization goes back to
the spring of 1836 when he commented on "Goethe the
observer": "What industry of observation! What impatience of words! To read Goethe is an economy of Time; for
you shall find no word that does not stand for a thing . . ."
(*JMN*, V, 133). Contrary to most Emersonian passages, the
suggestion here is of words fastened to things in a scientific
or descriptive sense. Goethe was a respecter of surfaces
and of exhaustive details: Emerson, who believed that the
arcs of his circle could never be joined, chided Goethe in

1837 for thinking it necessary to "dot round as it were the entire sphere of knowables" (*JMN*, V, 306), but when he began to think about the continuity of the whole, he looked to Goethe as "the philosopher of this multiplicity" (IV, 271). For Goethe was not a mere collector, like Bacon in Emerson's view (*EL*, I, 335). Goethe saw all the dots and the connections between them; "he never stopped at surface, but pierced the purpose of a thing" (XII, 324). In the 1840s, when all was in flight, connections were paramount: with "everything undressing and stealing away from its old into new form, and nothing fast but those invisible cords which we call laws, on which all is strung . . . the interest is gradually transferred from the forms to the lurking method" (VIII, 5).

Goethe's scientific method is predicated on the notion of constancy or homogeneity in nature, the assumption of continuous series without breaks, and the authority of Goethe together with the impact of Charles Lyell's *Principles of Geology* may have moved Emerson away from the catastrophism implied in his early lectures on science. Goethe's principle of development in individual organisms is one of repeated variations on an original, simple archetype, as in the hypothesized *Urpflanze*, and these, as the *Metamorphoses of Plants* makes clear, occur in polar stages of expansion and contraction. Pointing to the similarities between Goethe's model and the seven qualities or spiritual stages of Boehme, Ronald Gray has suggested that Goethe's theories are the outgrowth of his youthful alchemical and mystical studies, and Emerson's passage from Swedenborgian correspondence to a metamorphic view of nature appears to be a parallel route.[4] "Polarity is the law of all being," Emerson wrote in his journal in April 1837 (*JMN*, V, 304), when he was studying Goethe most intensively, and "the great principle of Undulation" is central to the American scholar who "now thinks, now acts" in order to maintain the wholeness or totality of his being (I, 98–99).[5] When he later explained what he called "the poetic curve of Nature" Emerson cited Goethe as a naturalist of imagination (VIII, 10–11).

> The electric word pronounced by John Hunter a hundred years ago, *arrested and progressive development*, indicating the way upward from the invisible protoplasm to the highest organisms, gave the poetic key to Natural Science, of which the theories of Geoffrey Saint-Hilaire, of Oken, of Goethe, of Agassiz and Owen and Darwin in zoology and botany, are the fruits. . . .
>
> Identity of law, perfect order in physics, perfect parallelism between the laws of Nature and the laws of thought exist. In botany we have the like, the poetic perception of metamorphosis,—that the same vegetable point or eye which is the unit of the plant can be transformed at pleasure into every part, as bract, leaf, petal, stamen, pistil or seed.
>
> (VIII, 7–8)

Emerson's eclecticism on this point defies precision. Coleridge probably led him to Hunter, whose museum Emerson visited first in 1833, and then again with Richard Owen in 1848, but the "electric word" has not been found in Hunter's writings. Emerson defined, in a fairly loose sense, two primary concepts of evolution or development: first, Hunter's idea, defended by Coleridge, of a "germ" or principle of life prior to organization; and secondly, a theory of development in which the arrest or progress of given tendencies produced an increasingly differentiated organism. Emerson probably regarded both these "laws" as approximations of Goethe's own theories of archetypal and polar development, and his account of metamorphosis, given above, is certainly derived from Goethe's study of plants.[6]

This passage from "Poetry and Imagination" was probably written after 1860, but, significantly, by 1849 Emerson's evolutionary verses had replaced a quotation from Plotinus as the motto for *Nature*:

A subtle chain of countless rings
The next unto the farthest brings;
The eye reads omens where it goes,
And speaks all languages the rose;
And, striving to be man, the worm
Mounts through all the spires of form.

(I, 1)

Striving—in Faust's own words, *"das Streben meiner ganzen Kraft"*—is the mark of a Faustian spirit, and an evolution similar to that of Emerson's worm is ironically promised to the alchemical Homunculus by Thales and Proteus in Part II of *Faust* (Act II); but the fate of Euphorion, child of Helena and Faust, a messianic poet and an Icarus-figure, makes clear by contrast that Faust's real strength lies not in flight, but in the most refined use of the earth.

At the summit of Emerson's natural history is man joining poetry and science, for poetry re-creates nature in a conscious act of the mind (VII, 37–39). In all poetry he found "metonymy," which he probably intended to mean the act of relating a part to the larger whole: ". . . the poet listens to conversation and beholds all objects in Nature, to give back, not them, but a new and transcendent whole" (VIII, 17). It is difficult to disentangle Emerson from Coleridge and Schelling at this point, and there is a remarkable analogy between Schelling awaiting the new Homer in 1811 and Emerson and Whitman longing for an American messiah a generation later.[7] But, as Goethe tempered the spirit of Romantic poetry, so the heroic and messianic qualities of Emerson's poet-figure are tempered throughout the 1840s by his role as mediator within the polar development and organization of nature. Emerson's figure emerges as the poet "described in *ideal* perfection" in the *Biographia Literaria*, who "diffuses a tone and spirit of unity, that blends, and (as it were) *fuses*" human faculties through the imagination, "that synthetic and magical power . . . [that] reveals itself in the balance or reconciliation of opposite or

56

discordant qualities."[8] Emerson's poet "is the person in whom these powers [of perception and of articulation] are in balance," and he "represents beauty" because "Beauty is the creator of the universe" (III, 7). The Orphic poet of *Nature* coveted truth and imposed upon the natural world his transcendent power of Reason; this poet, aware that he works as an integral part of an unfathomable, fluid whole, expresses that transcendent whole through an immanent, mediatory power analogous to that by which nature itself operates. Thus the poetic power, "while it blends and harmonizes the natural and the artificial, still subordinates art to nature."[9]

Man at the summit of the process is still part of the process. He must listen to nature, because the magic in art is simply the method of nature. Resisting the corpuscular universe of Newton, Coleridge insisted upon the interpenetrability of forces in nature, a conception that Goethe and Carlyle expressed poetically as *"der ewigen Weberin Meisterstuck,"* the eternal Weaver's masterpiece woven on the Loom of Time.[10] In *The Conduct of Life* Emerson appropriated this motif for the natural order, and in his metonymic view the "convertibility of every thing into every other thing" makes "Eleusinian mysteries" of ordinary facts (VI, 304). We may not know the exact laws of translation, Emerson wrote in the essay on "Beauty," but he quoted Goethe's assurance that " 'the beautiful is a manifestation of the secret laws of nature' " (VI, 288). In general, however, Emerson understood beauty as an expression of evolution and dynamic equilibrium in nature. It is the adaptation of form to purpose or function (VII, 53) and always "the mean of many extremes" (VI, 289); it is the more excellent symmetry achieved in moving or developing forms, which all follow the theory of dancing, seeking to "recover continually in changes the lost equilibrium, not by abrupt and angular but by gradual and curving movements" (VI, 292). The hero who reveals nature does not fix himself on a center but flows in the middle of the stream (*JMN*, VIII, 331); the reality he unfolds is neither pure action nor pure thought:

> The nearsighted people have much to say about action. But I can well say that the singing Iopas seems to me as great as the sworded Hector. It is by no means action, which is the essential point, but some middle quality indifferent both to poet & to actor, and which we call reality. . . . Not action, not speculation imports, but a middle essence common to both.
>
> (*JMN*, IX, 242)

In assigning the aesthetic process to a "middle place," mediating between extremes, Emerson was probably following Coleridge,[11] who in turn had followed Schelling back to the Renaissance NeoPlatonists. Ficino, for example, had cited Plotinus in explaining how the ancient magus manipulated images in a middle realm to draw the divine spirit toward the world of sense, and, influenced by Cusanus, he tended to identify the idea of Christ with the mediation implied by man's comprehension of beauty: both are coincidences of the infinite and the finite.[12] The idea that historical Orphism was originally a cult reconciling the worship of Apollo and Dionysus may be the product of later nineteenth-century interpretations, but the mythic Orpheus used art to make his way into the realm of spirits, and Emerson was probably aware of the mediaeval iconography of Orpheus-Christos, the good shepherd, civilizer of men in this life and intercessor in the life to come; he certainly must have known Carlyle's reference to "our highest Orpheus" in *Sartor Resartus*. Emerson's American contemporaries had rejected the old doctrine of vicarious atonement and placed new emphasis on the mediatorial Jesus, quite consciously merging Orphic and Christian allusions as in Thoreau's symbolic elaboration of Walden Pond.[13]

However, Emerson's image of the Whole Man moved away from the person of Jesus Christ, partly for the reasons given in the *Divinity School Address,* but primarily, I think, as a result of his own experience and interpretation of the lords of life. Although he called Jesus one of the true prophets, he had written in 1835 that Jesus was too limited and exclusive to fill the role of Universal Man (*L*, I, 450). The difficulty involved both the mythus of Christianity that had grown up around Jesus and the antinomian spirit that Emerson attributed to him in 1838 with approval but treated somewhat cautiously in 1840, significantly in relation to the mythical character of Prometheus:

> Prometheus is the Jesus of the old mythology. He is the friend of man; stands between the unjust "justice" of the Eternal Father and the race of mortals, and readily suffers all things on their account. But where it departs from the Calvinistic Christianity and exhibits him as the defier of Jove, it represents a state of mind which readily appears wherever the doctrine of Theism is taught in a crude, objective form, and which seems the self-defence of man against this untruth, namely a discontent with the believed fact that a God exists, and a feeling that the obligation of reverence is onerous. It would steal if it could the fire of the Creator, and live apart from him and independent of him. The Prometheus Vinctus is the romance of skepticism. Not less true to all time are the details of that stately apologue.
>
> ("History," II, 30–31; cf. *JMN*, VII, 508)

Aligning Prometheus and Jesus as antinomian heroes, Emerson acknowledges a compensatory law in history by which every crude imposition begets an equal resistance, but he does not involve himself in the underlying question, whether the realization of vision demands Promethean defiance and revolt from heroes like Jesus or an Orphic poet. The answer appears, however, epitomized in the fate of Uriel, who withdrew after his prophetic announcement, and on a broader scale in the ongoing portrait of the poet-hero that Emerson began to delineate after the *Divinity School Address* of July 15, 1838.

This Orpheus of the mid-world is born out of personal experience, and his work of mediation presupposes an enduring "discrepance" between the actual world and the world of thought. The germ probably lies in several journal entries for 1838:

> How true was the antique idea of Beauty expressed in all statues, "the tongue on the balance of expression" if I read the sense of that word aright. For, in life, actions are few, opinions few, prayers few, loves, hatreds, or any emissions of the soul. All that life demands of us through the greater part of the day, is composure, an equilibrium, a readiness, open eyes & ears, & free hands, a Sympathy. Society asks this & Truth & Love & the Genius of our Life. There is a fire in many men which demands an outlet in some vigorous action. They betray their impatience of quiet in an irregular Catalinarian walk; in irregular, faltering, disturbed speech too emphatic for the occasion. They do trifles with a tragic air. This is not beautiful. Let them split wood & work off this superabundant irritability.
>
> That which is individual & remains individual in my experience is of no value. What is fit to engage me & so engage others permanently, is what has put off its weeds of time & place & personal relation. Therefore all that befals me in the way of criticism & extreme blame & praise drawing me out of equilibrium,—putting me for a time in false position to people, & disallowing the spontaneous sentiments, wastes my time, bereaves me of thoughts, & shuts me up within poor personal considerations. Therefore I hate to be conspicuous for blame or praise. It spoils thought.
>
> *(JMN,* VII, 63–65: dated September 5th and 8th)

These are the deeper personal responses to the controversy breaking out over his *Address,* although they may be modelled on the renunciation of Teufelsdröckh and Wilhelm Meister, both of whom occupied Emerson's attention during this year.

The original Orphic poet, in the architectonic context of *Nature,* assumed a task of heroic construction and the apocalyptic, linear history of Prometheus. The act of his final song is the spirit's building outward from its first

house to a finished kingdom. Emerson's world after 1840
called for a different orientation:

> The philosophy we want is one of fluxions & mobility; not a
> house but a ship in these billows we inhabit. Any angular
> dogmatic theory would be rent to chips & splinters in this
> storm of many elements.
>
> (JMN, IX, 222)

In "The Method of Nature" (1841) genius is still identified
with heroic action, but Emerson distinguishes the "work of
ecstasy" as circular and beyond the straight line of intention
(I, 201). The role of man is specifically to reconcile what
history has proven to be irreconcilable: "a link was wanting
between two craving parts of nature, and he was hurled
into being as the bridge over that yawning need, the
mediator betwixt two else unmarriageable facts" (I, 207).
The essays of 1844 suggest that this work of reconciliation
is possible only in an aesthetic privacy. "A private fruit" is
sufficient in "Experience" (III, 83), and "The Poet" ends on
a note of abdication from high achievement: "The world is
full of renunciations and apprenticeships" which the poet
must undergo; his reward, finally, is a state of mind in
which "the ideal shall be real to thee, and the impressions
of the actual world shall fall like summer rain, copious, but
not troublesome to thy invulnerable essence" (III, 41–42).

Beginning in the 1840 journals Emerson sketched fragments of a fictive hero under the name of Osman or Saadi:
simple, charitable, affable but reticent, he is a renunciant
serene in his poverty and obscurity; he is temperate to the
point of a vegetable diet and instructed only in common
household tasks (*JMN*, VII, 502–503). In "Manners"
Osman appears as a pariah-figure to demonstrate the
abundant recompense of the heart in relation to the external world:

> The king of Schiraz could not afford to be so bountiful as
> the poor Osman who dwelt at his gate. Osman had a hu-
> manity so broad and deep that although his speech was so

bold and free with the Koran as to disgust all the dervishes,
yet was there never a poor outcast, eccentric, or insane
man, some fool who had cut off his beard, or who had been
mutilated under a vow, or had a pet madness in his brain,
but fled at once to him; that great heart lay there so sunny
and hospitable in the centre of the country, that it seemed
as if the instinct of all sufferers drew them to his side. And
the madness which he harbored he did not share. Is not this
to be rich? this only to be rightly rich?

(III, 154)

A similar transvaluation is afforded the drudges of
"Spiritual Laws" (II, 166) and "Art" (IX, 287); it is accomplished mythopoetically in "Saadi" when time is over-
thrown and the stooped crones who scour the poet's cot-
tage are suddenly transformed into gods.[14] Saadi himself is
a prophetic poet who avoids worldly and philosophical
conflicts because God gave him the lyre on the condition
that he "sit aloof." Thus "gentle Saadi" dispenses sunshine from his place in the middle, and this cheerful contribution to men makes them his doors to the "perfect
Mind" (IX, 129–135).

It has been said that Emerson drew upon Jones Very and
Thoreau's Orphic discipline for this portrait of the poet,
and also that it is autobiographical, just as the solitary
Wordsworthian youth of his early verses was probably a
version of himself. But certainly one other line of inspiration runs through the Persian poets and Emerson's general
view of the Orient, both of which can be again traced back
to Goethe. Goethe's *West-Eastern Divan* first prompted
Emerson to read the poetry of Hafiz and Saadi, and while
he admired them for their freedom, in several senses, the
complex polarity of East and West in Emerson's mind
made the Orient a symbol for timeless infinity as well as for
human acquiescence, an end to desire and a denial of progress.[15] Emerson meant to criticize Goethe in 1840 by calling
him a "poet of the Actual, not of the Ideal," whose "thinking was of great altitude, and all level; not a succession of

summits, but a high Asiatic table-land" (XII, 326, 331). But aiming toward reconciliation, Emerson himself was drawn toward the actual. And the best that men can expect in the mid-world might be described more accurately as a plateau between earth and heaven than as a succession of visionary summits.

The emerging ideal is emblemized in lines of Goethe translated by Emerson on July 15, 1840, with this comment:

> An able man is always an equilibrium to balance the extremes of the volatile around him.
>
>> "Sunshine was he
>> On the cold day
>> And when the dogstar raged
>> Shade was he and coolness"
>
> says the Arabic poet translated by Goethe, vol 6 p. 13.
>
> (*JMN*, VII, 384)

The following January these lines anchored Emerson's portrait of "Man the Reformer" in an address delivered to the Mechanics' Apprentices' Library Association of Boston. Sketching a simple yeoman of Jeffersonian and Thoreauvian dimensions, Emerson insisted upon practical and domestic arts as a proper counterweight to the usual indulgences of poets and philosophers.

> The mediator between the spiritual and the actual world should have a great prospective prudence. An Arabian poet describes his hero by saying,
>
>> Sunshine was he
>> In the winter day;
>> And in the midsummer
>> Coolness and shade.
>
> He who would help himself and others should not be a subject of irregular and interrupted impulses of virtue, but a continent, persisting, immovable person,—such as we have seen a few scattered up and down in time for the

blessing of the world; men who have in the gravity of their nature a quality which answers to the fly-wheel in a mill, which distributes the motion equably over all the wheels and hinders it from falling unequally and suddenly in shocks. It is better that joy should be spread over all the day in the form of strength, than that it should be concentrated into ecstasies, full of danger and followed by reactions.

(I, 255–256)

No doubt the orator chose his words and images shrewdly for the occasion; nevertheless, he spoke his own part and tendency. The work of reformation, of taming mankind, demanded a more equitable distribution of energy than momentary vision or ecstasy allowed. The poet as mediator would have to lower his pitch, and like Emerson's Transcendentalist be ready to exchange "the flash-of-lightning faith for continuous daylight, this fever-glow for a benign climate" (I, 352–353). The best way to survive the nightmare of "Experience" would not be to dream of the Central Man—Emerson still did, but when the dream subsided he found himself deceived and alone (*JMN*, IX, 395)—but to lower one's sights and keep moving in the middle: split wood, Emerson tells us, learn to swim amid these waves, learn to skate and we will stay up on this icy isthmus of the present state.

In *Representative Men* Emerson's interest appears to have shifted from the common man to the great man, the one who actively imposes upon nature and history.[16] The larger state of affairs in 1845 and 1846, when he wrote these lectures, had also moved him to write, "Things are of the snake," and there is a brief resurgence of messianic fervor in his journals for the same year. Emerson, however, was not one to be deceived by heroes, and his aim is signalled in the title of the introductory essay, "The Uses of Great Men." There he indicated "human nature's indispensable defence" against the abuses of their influence: great men are "counterweights and checks on each other." "The cen-

tripetence augments the centrifugence. We balance one
man with his opposite, and the health of the state depends
on the see-saw" (IV, 27). The representative heroes themselves are only hints of the Whole Man, and Emerson was
quick to record their limitations. Goethe and Napoleon are
treated, much as Jesus had been, as appropriate counterweights to the downward tendencies in their times; moreover, they balance each other, one the external, the other
the internal half of a new spirit in the century, and together
they are called "representatives of the impatience and reaction of nature against the *morgue* of conventions" (IV, 270,
289). The essay on Swedenborg is nearly a recantation of
Emerson's earlier admiration and specifically rejects any
rigid interpretation of correspondence. Some sense of the
limitations of Emerson's own work of 1836 might be seen
in his criticism of Swedenborg's system: "It is dynamic, not
vital. . . . The universe is a gigantic crystal, all whose
atoms and laminae lie in uninterrupted order and with
unbroken unity, but cold and still" (IV, 133). If Swedenborg was too introverted and too much the priest, he is
counterbalanced by Shakespeare, the cheerful extrovert
and player-poet, whose partiality was to have been too
much an entertainer. And in the conclusion to
"Shakspeare; Or, The Poet," the great men of the world
begin to fade before Emerson's dream of a new Orpheus:

> It must be conceded that these are half-views of half-
> men. The world still wants its poet-priest, a reconciler, who
> shall not trifle, with Shakspeare the player, nor shall grope
> in graves, with Swedenborg the mourner; but who shall
> see, speak, and act, with equal inspiration.
>
> (IV, 219)

Plato and Montaigne, the two remaining heroes, are the
most equitable of the great men and the best representatives of Emerson's Orphic image. In each the mark of
greatness is a comprehensiveness or self-containment that
imitates nature itself. Emerson would probably have

ranked Plato at the head of all philosophers and poets; his notes, later incorporated into the essay on Plato, explain that primacy:

> Pherecydes Syrus wrote, "Jove is a circle, triangle, & square, centre & line & all things before all," which indicates profoundness of perception. We say then of a Jove-like soul like Plato, that he at once shows the evanescence & the centrality of things. Things are in a flood and fixed as adamant. . . .

> Synthesis of the two elements
Coin of Jove

> It is as easy to be great as small. Now came a balanced soul. Precisely as high as he soared so deep he dived. If he loved abstract truth he saved himself with the most popular of all principles, the absolute good which rules rulers and judges the judge. If he made transcendental distinctions above the vision of ordinary mortals he fortified himself by drawing all his illustrations from sources disdained by orators & conversers: from mares & soupladles, from cooks & criers, potters & shoemakers.

> Herein following Nature, jealous of partiality, if he plants his foot here & says one thing, he is sure to plant his foot there, & make the counter-weight, resolved that the two poles shall be manifest; the two poles still appear & with him become two hands & grasp their own.
>
> (JMN, IX, 184, 328, 331: the quotation from
Taylor's "Introduction" to The Works of Plato, 1804,
I, xxvii)

Emerson balanced Plato, in part, by making him with Socrates a "double star" (IV, 70). Socrates is given the qualities of Saadi and Osman (IV, 72), and to the whole he brings the skepticism and earthiness that made him beloved by Montaigne. Although Emerson was heavily indebted to the interpretations of Taylor, he also claimed to have detached Plato from Platonism, that is, from the commentators and Platonists who would systematize and so shrink the great range of Plato's ideas. Thus Plato himself can be seen as embracing both sides of every great question; he is the most centered of men, and he is the only historical figure Emerson described as having accomplished the Orphic task. Plato "marries the two parts of nature," and the myth of "a god leading things from disorder into order" in the *Timaeus* illuminates the balance of nature and the relation between spiritual and material poles. As a philosopher Plato apprehended the dual cardinal facts, unity and variety; as a poet he combined lofty speech with low phrases; as a man he joined the symbolic heritages of Europe and Asia. It is apparent, in both the finished essay and the journal preparations, that Emerson worked consciously to make Plato a "balanced soul" in every detail; of all his partial portraits no other so closely approximates his Orphic ideal and "the wonderful synthesis" we see in nature.

"Montaigne; Or, The Skeptic" is less a portrait than an act of extraordinary legerdemain, for as the essay develops, its focus shifts away from the person and to the argument. Emerson's skeptic is as elusive as Proteus because, much more obviously than Plato, he inhabits the fallen world of "Experience." In the game of life, where everything has two sides, the skeptic takes "the middle ground" between idealists and materialists and keeps "this position of equilibrium" (IV, 155, 166). His balance is defensive:

> He is the considerer, the prudent, taking in sail, counting stock, husbanding his means, believing that a man has too many enemies than that he can afford to be his own foe; that we cannot give ourselves too many advantages in this unequal conflict, with powers so vast and unweariable ranged on one side, and this little conceited vulnerable popinjay that man is, bobbing up and down into every danger, on the other. It is a position taken up for better defence, as of more safety, and one that can be maintained; and it is one of more opportunity and range: as, when we build a house, the rule is to set it not too high nor too low, under the wind, but out of the dirt.
>
> (IV, 159–160)

The figure of a small bird bobbing in the storm is to become the symbol of a new adjustment between the poet and nature. Emerson's Montaigne does not soar like Plato (*JMN*, IX, 326), but he knows that he cannot settle into the dirt, either, and must keep moving in order to stay in the middle of the road. His philosophy therefore is "one of fluxions and mobility. . . . We want some coat woven of elastic steel, stout as the first and limber as the second" (IV, 160). The elasticity of this skeptic's clothes is demonstrated by Emerson in the latter part of the essay when he juggles facts and stretches words so that skepticism comes to mean a self-reliant faith and Montaigne is eased—or perhaps bent over backwards—into the company of believers. Expand the perspective from hours to years and disbelief becomes "structural" (IV, 175), a phase that superior minds pass through and an assurance that they will eventually attach themselves to "the permanent in the mutable and fleeting" (IV, 186). Time, deceiver and "perpetual Belly" though it may be, is still Emerson's chief hope; and here, as in "Experience," his counsel is, in effect, "Patience and patience, we shall win at the last," while his rhetorical magic displays the infinite convertibility of present words and things.

Neither of these two spherical figures, Plato and Montaigne, is a hero of action or imaginative vision: Plato has the common sense "to reconcile his poetry with the appearances of the world" and "never writes in ecstasy, or catches us up into poetic raptures" (IV, 61). Montaigne, attuned to a beneficent necessity in the succession of ordinary moments, is content in his saddle with "the potluck of the day" (*JMN*, VIII, 322); he would assent to Emerson's conclusion, that man is here "not to work but to be worked upon" (IV, 186). Both follow the rhythms of natural gradation and compensation, so that their lives and writings are the expression of unique mediatory powers. Emerson places them where he would place Iopas, the Orphic singer who tells the secrets of nature in Book I of Virgil's *Aeneid*, in a "middle essence," halfway between actuality and imagination, and they define, as well as any of his heroes do, the mid-world that is best. Thus the image of Emerson's ideal poet, even in *Representative Men*, is consistent with the milder Orpheus who tames men and harmonizes things, not directly but through the dexterous movements of his song.

Emerson's Orpheus—this composite portrait drawn from the essays and journals—is the culmination of his long quest for artistic form. It can be summarized in this way: the principle of beauty in nature, the perfect whole, becomes the artist, in his work and in his character. When the character of the poet merges with the shape of his art, Emerson approaches his own Orphic goal: the higher work of art is to make new artists who are more complete men; the true Orpheus "writes his ode, not with syllables, but with men." The poet-figure as mediator, as balanced and balancing soul, is an outgrowth of the countless vacillations and antitheses recorded by Emerson in the years between the preparation of *Essays: First Series* and the publication of the 1847 *Poems*.

More generally, the Orphic figure, as it is traced through Emerson's work, follows a characteristic Romantic course from Prometheus to Orpheus: it transforms the energy of a revolutionary prophet and builder into that of the artist proper. The difference between the two figures is summarized by Walter Strauss in his study of Orphic themes in modern poetry:

> Prometheus and Orpheus are readily contrastable as half-gods and as mythological culture-heroes. Prometheus defies Zeus in behalf of mankind and is martyred for his deed; as a fire-stealer, he is at the same time the eternal rebel (joining forces with Faust, Satan, and Cain) and the representative of a "progressive" Romantic humanism. Orpheus does not rebel; he refuses to accept the world as it

is; he does not lead the people, he charms them. Prometheanism aims for an outer transformation of society; it proposes to ameliorate man's lot by external action. Orphism proposes to transmute the inner man by a confrontation with himself and to alter society only indirectly, through the changes that man can effect within himself.[17]

Lewis Mumford used these contrasting myths to represent the technical and the artistic sides of man. Prometheus is identified as the hero of civilization, a giant and liberating strength in the external world. Orpheus, on the other hand, is an expression of what Mumford in his own *Conduct of Life* called the "superfluous," the excess of energy beyond what is biologically necessary for the organism's survival. This exuberance or vital impulse reaches back to the Demiurgos of the *Timaeus*, probably through Schiller's *spieltrieb* and Emerson's "ecstasy" or "plus" as defined in "The Method of Nature" and again in "Power."[18] It begins as play and develops as language, ultimately to form the ethical-aesthetic superstructure of civilization which we call culture. Thus Mumford's Orpheus is also identified with the "axial" stages of human development, those crucial points in history when man turned inward, so to speak, and new religions arose by focusing upon meek, introverted, saintly figures like Buddha, Mahomet, or Jesus. Emerson's fictive poet-saints, Osman and Saadi, belong to this line. Within Mumford's scheme of history nineteenth-century Concord might be another axial moment, and Emerson's improvised prophet a fresh substitute for the tarnished figurehead of Christianity. In his 1957 introduction to *The Golden Day*, where Mumford reconsidered the era from the perspective of *The Transformations of Man*, the New England Renaissance is a brief but doomed post-axial synthesis of the sort the twentieth century desperately needs. By 1845 the primitivist strain in American culture had strengthened the weaker of two dominant nineteenth-century ideologies and produced "the image of a new kind of personality . . . in whom an unstable synthesis of the romantic and utilitarian elements was actually effected."[19] Mumford calls this synthesis post-axial because it embraces axial inwardness without relinquishing the ideals of personal freedom and equality that the industrial revolution has made realizable. The conception of a new personality that balances the romantic against the utilitarian (Thoreau and Audubon are the examples) points to Emerson's ideal of Orpheus as a mediator between imagination and science. Such a character is the necessary actor in Mumford's speculations about a modern drama of renewal in *The Conduct of Life*. In a world weighed down by functional mechanization, renewal can begin only when a man takes the axial step of withdrawal and rejection in order to establish a new inner equilibrium. The lower way of "Experience" leading to the mid-world is, like the solitary discipline of *Walden*, a literary version of such a step, and the new man that Mumford requires is, like Emerson's, a "Whole Man" or balanced man emerging from the "repolarizing" or compensatory processes of nature and history in which he himself has played a part.[20]

Both *Walden* and "Experience" drive their protagonists inward: the private fruit of "Experience" is also the consciousness of self, that "certain doubleness" that makes Walden a beloved, "companionable" solitude for Thoreau. In this sense, the self-consciousness that shrouded the spontaneous, unconscious centers of personality for the younger Emerson becomes a means of restoring health: the remedy for the Romantic disease is homeopathic, to paraphrase Carlyle and Hegel, and there is an element of danger in these cures. Mumford is in many ways the modern American thinker closest to Emerson, but it is fair to say that in writing about the Orphic aspirations of man he neglects this Romantic dilemma and its attendant agonies. Perhaps that is why he can abandon Promethean energies

with such ease when in fact he looks to the eventual transformation of society at large. Though Emerson was prone
to the same oversight, he did not so readily give up the
Promethean mode, and when he did he also discarded
much of the cultural progressivism that Mumford retains.
In short, Emerson wrestled with the angel Art and knew
the threat of maiming in a way that parallels the experience
of his great English contemporaries.

In his analysis of Romantic poetry as internalized
romance-quest, Harold Bloom distinguishes a passage between two stages or modes of energy, the organic and the
creative, which he names "Prometheus" and (in Blake's
term) "the Real Man, the Imagination."[21] In the first stage
the poet allies himself with nature and with the social
struggle against repression; in the second he disengages
from the world and recognizes that nature is an antagonist,
though not the ultimate antagonist, which is a recalcitrance
in the self, the demonic solipsism of an acutely self-
conscious imagination. The great dramas of Romantic
poetry are acted on the second stage where the self-
conscious power, the imagination, shines inward to encounter the poet's other self, the shadow that must be
brought to light if he is to regain an original wholeness.
The dialectic of Emerson's prose moves in analogous
stages: true, the Orphic quest under the guise of Reason or
imagination is opposed to nature, or uses nature to go
beyond nature, but it is for a time allied with Promethean
energy that seeks to impose its order upon the natural
world. Then there is a moment when mythically, as we
shall see in Emerson's poem, the riddle of the Sphinx appears to be unanswerable, when the marriage of energy or
spirit with matter seems impossible, and the labyrinthine
world of "Experience" turns the poet in upon himself.
Emerson was not the kind of artist to stare, inwardly and
obsessively, at this abyss, and his artistic response was to
redefine the imagination in terms of nature and eventually

establish his way station on a tableland or middle ground.

Once again the exemplar for Emerson and for the Romantic conception of aesthetic space in America is Wordsworth, descended from the Simplon Pass, and even from his Snowden vision, in *The Excursion*. Not an influence, but most clearly a type for the American experience is the first book of "The Recluse," "Home at Grasmere," which was not published as a whole until after Emerson, Thoreau, and Hawthorne were gone. It concludes with the lines printed as the Prospectus in 1814, and the essence of what precedes them is that the happy valley of Grasmere is the necessary condition for those or any other spousal verses. There the poet is admonished, " 'Be mild and cleave to gentle things, / Thy glory and thy happiness be there,' " and in this perfect whole the actual and the imaginary mingle:

> Dreamlike the blending also of the whole
> Harmonious landscape; all along the shore
> The boundary lost, the line invisible
> That parts the image from reality;
> And the clear hills, as high as they ascend
> Heavenward, so piercing deep the lake below.

Grasmere in Wordsworth's description becomes an English Walden, an oxymoronic frontier-space that is both boundary and center and yields a unique aesthetic sensation:

> 'Tis, but I cannot name it, 'tis the sense
> Of majesty, and beauty, and repose,
> A blended holiness of earth and sky,
> Something that makes this individual spot,
> This small abiding-place of many men,
> A termination, and a last retreat,
> A centre, come from wheresoe'er you will,
> A whole without dependence or defect,
> Made for itself; and happy in itself,
> Perfect contentment, unity entire.[22]

Emerson, unlike Shelley or later Yeats, had no quarrel with what Yeats called the primary wisdom of Wordsworth's wanderer. Walter Strauss intelligently suggests that Orphic orientation had become twofold by the middle of the nineteenth century,[23] and we should probably distinguish the naturalized way of Goethe and Wordsworth from the way of Blake and Yeats, Mallarmé and Rilke.

Emerson led his American contemporaries into the former way, the tableland between heaven and earth where they might keep the balance observed in nature. Thoreau, as Mumford has indicated, took this ground, and so did Hawthorne, who in 1855 found Grasmere and Wordsworth's grave a testament to the simple beauty of nature as opposed to art; characteristically, he wrote in his diary, "I rather wonder that people of real taste should help Nature out. . . ."[24] For in 1849 Hawthorne had encamped in the neutral territory, resolved never to trespass against "our great creative Mother" as Aylmer and Ethan Brand had. Melville's dialectic reached its midpoint in the next two years, as Ishmael becomes Emerson's Montaigne, following the white whale of his own "equal eye," not the one in Ahab's Promethean imagination. The whale itself is a model of Goethe's perfect whole: in the language of the West-Eastern poet, he is warm in ice and cool at the equator, and like Emerson's Plato he is a "wonderful synthesis," a creature who "can see two sides of a thing."[25] No doubt Blake would have found in all this the God of Melville's "Conflict of Convictions"—what Blake called "the divinity of yes and no too—the yea, nay, creeping Jesus." He would have thought that Emerson like Wordsworth must know better, and he might have added the memorable comment made on Sir Joshua Reynolds: "Any fool can concentrate a light in the middle."[26] Emerson's mature Orphic voice is the end, not the beginning of Blakean Romanticism in America, and what we begin with Emerson is a new, peculiarly modern alliance between poetry and natural history.

PART TWO:
The Major Poems

——

I hung my verses in the wind,
Time and tide their faults may find.
—EMERSON, ''The Test''

First Poetic Fruits

———

There is no architect
Can build as the Muse can;
She is skilful to select
Materials for her plan.
—EMERSON, "The House"

EMERSON'S POETRY, though it was literally scattered over five decades of his life, is of a piece and represents his second major encounter with art because it has a justification of its own, apart from everything else that he wrote. First, though he realized that his singing, for all practical purposes, was to be in prose, all his life Emerson aspired to a place among the poetic bards: poetry he thought the vehicle of Reason, prose carried the Understanding. Secondly, he undertook the major phase of his poetic career because he recognized the primacy of poetry in a new and startling sense. He always said that he collected his poems for publication in 1846 because various friends pressed him to do so, and that is somewhat true; truer still was the underlying recognition that the dark and indirect way of poetry is the necessary means to any Orphic achievement:

> As the musician avails himself of the concert, so the philosopher avails himself of the drama, the epic, the novel, & becomes a poet; for these complex forms allow of the utterance of his knowledge of life by *indirections* as well as in the didactic way, & can therefore express the fluxional quantities & values which the thesis or dissertation could never give.
>
> (*JMN*, VII, 190)

Here, in the broadest sense, is why Emerson became a

practicing poet after 1839, and why his prose can accurately be called a prelude to his poetry. Whatever their merits or faults, his poems are central because they reflect and foreshorten, to our advantage, the contours of thought and form that have made Emerson not just an influence but a measure for subsequent American literature. Stephen Whicher's brief and invaluable introduction to the poems[1] accepts the traditional view that Emerson never found his proper style as a poet and sums him up as a "transitional and divided figure." His search for style was, in Whicher's words, "confused, never quite successful" and "yet seminal"—"seminal," I would add, because the divisions that plagued Emerson have been the continuous burden of Romantic poetry in America.

Emerson's awareness of his own divided self spurred the major phase of his poetic activity. "Life is not dialectics" (III, 58), and the expression of life he sought was not the "didactic way," but the method of indirection he discovered through the dialectics of his prose. The prose itself leans toward poetry after 1840, when the thread of argument slackens and imagery begins to organize instead of being subordinated to a frame. The speaking voice becomes less assertive, and no longer so homiletic or philosophical, but often multiple and nearly fictive. But it is in poetry or mythopoesis that Emerson's inherent fable finally comes to life. There the shadowy hero of the essays moves to the foreground and the drama implicit in the prose is acted out in verse. The great polar forces hypostatized in the essays are personified in encounters of the two played on a single stage—that is, the setting for Emerson's poetry is, as a rule, natural, of one world, and not hierarchical or supernatural. His poems are often like Renaissance portraits or emblems, and they are Orphic work in the sense that they attempt to make giant men in "dark" fables, poetry in Bacon's "parabolic" sense that clarifies by obscuring. The poetic fable, a brief but powerfully illuminating narrative, like a small gem or crystal, and the fragmentary monologue, a true version of living thought, were right forms for a husky-voiced, inconsecutive Orphic poet. And in the heroes of Emerson's poetry, we have, as it were, his last avatars for Orpheus.

His form is adequate to, because it is an expression of, himself—Emerson, I think, would have been pleased by such a response to the charge that his poetry lacked an adequate form. It is to the credit of an endless experimenter that he achieved superb instances—not just lines and couplets, but whole poems, and even groups of them—in a great variety of styles and forms. The first such achievement appears to center on the year 1834[2] and is somewhat fugitive from Emerson's Orphic concern. But in this group are some of his most admired poems, "Each and All," "The Rhodora," and "The Snow-Storm," and they make an instructive difference from the prosaic blank verse and free verse dotting the journals between 1827 and 1832, and from the more individually expressive forms of the later poetry. What prompted this sudden and successful venture is not known—certainly not the coinciding invitation to deliver the Phi Beta Kappa poem at Harvard, if we may judge from the platform couplets Emerson produced for that occasion. The poems themselves, which were not published until 1839, imply the self-same power that inspired *Nature*. Moreover, a common influence is in evidence, for the lines that reinforce the central, anthropomorphic truth of *Nature* are also a touchstone for Emerson's poetic style of 1834.

> Man is all symmetry,
> Full of proportions, one limb to another,
> And all to all the world besides.
> Each part may call the farthest, brother;
> For head with foot hath private amity,
> And both with moons and tides.
>
> (I, 68)

The idea of a relation between the forms of thought and matter, already implied by the marriage metaphors of Wordsworth and Swedenborg, was strengthened by Emerson's study of the seventeenth-century Metaphysical poets and chiefly among them of George Herbert. There—in the "Jordan" poems, for example—Emerson found an ideal of simple, heartfelt poetry similar to what he had felt in Wordsworth's rural verses. Herbert's contribution is larger, however, for Herbert provided a model, not merely for simplicity of speech and imagery, but for combining that simplicity with architectonic skill, with the concentrated and integrated structure that distinguishes the seventeenth-century meditative style. Emerson always placed Herbert in the first rank of poets, and his admiration culminates in the 1835 lectures on English literature where Herbert is praised for his simple and chaste expression of abstruse thought: "I should cite Herbert as a striking example of the power of exalted thought to melt and bend language to its fit expression" (*EL*, I, 350).

Most notable in the poems of 1834 is a precise and skillful organization, what Herbert called "neatness" and what Emerson at that time probably would have called "symmetry."[3] What they owe to Herbert is not always explicit but the debt is clear enough in another poem probably written about this time and later taken for Herbert's own work.

> How much, preventing God, how much I owe
> To the defences thou hast round me set;
> Example, custom, fear, occasion slow,—
> These scorned bondmen were my parapet.
> I dare not peep over this parapet
> To gauge with glance the roaring gulf below,
> The depths of sin to which I had descended,
> Had not these me against myself defended.
>
> ("Grace," IX, 359)

Here, as John Broderick has shown,[4] is a direct parallel with the first line of Herbert's "Sinne," "Lord! with what care hast thou begirt us round." Moreover, the retard effected by the naming or cataloging device in the third line is characteristic of Herbert and may also have been taken over from the catalog somewhat more extended in "Sinne" (though cataloging is a common enough technique among seventeenth-century poets, and Emerson may have found precedents in Milton, Robert Herrick, or even the American William Bradford). Personification of the defenses as "scorned bondmen" calls to mind Herbert's specific recommendation that "things of ordinary use" ought to illustrate "Heavenly Truth." New England has never forgotten this advice, and the bondmen of "Grace" reappear constantly in Emerson's poetry, importing truths well above their station. The "drudge in dusty frock" who appears in "Art," for example, has been compared to Herbert's servant in "The Elixir," a poem that Emerson especially admired and quoted in 1835. Thus there is no doubt about Herbert's influence. More generally—and here I think the poems of 1834 can be included as having the same qualities—Emerson had learned Herbert's "neatness": structuring a poem on a single metaphor or situation, as "Grace" is based on the figure of a fortress; the smoothness of tone and rhythm, conversational but always melodic, never jagged but sufficiently pointed and varied to gain the quality of speech, as in the catalog or in the stressed pronouns ("these me") which give the last line of "Grace" a peak before it falls off to the diminished feminine ending.

"The Rhodora" (IX, 37) displays the same neat structure and rhythm as "Grace," again modulated by a feminine rhyme that sets off the gnomic couplet, and by the deliberateness of the last line with its hyphenated adjective, monosyllabic parallelism, and pointed pronouns. "The Rhodora" conveys, too, the humility and intense dedication that Emerson and Herbert shared. One might draw further analogies between Emerson's poem and the struc-

tures of seventeenth-century meditation. It is probably
natural to associate Emerson with Augustinian illumination and the relatively free meditative modes of Vaughan
or Milton. That is, roughly speaking, the mode of Emerson's prose, even in such a disciplined way as "Experience," and the visionary moment described by Henry
Vaughan—

> I am so warm'd now by this glance on me,
> That, midst all storms I feel a Ray of thee;
> So have I known some beauteous *Paisage* rise
> In suddain flowres and arbours to my Eies,
> And in the depth and dead of winter bring
> To my cold thoughts a lively sense of spring.
>
> ("Mount of Olives")

—parallels such moments in Wordsworth and Emerson,
specifically in the climax of "Each and All." Yet in terms of
poetic structure Emerson in 1834 inclines toward the more
orderly discipline of Herbert and the Ignatian meditation,
beginning with a composition or focusing upon a concrete
situation and proposing of the spiritual problem therein
dramatized; following with an analysis of the problem; and
ending in the colloquy, an intimate conversation and union
between the poet and the object of his spiritual exercise.[5]

"The Rhodora" follows this pattern but with an essential
difference that sets Emerson apart from the Metaphysicals:
whereas the Ignatian formula is triadic, the structure of
"The Rhodora" is clearly binary, two sets of eight lines
each. In the first, the situation is posed and the question
implied (actually stated already in the subtitle of the
poem); in the second, an answer is given immediately,
without any deliberation, and the answer itself eschews
analysis:

> Rhodora! if the sages ask thee why
> This charm is wasted on the earth and sky,
> Tell them, dear, that if eyes were made for seeing,
> Then Beauty is its own excuse for being:
> Why thou wert there, O rival of the rose!

I never thought to ask, I never knew:
But, in my simple ignorance, suppose
The self-same Power that brought me there brought you.

(IX, 38)

The rhodora needs no reasoned argument, no "excuse" for its existence. In terms of the meditative formula, we have only composition and colloquy, two parts subtly inter-twined. The first part of the poem portrays the rhodora as a humble, self-sacrificing flower which, though equal to the celebrated rose, prefers obscure service to worldly fame. Sacrifice and service are implied, almost to the point of martyrdom, in the fallen petals. In the last eight lines the poet identifies himself with the same Christian virtues: his "simple ignorance" is faith, if not in Providence, certainly in a wise and sensitive Creator; the worshipful humility which the poet and the flower share explains their intimate rapport. The philosophical sages, on the other hand, are shut out; as the flower leans toward Christian sacrifice, the sages are associated with self-seeking, utilitarian interests, perhaps even cavalier interests, who see the flower's charm as "wasted." Thus a dramatic undercurrent—the subtle alliance of poet and flower against the sages—helps to create a mood of religious dedication that excludes the inquiring, analytical mind, and at the same time militates against a narrowly aesthetic, "beauty for beauty's sake" interpretation of the poem.

Quietist in manner and undisturbed by the notion of flux, "The Rhodora" descends along with Philip Freneau's "Honey Suckle" and William Cullen Bryant's "Yellow Vio-let" from eighteenth-century treatments of nature. It shares in the stability of Emerson's *Nature*, for both works illustrate the attention to structure, the eye for neatness and symmetry, that Emerson as scientific observer culti-vated during these years. And the well-known passage concluding the section of *Nature* on "Beauty" bears out the message of "The Rhodora":

"This element [Beauty] I call an ultimate end. No reason can be asked or given why the soul seeks beauty. Beauty, in its largest and profoundest sense, is one expression for the universe. God is the all-fair" (I, 24). Finally, the binary structure of the poem reflects, in its omission of any extended analysis, Emerson's attack on the Understanding in *Nature*.

"The Snow-Storm" divides as clearly into two parts: first, the composition or setting that explicitly invites meditation, and then a more intimate encounter with the storm that, if not a colloquy proper, nonetheless transcends commonplace awareness. Emerson's architecture here is as carefully contrived as in *Nature*, and builds on the same incline from "Commodity" to "Beauty." The poem might be subtitled, in the manner of "The Rhodora," "On Being Asked, Wherefore is the Storm?" The answer comes after a series of parallel stoppages: by halting all ordinary human activity, the imperious storm offers, in the oxymoron of "tumultuous privacy," a moment of aesthetic consciousness. Drawn closer by the simple invitation, "Come see the north wind's masonry," we watch as the creative energy of nature is loosed. Imagination in the second paragraph overwhelms the practical Understanding of the first, with its enlarged figurative range and its complicated, almost reckless syntax and rhythm that would sometimes defy "number and proportion." The storm conquers man, not merely in the practical sense, but by overwhelming him with the prolific power of a "fierce artificer" and by leaving him to gaze upon the bastions and turrets so swiftly built, to ponder the mockery of his intentions in the "frolic" work of the snow. The touch of humor in the storm suggests the ultimate beneficence of Nature, and once again the superiority of the purely aesthetic perspective, for all that the storm builds is round and tapering, and "a swan-like form invests the hidden thorn." No wonder, then, that art, or man's limited creative power, is astonished, as Goethe was by the creative force of nature ("*Zum Erstaunen bin ich da*"):

> And when his hours are numbered, and the world
> Is all his own, retiring, as he were not,
> Leaves, when the sun appears, astonished Art
> To mimic in slow structures, stone by stone,
> Built in an age, the mad wind's night-work,
> The frolic architecture of the snow.
>
> (IX, 42)

We are lost in this syntactical maze and in a suspension of rhythm ("the mád wiñd's níght-wórk"), until the last graceful line, a perfect iambic pentameter, resolves the poem and gently sets us down from a momentary Uriel-like vision. For art can only imitate "stone by stone" what nature has done overnight, and evil seems to bless only so long as the swan-like forms resist the morning sun. Like a parallel passage in "History" (II, 19), "The Snow-Storm" is based upon the view that art imitates the recurring archetypes of nature. The poem shares the foundation Emerson built on in 1836, when he wrote in the "Introduction" to *Nature* that man's "operations taken together are so insignificant, a little chipping, baking, patching, and washing, that in an impression so grand as that of the world on the human mind, they do not vary the result" (I, 5); unlike *Nature*, however, it avoids reaching out to the implications of the dissolving power, either in the sun or in the human imagination.

Both "The Snow-Storm" and "The Rhodora" are rather firm and controlled statements of the binary form that was Emerson's persistent model for philosophical inquiry. Given the soul and nature, the ME and NOT ME (I, 4), correspondence is the hidden alliance between the two that makes both the poet and the flower responsive to sentiments of beauty and sacrifice. Much of Emerson's poetry thus resolves itself into a binary, question-and-answer form, often dramatized as an encounter between the poet and nature personified as a whole or symbolized by a single object, a tree, stream, or mountain. According to Emerson's early faith, the poet needs only to put the question, or go to the window, and nature will awaken in him the answer. He does not analyze, he simply "apprehends" the truth of what he has already acted out (I, 3–4).

Like its companion-pieces of 1834, "Each and All" also focuses on the spontaneity of true insight and the "personal knowledge," in Sewell and Polanyi's sense, that is inseparable from acts and feelings. The climax of the poem is a nearly visceral rejection of false claims by the Understanding, and Emerson closes with a classic expression of the visionary moment: the poet realizes, in effect, what he has just acted out. His inner experience is more dramatically revealed than in "The Rhodora" or "The Snow-Storm," but "Each and All" is still elaborately structured, carefully divided into parts and then subdivided into instances or images. And again the poet's encounter with nature takes a binary form, given over first to his doubts or problem (in this case, the need for proof of nature's aphorism, "All are needed by each one; / Nothing is fair or good alone"), and then to nature's answer (the last ten lines in which the poet sees the truth without having it proved in any discursive way); and so conceived it shows, as "The Rhodora" did, the fundamental distinction between Emerson and the Metaphysicals: for Emerson, analysis is not the means to revelation. The long middle of the poem, which might be taken as an "analysis" of the type appropriate to the Ignatian structure, does not lead to the resolution, but curiously to a point where the poet would have discarded beauty in favor of truth.[6]

> Then I said, 'I covet truth;
> Beauty is unripe childhood's cheat;
> I leave it behind with the games of youth:'—
> As I spoke, beneath my feet
> The ground-pine curled its pretty wreath,

> Running over the club-moss burrs;
> I inhaled the violet's breath;
> Around me stood the oaks and firs;
> Pine-cones and acorns lay on the ground;
> Over me soared the eternal sky,
> Full of light and of deity;
> Again I saw, again I heard,
> The rolling river, the morning bird;—
> Beauty through my senses stole;
> I yielded myself to the perfect whole.
>
> (IX, 5–6)

Only in the end, when the poet is taken by surprise, does he realize that truth, beauty, and goodness are not isolated elements but aspects of the "perfect whole." Though rare, this experience is not unknown, for the poet exclaims, "Again I saw, again I heard," recalling lines from other visionary poets whose moments of insight counteract the light of common day. Like Wordsworth's in the "Immortality" Ode, and like Stevens' in "Martial Cadenza," Emerson's vision in "Each and All" counteracts the common experiences enumerated in the middle of the poem from which the poet infers that beauty is a cheat. The poet's inference is wrong, of course, but it may be a legitimate inference given the facts at hand, and his making it dramatizes the weakness and dangers inherent in the analytic method: inference or induction, that is, generalizing from a series of instances, is the way of the Understanding; only direct and intuitive experience "through my senses" brings the positive truth home.

All of these first important poems, then, show a sense of design founded in the order of correspondence or symmetry, and like the early essays their form implies the easy victory of imaginative insight over ordinary, mundane powers. Emerson appears to have taken Herbert as a specific model for poetic form, and we can see, in retrospect, that he was moving in the same direction as Coleridge and Wordsworth, joining the devotional forms of the seventeenth century with the descriptive genre and style of eighteenth-century nature poetry, which was his more obvious heritage in the literary climate of early nineteenth-century New England. "Each and All," moving as it does from the symmetry of illustrative or external instances to the personal, inward experience, exemplifies the more general transition of Romantic poets in search of an appropriate lyrical form.[7] Emerson, like the great English Romantics, believed that mythic personification was the essence and not the ornament of true poetry, and after 1839, when he decided that it was necessary to be a poet in more than a general sense, he tried to make the fable breathe—to write his ode "not with syllables, but men"—by dramatizing his representative encounters and the intricate process of Man Thinking.

V

Fables of Apocalypse

———

Wine is translated wit,
Wine is the day of day,
Wine from the veilèd secret
Tears the veil away.

His instant thought a poet spoke,
And filled the age his fame;
An inch of ground the lightning strook
But lit the sky with flame.

And as the light divides the dark
  Through with living swords,
So shall thou pierce the distant age
  With adamantine words.
                —EMERSON, fragments on
                    the poet and poetic
                    power

IN THE YEARS between 1834 and 1839 Emerson worked out
the artistic implications of what he called the "First
Philosophy," the core of ideas that is inspiration for his
early essays and for the primary fable of his poems. So far
as we know, he wrote little poetry (of his major poems,
only "The Humble-Bee," traditionally assigned to 1837)
and did not publish what he had written. Suddenly in 1839
he decided to publish some of his early poems, including
"The Rhodora" and "Each and All," which he sent to
James Freeman Clarke's *Western Messenger* along with a
note regretting that he had only a few new poems and
could not improvise verses "as freely as the wind blows."[1]
His journals at this time show an aroused interest in poetry
as distinct from poetic prose or eloquence, and it is clear

that Emerson, despite his diffidence, had begun a new experiment in form. Thesis or dissertation would not do; the old way was too constrained, too direct, for the complex life. Poetry, on the other hand, was free speech, a live performance where words were not merely "fossil poetry" but acts of the mind; poetry was the true expression of the world as metamorphosis.

This realization in 1839 sparked Emerson's most rhapsodic language in prose or verse. "Poets are thus liberating gods," he repeated in the dithyrambic essay "The Poet" (III, 30, 32), and the kind of verse he expected to issue from this concept of poetry is implied in the well-known journal entry of 1839 calling for "grand Pindaric strokes, as firm as the tread of a horse" or "the stroke of a cannon ball"—"I wish to write such rhymes as shall not suggest a restraint, but contrariwise the wildest freedom" (*JMN*, VII, 219). "The Poet" sketches a similar program, drawing on Emerson's early conviction that "abandonment" to vision and the deep, spontaneous self opens the doors of universality:

> It is a secret which every intellectual man quickly learns, that beyond the energy of his possessed and conscious intellect he is capable of a new energy (as of an intellect doubled on itself), by abandonment to the nature of things; that beside his privacy of power as an individual man, there is a great public power on which he can draw, by unlocking, at all risks, his human doors, and suffering the ethereal tides to roll and circulate through him; then he is caught up into the life of the Universe, his speech is thunder, his thought is law, and his words are universally intelligible as the plants and animals. The poet knows that he speaks adequately then only when he speaks somewhat wildly, or "with the flower of the mind;" not with the intellect used as an organ, but with the intellect released from all service and suffered to take its direction from its celestial life; or as the ancients were wont to express themselves, not with intellect alone but with the intellect inebriated by nectar. As the traveller who has lost his way throws his reins on his horse's neck and trusts to the instinct of the animal to find

his road, so must we do with the divine animal who carries
us through this world. For if in any manner we can stimu-
late this instinct, new passages are opened for us into nature; the mind flows into and through things hardest and
highest, and the metamorphosis is possible.

(III, 26–27)

Emerson's Platonic imagery defines ecstasy, the work of
man's superfluous, released energy, in terms of the divine
intoxication of the poet, whence his words become "uni-
versally intelligible" like the things of nature. In poems
that are so truly alive the poet comes closest to the Orphic
marriage of words and things.

The kind of apocalypse defined in "The Poet" is not,
however, what the Orphic poet prophesied in 1836. What
we should recognize here is a poetic apocalypse comparable to the tradition of the "paradise within" that descends
in English poetry from Milton to the great Romantics.[2]
Apocalyptic imagery attends Emerson's messianic poet: his
arrival, his words, mark a new second birth for every man
and the renovation of nature:

We know that the secret of the world is profound, but who
or what shall be our interpreter, we know not. . . . Mankind in good earnest have availed so far in understanding
themselves and their work, that the foremost watchman on
the peak announces his news. It is the truest word ever
spoken, and the phrase will be the fittest, most musical,
and the unerring voice of the world for that time.

All that we call sacred history attests that the birth of a
poet is the principal event in chronology. Man, never so
often deceived, still watches for the arrival of a brother who
can hold him steady to a truth until he has made it his own.
With what joy I begin to read a poem which I confide in as
an inspiration! And now my chains are to be broken; I shall
mount above these clouds and opaque airs in which I
live,—opaque, though they seem transparent,—and from
the heaven of truth I shall see and comprehend my rela-
tions. That will reconcile me to life and renovate nature, to
see trifles animated by a tendency, and to know what I am
doing. Life will no more be a noise; now I shall see men and

women, and know the signs by which they may be discerned from fools and satans. This day shall be better than my birthday: then I became an animal; now I am invited into the science of the real. Such is the hope, but the fruition is postponed.

(III, 11–12)

But the poet has not announced man's dominion over nature, nor the beginnings of a new heaven and earth. Rather his message is a telling or true tallying of nature's text; the power of song is revelation, not correspondent revolution. Emerson is very precise in describing the new heaven as "the heaven of truth," and his own liberation as one that will "reconcile" him to life and enable him to see the "tendency" animating things. And he ends the passage with the admission that "fruition is postponed." In the same way the Orphic apocalypse of song in Emerson's poetry is internalized as the mind's perception of truth and, in some instances, even this revelation is displaced temporally into an indefinite future. The development of this poetic motif is bound to a crucial ambiguity in the "correspondent revolution" of *Nature*, which allows both catastrophic and uniformitarian interpretation: it can mean that the power of the spirit will change the world and erase alienation, or that the discovery of law will show that the world as idea renders "disagreeable appearances" meaningless or trivial. Emerson's early essays seemed to presume the first, but the hero of the "mid-world" essays works at the rough edges, patching particulars, joining the opposites that nature provides, but never imposing on nature as a whole. His method is nature's own, slowly and uniformly progressive, no longer catastrophic as it was in "The Snow-Storm." Similarly Emerson's poetic Orpheus will liberate by revealing the secret law of nature, or by savoring the present moment and leaving apocalypse to some distant, disregarded future. Wordsworth, "long before the blissful hour arrives," chants the consummation in words that speak of present facts, and Emerson writes from the same perspective in key passages of his poetry. Apocalyptic break-through or disruption occurs only as poetry reflects the life of the mind, and the only natural catastrophes are those of inward illumination.

Emerson's central poetry, then, is organized around the primary fable of a poet-hero who accomplishes the messianic prophecy by simply revealing the secret of nature. In this sense he "conforms things to his thoughts" (I, 52), and, like Orpheus, solves the riddle of nature or dissolves the solid world. The essentially Orphic character of Emerson's fable is clearest in a rarely noticed passage from "History," in which two branches of the Orphic tradition, the line of the *prisca theologia* and the Ovidian theme of metamorphosis, are drawn together. History, Emerson has suggested, is the repetition of "universal verities" that are compressed in fables; significantly, from Prometheus, the defier of fixed order, he turns to Orpheus, the interpreter of the free and the true:

> The power of music, the power of poetry, to unfix and as it were clap wings to solid nature, interprets the riddle of Orpheus. The philosophical perception of identity through endless mutations of form makes him know the Proteus. . . . I can symbolize my thought by using the name of any creature, of any fact, because every creature is man agent or patient. . . . The transmigration of souls is no fable. I would it were; but men and women are only half human. . . . Ah! brother, stop the ebb of thy soul,—ebbing downward into the forms into whose habits thou hast now for many years slid. As near and proper to us is also that old fable of the Sphinx, who was said to sit in the road-side and put riddles to every passenger. If the man could not answer, she swallowed him alive. If he could solve the riddle, the Sphinx was slain. What is our life but an endless flight of winged facts or events? In splendid variety these changes come, all putting questions to the human spirit. Those men who cannot answer by a superior wisdom these facts or questions of time, serve them. Facts encumber them,

tyrannize over them, and make the men of routine, the men of *sense*, in whom a literal obedience to facts has extinguished every spark of that light by which man is truly man. But if the man is true to his better instincts or sentiments, and refuses the dominion of facts, as one that comes of a higher race; remains fast by the soul and sees the principle, then the facts fall aptly and supple into their places; they know their master, and the meanest of them glorifies him.

(II, 31–33)

The special role of Orpheus is to reconcile identity with endless mutation, and to solve the riddle that confronts him, which is the riddle of Proteus or the Sphinx. By 1839 Emerson knew enough of poetry, and of primitive poetry in particular, to imagine its origins in the ritual *ratsel-wettkampfe*.[3] Thus his hero is a riddle-solver, and more specifically in the figure of Orpheus a mediator or reconciler of contradictions, dilemmas, and paradoxes. The "riddle of Orpheus" is the eternal problem of the One and the Many, which Emerson recorded in his journal for December 1842:

> In Orpheus, the Demiurgus interrogates Night, thus,
>
>> "Tell me how all things will as one subsist
>> Yet each its nature separate preserve."
>> (*JMN*, VII, 474)

Emerson's source was probably Taylor's *Hymns of Orpheus*, though these lines are also quoted by Proclus and by Cudworth, who cited them in his argument that the Orphic theology reconciles monotheism and polytheism.[4] For Emerson, of course, this version of Orpheus would be a prototype for all thinkers who have, like Emerson's Plato, fully acknowledged the two cardinal facts of Unity and Variety. Orpheus designates the power poetry has to take us back to the "holy place" of our origins, into the realm of the Mothers to which Faust descends (or ascends, as they are the same) in Part II of Goethe's drama: then "we stand before the secret of the world, there where Being passes into Appearance and Unity into Variety" (III, 14). Our world, in the mysterious form of Proteus or Sphinx, is an endless succession of questions and choices, as in "Experience" or the poem "Days"; and man, "the broken giant" (II, 31), suffers Ovidian changes until he can assume his true form by exercising the exemplary power of Orpheus.

As Orphic fable, the binary encounter in Emerson's poetry is distinctly changed. When nature is identified with the Sphinx or with the Orphic Night, the mild, intimate union of the poet with the Rhodora no longer serves; the poet leaves Beulah for a new marriage in which nature is something alien and must be tamed in a poetic apocalypse of the mind. Thus, in his first surge of verse after 1840, Emerson transformed the relatively abstract and stable forms of his early poetry into more dramatic riddle-solving encounters in poems like "The Sphinx," "Wood-notes," "Monadnoc," and others that focus upon secret knowledge, an inexplicable paradox, or an object that is an "eternal fugitive" (IX, 89). When the poet solves the riddle he generally succeeds through the magical power of some draught or song.

Both these motifs are Orphic: Emerson undoubtedly associated the potent song with Merlin and the Welsh bardic tradition,[5] but he did so because the bard as "prophet & priest" stood closer to "the primitive and permanent sources from which the human mind draws excitement and delight" (*EL*, I, 273) and to the time when words were things (VIII, 57). The bard, then, is assimilated into the poetic priesthood, and his miraculous song draws upon the general powers represented by Orpheus. In 1841 Emerson wrote,

> I do not wonder at the miracles which poetry attributes to the music of Orpheus, when I remember what I have experienced from the varied notes of the human voice. They are an incalculable energy which countervails all other

forces in nature, because they are the channel of supernatural powers.

("Lecture on the Times," I, 263)

And in many of his verse-fragments the power of the Muse
is allied with the Creation itself—"Take me out, and no
world had been / Or chaos bare and bleak"—and matter
charmed by the poet's song falls into step and hums his
tune (IX, 476–477). "Destiny" proclaims that music is its
own offspring and stands before all the gods:

> There's a melody born of melody,
> Which melts the world into a sea.
> Toil could never compass it;
> Art its height could never hit;
> It came never out of wit;
> But a music music-born
> Well may Jove and Juno scorn.
>
> (IX, 31)

This power remains in the world as the *magia naturalis* of
Ficino and the Renaissance synthesizers of Plato and Her-
meticism. It can cure disease—"The music that can deepest
reach, / And cure all ill, is cordial speech" (IX, 219)—and
tame the angers of beasts and men. Thus the formula of the
Runic bard that the young Emerson copied into his
notebook points to the explicitly Orphic work of reconciliation and peace-making that is given to Emerson's Merlin:

"I know a song by which I soften and inchant the arms of
my enemies. . . ."[6]

> Merlin's mighty line
> Extremes of nature reconciled,—
> Bereaved a tyrant of his will,
> And made the lion mild.
> Songs can the tempest still,
> Scattered on the stormy air,
> Mould the year to fair increase,
> And bring in poetic peace.
>
> (IX, 122)

Along with music, wine was especially recommended by Ficino for purifying the human spirit as well as for attracting and absorbing the divine.[7] "The Poet" obviously subscribes to a doctrine of intoxication or *"ecstasy,"* both in Emerson's special sense of an extra energy and in the etymological sense of standing outside oneself in the visionary moment. But, "The Poet" adds, the true bard accepts no coarse substitute in place of the true nectar, "for poetry is not 'Devil's wine,' but God's wine" (III, 29). Emerson's distinction is perpetuated in New England by Thoreau's "thought of an older, a newer, and purer wine, of a more glorious vintage" than his neighbors could buy (in the conclusion of *Walden*); by Hawthorne, whose vine is an emblem for Priscilla in *The Blithedale Romance*, yielding not wine for "bacchanalian ecstasies," but what Miles Coverdale belatedly recognizes as the rich and natural juices of the heart (XXVIII); and, of course, in Dickinson's variations (J214, J383) on the Emersonian whim that air is sufficient for inspiration and the poet "should be tipsy with water" (III, 29). It is a distinction derived from the Orphic and Pythagorean discipline of temperance, and probably from Taylor's particular interpretations in *The Eleusinian and Bacchic Mysteries*. In the Orphic theogony[8] Dionysus was one of a number of names, including Eros and Phanes, for the androgynous first of the gods, who is said to have emerged from an egg and created the world. Phanes must have quickly taken on male attributes, since in this work he was assisted by his daughter-consort Night, to whom he gave great powers, including the gift of prophecy. Zeus, descended from the children of Night, was the Creator only in the sense that he later swallowed Phanes and thus enclosed all things. Dionysus was also the name for a child of Zeus, torn to pieces by the Titans and later restored by Apollo, and this Dionysus has been regarded in Orphic literature as the reborn Phanes. In his commentaries Taylor appears to have identified the sparagmos of Dionysus with the various myths of the human condition as fragmented and yet retaining a spark of the original whole, and Taylor emphasized the role of Apollo as "savior of Dionysus" and the necessary qualification of Dionysian impulses by Apollonian restraint in the Orphic life.[9] The Orphic Dionysus, then, is that which was in the beginning and which is reborn, not the god that traditionally passes as Bacchus.

Thus while Emerson looked on the vine as a means of emancipation from the Understanding, he steadfastly interpreted it as spiritual and as a symbol of harmony and symmetry, even in what he called the "bacchanalian songs of Hafiz" (VIII, 249). To the poet who comes to solve Monadnoc's riddle, the mountain offers, from its apparently barren summit, a vintage that is distinct from any earthly wine:

> When he cometh, I shall shed,
> From this wellspring in my head,
> Fountain-drop of spicier wroth
> Than all vintage of the earth.
> There's fruit upon my barren soil
> Costlier far than wine or oil.
> There's a berry blue and gold,—
> Autumn-ripe, its juices hold
> Sparta's stoutness, Bethlehem's heart,
> Asia's rancor, Athen's art,
> Slowsure Britain's secular might,
> And the German's inward sight.
>
> (IX, 70–71)

This mountain is very like a whale, whose gray head and body hold spicy riches, and the juice it ferments is the true nectar Emerson wrote of in "The Poet," the wine of the renewed imagination that dissolves the solid world.[10] With Pan's food it nourishes the original creative power that makes not forms or images but the things themselves:

I will give my son to eat
Best of Pan's immortal meat,
Bread to eat, and juice to drain;
So the coinage of his brain
Shall not be forms of stars, but stars,
Nor pictures pale, but Jove and Mars.

(IX, 71)

The Orphic imagination writes not syllables, but men.

"Bacchus," despite the fact that it was not written until 1846, has been justly celebrated as the most authentic expression of Emerson's bardic mood and idea of poetic intoxication. It comes at a time when the poet had certainly passed his own ecstasies, and when losses and the larger events of the day perhaps represented something like the "nadir's floor" (IX, 122) for Emerson; but at that moment he thought to converse again with the Central Man (*JMN*, IX, 395), and in his journals searched desperately for the "new man" in contemporary and rather implausible figures like Father Taylor or Parker Pillsbury. "Bacchus," then, speaks for a resurgence of hope and is, in a formal sense, an echo of *Nature* ten years earlier because of the way it grafts the energy of vision onto a stable framework. Emerson had already experimented with the short lines and variable stresses that predominate in the *Poems* of 1847, and these together with exhortations and the imagery of thrust and direction give "Bacchus" its sense of energy unrestrained. The poet abandons himself, lets his intellect take direction from its celestial life, and paradoxically in this "wildest freedom" discovers the underlying symmetry of nature in the ample and radiating shape of the vine: the framework for "Bacchus" is the inclusiveness of polar and antithetical extremes. E. W. Emerson aptly commented on the range of the poem when he noted in the Centenary Edition, first, the motto from the *Phaedrus* that Emerson wrote in his own copy—"*The man who is his own master knocks in vain at the doors of poetry*"—and then this passage, presumably from an early version of "Poetry and Imagination":

> For a wise surrender to the current of Nature, a noble passion which will not let us halt, but hurries us into the stream of things, makes us truly know. Passion is logical, and I note that the vine, symbol of Bacchus, which intoxicates the world, is the most geometrical of all plants.
>
> (IX, 443–445; cf. J, VIII, 34)

The geometry of the vine suggests that the appropriate Bacchus for this poem is the reborn Dionysus-Phanes, symbolizing the participation of all things in the whole.[11] In another version Emerson associated Bacchus with the Demiourgos (IX, 444), and in a later poem the "infant Bacchus in the vine" marks the beginning of the evolutionary process (IX, 230).

To the poet the true wine gives a range of cosmic consciousness as extensive as Whitman's in "Song of Myself"—

> That I intoxicated,
> And by the draught assimilated,
> May float at pleasure through all natures;
>
> . . . .
>
> That I, drinking this,
> Shall hear far Chaos talk with me;
> Kings unborn shall walk with me;
> And the poor grass shall plot and plan
> What it will do when it is man.
> Quickened so, will I unlock
> Every crypt of every rock.
>
> (IX, 126)

And the universal plan of ascension dissolves the fixed walls of the world conceived as commodity, marrying heaven and hell in Orphic imagery descended from earliest sources through Milton, Swedenborg, Blake, and Wordsworth's Prospectus. The vine of "Bacchus" descends to darkness and soars high in light:

> . . . its grapes the morn salute
> From a nocturnal root,
> Which feels the acrid juice
> Of Styx and Erebus;
> And turns the woe of Night,
> By its own craft, to a more rich delight.
> . . . .
> [Its] ample leaves and tendrils curled
> Among the silver hills of heaven
> Draw everlasting dew.
>
> (IX, 125)

It reconciles pagan and Christian versions of the man-god who redeems us all from the crypt of death, and it is a compensation or "antidote" for the false wine of use and trade that makes us forget our origins. Thus the poet of "Bacchus" would restore man to the full stature of his "ancient being": on the day of renewal the lost Pleiad, which some say is Emerson's Uriel banished by a "forgetting wind,"[12] will take its place again in the blue firmament, and the giant forms, primitive and perfect as an orb, will return to inhabit the earth.

> The winds took flesh, the mountains talked,
> And he the bard, a crystal soul
> Sphered and concentric with the whole.
>
> (IX, 322)

Clearly in "Bacchus," and even more so in the manuscript trial (IX, 443–445), Emerson's fable of renewal depends upon the concept of creative metamorphosis, and his insistent spiritualizing of Bacchus makes his wine interchangeable with water, as indeed it is in "Bacchus" where water as well as wine "needs no transmuting." To doctrinal transubstantiation Emerson opposed the natural law of transformation, so that the metaphor of dissolution and circulation assumes an essential role in almost every one of his poetic encounters. Thus poetry is a true alchemy worked by the universal solvent upon the impure substances of the earth:

Mountains and oceans we think we understand;—yes, so long as they are contented to be such, and are safe with the geologist,—but when they are melted in Promethean alembics and come out men, and then, melted again, come out words, without any abatement, but with an exaltation of power!

(VIII, 16)

Here Emerson links poetry to the Promethean fire and the assailing waves of his early antinomian attacks upon the Understanding. Things dislimn in the sea and mountain imagery of "Monadnoc" and "The Seashore," and in sections of the unfinished "Poet" where "the mountains flow, the solids seem," "the solid mountain swims / In music and uplifting hymns" (IX, 315, 325). Like melodies the sun is an agent of Apollo, melting solids and thawing snow-drifts into flowers, and the song of the wind in the pines tells of metamorphosis that

> dissolving all that fixture is,
> Melts things that be to things that seem,
> And solid nature to a dream.
>
> (IX, 52)

Under the questioning of the poet the Sphinx in its penultimate stanza dissolves into a shower of color and light (IX, 24–25) that suggests the alchemical *cauda pavonis*, the peacock's tail of many colors symbolizing the division of elements. [13] Since Emerson associated the Sphinx with the stone face known as "the Old Man of the Mountain" in Franconia Notch, New Hampshire (*L*, II, 221), it is not surprising that the fate of the Sphinx and the prophecy the mountain makes for itself in "Monadnoc" are essentially the same: since "adamant is soft to wit," the great rock-cone will "spin" and "pass" when the hero comes (IX, 69). Merlin comes to release the "ice-imprisoned flood" (IX, 120), and the words of Saadi set the world vibrating in presage of the dawn. Emerson's verbs show how the work

102

of water steals into his crucial passages:

> *Swims* the world in ecstasy,
> The forest *waves*, the morning *breaks*,
> The pastures sleep, *ripple* the lakes,
> Leaves twinkle, flowers like persons be,
> And life *pulsates* in rock or tree.
>
> (IX, 134; my italics)

Morning and of course Spring, for Emerson as for Thoreau, are the natural archetypes of renewal; once he had perceived the world as metamorphosis Emerson would have had difficulty, I should think, writing a poem like "The Snow-Storm." The diffuse "May-Day" of 1867 might be conceived as an answer to the winter architectonics of 1834 in both imagery and form, but it holds little in the way of poetic heat or light. Emerson knew better, eschewing long poems and condensing tuns to drops like the brilliantly compressed quatrain titled "Nahant" or the short poem "Rubies" that fairly bursts with images of apocalypse.

> They brought me rubies from the mine,
>   And held them to the sun;
> I said, they are drops of frozen wine
>   From Eden's vats that run.
>
> I looked again,—I thought them hearts
>   Of friends to friends unknown;
> Tides that should warm each neighboring life
>   Are locked in sparkling stone.
>
> But fire to thaw that ruddy snow,
>   To break enchanted ice,
> And give love's scarlet tide to flow—
>   When shall that sun arise?
>
> (IX, 217–218)

This is an astonishingly powerful poem if we see in it, as we do in Blake, the cross-fire of inward and outward revolution, and Emerson's Promethean alembic that changes mountains into men and finally into the hot words of vision. The twelve lines of advancing, martial cadences review a whole array of dissolving images deftly intertwined: the rock or stone, the sun melting ice and snow, wine or blood acting like the tide of the sea to nourish life, and a reminiscence of paradise or the golden age when the ruby of today was newly fermented wine. A dramatic situation, briefly evoked, separates the poet from other men who bring him stones to interpret. Twice the poet-seer sees with imaginative vision: the somewhat cryptic, poetic vision of the first stanza becomes a vision fully moral and prophetic in the second. The second look is with the mind's eye, unfreezing the metaphor of the first, opening, but only obliquely, the way between the actual and the possible. Emerson looks through, not with, the eye, and the apocalyptic question that ends the poem is Blake's also, for here Emerson's poetry comes close to Blake's; but the enormous difference is that Blake's "Golden Net" is what became the web of life for Emerson.

This fable of the poet dissolving and solving nature runs through Emerson's poetry, and there are so many lines or fragments that do not make real sense without it that at times it seems Emerson, like a parrakeet trained to a single note, had only one thing to say. Love of unity notoriously breeds a perfect repetition, and so Emerson stuck in his fable. Merlin, the neat union of magician and bard, with his music pulsing to nature's own heartbeat, and his temperance ("He has not tasted wine impure," IX, 237), and his peace-making role, is probably Emerson's fullest poetic incarnation of Orpheus confronting the Proteus. In Merlin the bard, as in his concept of the Orphic poet in *Nature*, Emerson at first carried out the Renaissance aim of getting at the source or beginning of things through an unbroken line of prophets. But Merlin lives and has a whole history in Emerson's poetry, that incidentally turns once more toward Blake—mythically if not formally—because both

Emerson and Blake brooded on the enchantment of Merlin, which is a type for the fall of Albion. The eternal abides, yet changes, according to the law of metamorphosis, and we shall see, in an arc continued from the prose, Emerson's own curve traced again in the development of his poetic form and the later versions of his primary fable.

Metamorphoses;
or, The Beautiful Changes

———

I suppose if verses of mine should be compared with
those of my friends, the moral tendency would be
impressed on all mine as an original polarity; that all
my light is polarized.
> —EMERSON, on his *Poems* (1847)
> published Christmas Day 1846

If a man has a see-saw in his voice, it will run into his
sentences, into his poem, into the structure of his
fable. . . .
> —EMERSON, "Fate"

I HAVE SPOKEN of a notable variety of achievement in Emerson's poetry, and in nature, conceived as a progressive experiment, variation and freedom are necessarily related. Metamorphosis in liberating the poet assured him that in art as in nature the beautiful changes, and whatever Emerson meant, exactly, by his remark on the *Poems* of 1847, "an original polarity" rightly describes the law of changes in all his work.

In one sense polarity is just the opposite of "a foolish consistency"; it is the ability to see that "everything has two sides." This is the advantage of yielding to whim or the succession of moods, and one of the early poems shows how Emerson could capitalize, as an artist, on "our moods [that] do not believe in each other."

> By fate, not option, frugal Nature gave
> One scent to hyson and to wall-flower,
> One sound to pine-groves and to waterfalls,
> One aspect to the desert and the lake.

It was her stern necessity: all things
Are of one pattern made; bird, beast and flower,
Song, picture, form, space, thought and character
Deceive us, seeming to be many things,
And are but one. Beheld far off, they part
As God and devil; bring them to the mind,
They dull its edge with their monotony.
To know one element, explore another,
And in the second reappears the first.
The specious panorama of a year
But multiplies the image of a day,—
A belt of mirrors round a taper's flame;
And universal Nature, through her vast
And crowded whole, an infinite paroquet,
Repeats one note.

("Xenophanes," IX, 137)

"Xenophanes" is explicitly dated 1834, for otherwise its
theme and tone would argue persuasively that it was written after 1842 as were its companion-pieces (in the 1847
edition) "Blight" and "A Day's Ration." It clearly antici-
pates an essay like "Circles" by setting against the dominant order of correspondence—the order that, in the
poem, unifies a catalogue of diversities—a personal response to that order, haunted by spectres of indifferency
and antagonism. It is Xenophanes, the dramatized persona, who brings down Emerson's sublime architecture of
1836 in this poem. To him plenitude is a crowd of
anonyms, and the appearance of variety simply the deceit
of a designer who works under a stern and parsimonious
necessity. Unity, on the other hand, is dull and grating,
and the meaning it appears to give to nature is also decep-
tive, like the mimicry of the parrakeet. After the reverberat-
ing sound of "one" throughout the first twelve lines and
the slow beats of the catalogue, the poem rises in the suspended phrases of its last sentence, and we might expect a
resolution like the perfect pentameter in "The Snow-
Storm"; but it is instead cut short by the abrupt "one

note," a hollow echo of what has already been heard several times over. "Xenophanes" is Emerson's palinode of 1834, a tightly organized, blank-verse meditation, in that respect like "The Snow-Storm," but without any recognition of nature as gaily myriad-handed.

In the poetry of his major phase (roughly from 1839 to 1847) Emerson moved, appropriately for the expression of what is free and flowing, toward a much looser form of meditation than that of the 1834 poems. He began to favor shorter, more compressed units of thought, reflected in the choice of meters and the often cryptic or elliptical syntax; his rhythms and language grow easy and informal; and the arguments are less explicit, often depending more on imagery than on direct and logical statement. Sometimes it seems, in fact, that Emerson was trying to bring his poetry closer to the actual processes of thought, to create what we today might see as a rudimentary "stream of consciousness" technique.

Such a change can be seen by comparing "Each and All" with another well-known poem, "The Problem," which was written in 1839. In the Herbertian style of 1834, "Each and All" is precisely worked out, an arrangement of discrete parts in a deliberate pattern. Admirable as it is, this formal coherence does have its price—a felt loss in vitality, perhaps, and the friction of such deliberateness in method rubbing against the spontaneity finally endorsed by the poem. As obviously as "Each and All" is composed, "The Problem" is a casual arrangement, its parts more like beads loosely connected on a string. It is a poem of meditation on a matter of great personal concern to Emerson, contrasting again with "Each and All" where, despite the dramatization of inner experience, the theme is more philosophical and objective. From its beginning "The Problem" strikes a note of sincerity and simplicity, of the direct rendering of personal feeling:

> I like a church; I like a cowl;
> I love a prophet of the soul;
> And on my heart monastic aisles
> Fall like sweet strains, or pensive smiles:
> Yet not for all his faith can see
> Would I that cowled churchman be.
>
> (IX, 6)

So brief and straightforward a statement is underlined by the simple, balanced tetrameter and the easy rhymes, and the impression of unreserved candor is always enhanced when one admits liking what one cannot approve. Set beside these the first lines of "Each and All," and the relative contrivance of the latter is evident: "Little thinks, in the field, yon red-cloaked clown / Of thee from the hill-top looking down." Despite the rhyme, the movement here is of studied blank verse, complicated by inversions and enjambment. Development in "The Problem" strengthens the impression that the poem is working out an explanation, not dramatizing one already made. Questions help to break up the pattern of assertion, the arguments are cumulative rather than logical, and the conclusion falls off instead of rising, an abrupt repetition of the opening lines that seems to say, "Even if the explanation has been incomplete or logically unsatisfactory, my conviction remains unchanged." Again, by comparison, the conclusion of "Each and All" is staged, more theatrical than dramatic.

Both poems touch upon the relation of beauty to truth, which is perhaps the inevitable crux of the metamorphic view. "Each and All" reflects Emerson's early faith in a perfect whole that unites beauty with truth and goodness; it suggests the same predilection for symmetry or unity observed in the doctrine of correspondence and *Nature*. "The Problem," like the 1839 journal passage in which the philosopher becomes a poet (*JMN*, VII, 190), shifts from philosophical to aesthetic, from transcendent to natural

109

standards.[1] Revelation, according to the argument summarized in the couplet "one accent of the Holy Ghost / The
heedless world hath never lost," is available at all times
and to all creeds; it is natural rather than sectarian, identified with passionate acts of creation rather than with
statements of belief or dogma. The point of accumulating
examples in the body of the poem is to grant "an equal
date," that is, equal authority, to both pagan and Christian
forms in every era. Emerson's aim here is as syncretic as in
"Bacchus," and he praised Jeremy Taylor by calling him at
his best a "Christian Plato" (IX, 407). The assertion that
revelation is equally available throws new light on the
question Emerson asks himself: why must he insist, in the
poem, upon his difference from the bishop, or why, in
actual life, did he resign from the church if the way of the
priest and the way of the seer are just different paths to the
same truth? The answer is that Emerson's touchstone here
is beauty, not truth, and not the secrets of any priesthood
ancient or modern; he likes the rhythm of church aisles and
Taylor's words "are music in my ear." The revelation
available to Phidias, the Delphic oracle, and Michelangelo,
as well as to divines, is really artistic inspiration drawn
from natural forms. Emerson might still have squared with
the bishop if he had introduced the analogy between man's
art and God's divine creation; but he inclined to the view
that art does not create nature, rather nature creates works
of art:

> These temples grew as grows the grass;
> Art might obey, but not surpass.
> The passive Master lent his hand
> To the vast soul that o'er him planned;
> And the same power that reared the shrine
> Bestrode the tribes that knelt within.
>
> (IX, 8)

A "passive Master" fills the role of Emerson's artist, not an
orthodox Jesus nor the more dynamic creator-gods of older

theologies. Art and the artist must find their place within the order of nature, and that order, illustrated on all levels in the poem, is development from inside outward and from below upward. "Up from the burning core below" all things are "outbuilt." The individualistic and evolutionary implications of such an order are difficult to reconcile with episcopal office, and this imagery of direction or thrust justifies Emerson's making his churchman specifically a bishop.

The structural and conceptual changes illustrated by "The Problem" reflect, in part, Emerson's newly found enthusiasm for the art of poetry in 1839. Yet one would hardly call the protagonist of that poem "bardic," and one listens in vain there for the hammer strokes of Merlin. The poetic program of 1839 to 1841 demanded more radical innovations and clearly displaced Herbert or Wordsworth as models. To find a suitable aesthetic form, Emerson would turn willingly to beauty that was in the beginning and had never been lost—for him personally, the earliest rhythms he had known, the hymnal meters that sounded instinctively in every nineteenth-century New England ear, and the freer rhymes of the amateur household verse his family practiced as well as his own bold experiment in "Gnothi Seauton."[2] He looked to sources that corroborated his ideas about poetic freedom, mainly to the older traditions, the poetry of Saadi and Hafiz, the Vedas, and the ancient British bards. The last, in particular, offered an important source for explicit ideas about the poet and poetic technique. In his 1835 lectures Emerson commented on the revered place of the poet in the earliest British societies and quoted extensively from Welsh and Anglo-Saxon lyrics (avoiding battle epics) which he compared formally to the psalms of David (*EL*, I, 248). Here was material for his portrait of the poet as riddle-solver and peace-maker. Moreover, from one of his sources, Sharon Turner's *History of the Anglo-Saxons*, Emerson would have learned that

abrupt transitions, clipped syntax, periphrasis, and repeated epithets were all characteristic devices of the ancient bards, and that they used no rules for meter, "con-
sulting only the natural love of melody."[3] Very likely he
also read Longfellow's anthology of European poets published in 1845. In an essay introducing his own translations
of Anglo-Saxon lyrics, Longfellow noted especially

> the short exclamatory lines, whose rhythm depends on al-
> literation in the emphatic syllables, and to which the gen-
> eral omission of particles gives great energy and vivacity.
> Though alliteration predominates in all Anglo-Saxon
> poetry, rhyme is not wholly wanting. . . . [Rhyme and al-
> literation,] brought so near together in the short, emphatic
> lines, produce a singular effect upon the ear. They ring like
> blows of hammers on an anvil.[4]

Much that Turner and Longfellow describe appears fre-
quently in Emerson's poems, and especially as nature's
riddle in the earth-song of "Hamatreya" and the original
opening lines of "Woodnotes II" (1847 edition). Perhaps
the best evidence that he imitated the metrical half line,
periphrasis, and alliteration of the Anglo-Saxons is in a
manuscript trial beginning, "Poet of poets / Is Time, the
distiller, / Chemist, refiner."

> All through the countryside
> Rush locomotives:
> Prosperous grocers
> Posing in newspapers
> Over their shopfires
> Settle the State.
> But, for the Poet,—
> Seldom in centuries
> Comes the well-tempered
> Musical Man.
> He is the waited-for,
> He is the complement,
> One man of all men.
> The random wayfarer
> Counts him of his kin

This is he that should come
The Tongue of the Secret
The Key of the casket
Of Past & Future.

. . . .

True bard never cared
To flatter the princes
Costs time to live with them.
Ill genius affords it,
Pre-engaged to the skies
Foremost of all men
The Poet inherits
Badge of nobility,
Charter of Earth;
Free of the city,
Free of the [field] [meadow] forest
Knight of each order,
Sworn of each guild
Fellow of monarchs,
And, what is better
[Fellow] Mate of all men.[5]

The corrections show that Emerson consciously sought al-literation, and the general mood and descriptive effects of this passage are reminiscent of the Old English lyric. If the passage were written as full four-stress lines (instead of half lines) and given rhyme, which Emerson thought an essential and primitive quality of poetry (VIII, 45–48), the result would be similar to the staccato tetrameters that are so common in the *Poems* of 1847.

What Emerson did, essentially, was to roughen the familiar octosyllabic couplet, using a free foot and such devices as alliteration, anaphora, and catalexis to hammer out what he conceived to be an energetic and compressed poetic line. If he needed contemporary precedent, he had Bryant's early defense of trisyllabic variations behind him, and, more important, the examples of Coleridge in *Christabel* and the whole body of Goethe's verse.[6] Since Emerson drew upon Goethe's Orientalism for his idealized poet-figure, it is likely that he was particularly attracted by the epigrammatic or aphoristic style of the *West-Eastern Divan*, which is as much Goethe as it is Persian. Poems need not be long, Emerson was convinced (*J*, V, 441; *L*, II, 415); the poetic work, like the *opus* of the alchemical tradition that lay behind both Emerson and Goethe, was to compress the universe into a quintessential or mercurial droplet. Like many of his Romantic contemporaries, Emerson ran into difficulties with any project over a hundred lines, and he even tried to distill his short poems with gnomic summaries in a couplet or quatrain, such as those in "To Rhea" or "Uriel."[7] Clearly, the famous idea of a poem as a "metre-making argument" (III, 9) had little to do with logical or tight structure. Again Emerson was turning away from Herbert when he imitated the ancients' periphrasis, and he found further justification for his own practice in the "inconsecutiveness" of the Persians:

> The Persians have epics and tales, but, for the most part, they affect short poems and epigrams. Gnomic verses, rules of life conveyed in a lively image, especially in an image addressed to the eye and contained in a single stanza, were always current in the East: and if a poem is long, it is only a string of unconnected verses. They use an inconsecutiveness quite alarming to Western logic, and the connection between the stanzas of their longer odes is much like that between the refrain of our old English ballads . . . and the main story.
>
> (VIII, 243)

It is not at all inaccurate, then, to think of Emerson's longer poems of the 1840s as successions of polished gems worked onto fairly insubstantial strings. Emerson himself used the image, though we should remember that he often thought of the string as the inexpressible Law that relates all things.

This compressed and heroic style, Emerson thought, appropriately clothed his familiar main story. The "well-tempered Musical Man" of the manuscript trial just quoted is a new Orpheus who is the fulfillment of the natural evolutionary process and who shares Time's power to dissolve "towns into melody." In what appears to be the conclusion of this trial poem, he is the one to tell what nature is, and he will tame men and move things with his speech:

> He will come one day
> Who can articulate
> That which unspoken
> Vaults itself over us,
> Globes itself under us,
> Looks out of lovers' eyes,
> Dies, & is born again;—
> He who can speak well;
> Men hearing delighted
> Shall say, *That is ours*.
> Trees hearing shall blossom,
> Rocks hearing shall tremble,
> And range themselves dreamlike
> In new compositions,
> Architecture of thought.
> Then will appear
> What the old centuries,
> Aeons were groping for,
> Times of discomfiture,
> Bankrupt milleniums.
>
> Thought is the sole price
> For which I sell days
> And willing grow aged
> Melting matter to pictures
> And life into law.

Explicitly Orphic, these lines are also an explicit internalization of apocalypse. In the last five lines Emerson's own self—an "I" like the "I" of "Experience"—breaks in upon the prophecy, and the gap between the actual and the visionary is suddenly recalled; reminded of his own wearing away, the poet is willing to barter the external "days" and the hope of a correspondent revolution there for the thought that reconciles him to nature. In another version of the same poem the internalization at this point is just as explicit:

Teach him gladly to postpone
Pleasures to another stage
Beyond the scope of human age
Freely as task at eve undone
Waits unblamed tomorrow's sun.
(J, VIII, 68)

This swerving from apocalypse points to a second important development in the major phase of Emerson's poetry, and that is the way he modifies the situation and tone in his central encounter between the poet and nature. Just as he managed to balance the later essays, by polarizing antitheses or (as Whicher first pointed out) by allowing different voices to speak for opposing sets of ideas, so Emerson gradually loosened the identification between himself and the questing poet-figure he created, removing to his own neutral territory and often leaving the encounter as a standoff or certainly something less than a clear-cut victory of the imagination.

In the earlier bardic poems the poet-figure appears as an active and relentless seeker of truth. Whatever frustrations he encounters, there is nevertheless an air of certainty that he is on the right track, in verses like the "Dull uncertain brain, / But gifted yet to know" fragment (IX, 389–390). In "The Poet" he is the bard who will pierce through to central truth, and like the poet-figure of the *Ion* and Coleridge's *Kubla-Khan* is set apart from other men:

The gods talk in the breath of the woods,
They talk in the shaken pine,
And fill the long reach of the old seashore
With dialogue divine;
And the poet who overhears
Some random word they say
Is the fated man of men
Whom the ages must obey:
One who having nectar drank
Into blissful orgies sank;
He takes no mark of night or day,
He cannot go, he cannot stay,

116

He would, yet would not, counsel keep,
But, like a walker in his sleep
With staring eye that seeth none,
Ridiculously up and down
Seeks how he may fitly tell
The heart-o'erlading miracle.

(IX, 311–312)

Plagued by having heard only a "random word" and not the whole truth, this poet suffers prolonged periods of despair (the poem's original title was "The Discontented Poet, A Masque"). He complains, in effect, that the law of spirits is not kept as faithfully as the law that regulates nature. The Chorus of Spirits answer, first, that they and he are brothers by nature and no one can violate his own nature (IX, 319); second, that no one serves the spirit out of physical compulsion or simply to be rewarded, but out of penury and love:

Serve thou it not for daily bread,—
Serve it for pain and fear and need.
Love it, though it hide its light;
By love behold the sun at night.
If the Law should thee forget,
More enamoured serve it yet. . . .

(IX, 320)

Emerson took great pains with this poem and worked on it for some ten years, but he could never finish it. The reason may be that the poem moves insistently toward a final resolution, but Emerson was never satisfied by any of the answers he could write for the Chorus of Spirits. Perhaps, too, the overt, yet stylized dialogue of a masque drew him too far toward direct statement. He had already written in "The Over-Soul," "An answer in words is delusive." There the only answer is an exhortation that echoes Goethe and Carlyle: "work and live, work and live," so that "all unawares the advancing soul has built and forged for itself a new condition, and the question and the answer are one" (II, 285).

117

Renunciation of answers in the ordinary sense is a necessary if ambivalent aspect of Emerson's experience of revelation. At first it is simply a rejection of the Understanding that is part of the initiation into Reason, but later the absence of answers awakens uncertainties and anxieties in the poet. Then nature in her encounter with man takes on a secretive and antagonistic air, deliberately taunting us for our ignorance of her mysteries in "The World-Soul" and "The Sphinx." At the beginning of her poem the Sphinx is moody, brooding because man alone is alienated from beauty and joy; but she is also "merry" and, by the end, a little scornful of her overly confident interrogator.

> The old Sphinx bit her thick lip,—
>   Said, "Who taught thee me to name?
> I am thy spirit, yoke-fellow;
>   Of thine eye I am eyebeam.
>
> "Thou art the unanswered question;
>   Couldst see thy proper eye,
> Alway it asketh, asketh;
>   And each answer is a lie.
> So take thy quest through nature,
>   It through thousand natures ply;
> Ask on, thou clothed eternity;
>   Time is the false reply."
>
> Uprose the merry Sphinx,
>   And crouched no more in stone;
> She melted into purple cloud,
>   She silvered in the moon;
> She spired into a yellow flame;
>   She flowered in blossoms red;
> She flowed into a foaming wave:
>   She stood Monadnoc's head.
>
> Thorough a thousand voices
>   Spoke the universal dame;
> "Who telleth one of my meanings
>   Is master of all I am."

(IX, 24–25)

The Sphinx is the "slippery Proteus who will not be caught," the conception of nature that makes possible Emerson's metamorphosis and the fluid poetic symbolism it implies.

Placing "The Sphinx" in this context supports Thomas Whitaker's contention that the poet is rebuked and the poem dramatizes ultimate skepticism.[8] This is one of the first poems in which the "I," presumably Emerson, is separated from the poet-figure within the poem. Granted, what the poet says so cheerfully in the poem Emerson might at one time or in part have approved; but here Emerson turns dialectically on himself, admitting that something he might easily have written in 1836 seems only a partial view to him in 1840 and therefore an unacceptable version of the whole. Thus the last two lines of the poem, intentionally ambiguous, do not necessarily mean that the poet has mastered the Sphinx, but more likely that he has not been able to tell one meaning, since according to the organic view of things one cannot understand any part before he fully understands the whole. Thus the riddle is unsolved; what relieves the skepticism of the poem is not knowledge but appreciation—Emerson, despite his sympathy for the poet's quest, rejoices that nature transcends man's understanding, and is thrilled by the sheer beauty of the Sphinx's transformations at the end of the poem. A still more placid conjunction of ignorance with aesthetic awe appears at the end of "The Adirondacs," the poem Emerson wrote to commemorate a camping trip taken with James Russell Lowell, Louis Agassiz, and others in the summer of 1858:

> And Nature, the inscrutable and mute,
> Permitted on her infinite repose
> Almost a smile to steal to cheer her sons,
> As if one riddle of the Sphinx were guessed.
>
> (IX, 194)

But it hasn't been: the subjunctive underlines the negation, despite the nostalgic sentiments that have preceded it. The whole poem, moving through leisurely, good-natured narrative and digression, imitates the repose of nature in a subdued wisdom like that of the negative theology.

"Woodnotes," originally published as two poems in *The Dial*, 1840–1841, is Emerson's longest and least qualified celebration of metamorphosis; it modulates between the spirit of audacious truth-seeking in which the poet-figure sets out, as in "The Sphinx" or "The Poet," and the detached appreciation that tends to resolve the quest after 1840. The first part of "Woodnotes" is primarily a characterization of the poet-figure in the guise of a forester and specifically American hero. The second is the song of the pine tree, a natural aeolian harp, whose words work not discursively but magically as in the Orphic incantation or potent song. Thus together the two parts make up the question-and-answer encounter between the poet and nature.

Formally the poem moves well beyond the symmetries of "Each and All" and is founded (especially in the original version) on Emerson's heroic line, itself the subject of various transformations and counterpointings. Each of the numbered sections in "Woodnotes I," for example, establishes its own rhythmic pattern. In the first section that emphasizes mystic knowledge, strong trochaic beats predominate. Next, the learning of the forester is presented as more natural than occult, and the pattern is a more relaxed and regular iambic tetrameter. When the world begins to shape itself as an Augustan harmony, the line modulates into an appropriate form, the heroic couplet:

> Go where he will, the wise man is at home,
> His hearth the earth,—his hall the azure dome;
> Where his clear spirit leads him, there's his road,
> By God's own light illumined and foreshowed.

> (IX, 46)

In the last part of "Woodnotes I" this spatial panorama is transformed into a temporal frame, the moment of revelation—"One of the charmed days / When the genius of God doth flow." The poet is, like Stevens' singer at Key West, "the heart of all the scene," and in a roughened and metrically irregular speech he tells of the "secret sympathy" between nature and the natural man, a type like Natty Bumppo who lives and dies by the signs of the earth. The mazy rhythms emerge from the forest in the poet's straightforward affirmation of reciprocal faith at the end of the poem. Passages like this one or the "ecstasy" in "Saadi" (IX, 134) are assurance that Emerson treated metrical variation as Coleridge had when he wrote that it was "not introduced wantonly . . . but in correspondence with some transition in the nature of the imagery or passion."[9] Certainly Emerson's intentions in rhyme and meter were not understood by his American contemporaries, and one wonders, then, if the "good-humoredly puzzled smile with which he once confessed his inability to apprehend the value of accent in verse" was not the shrewd smile of Emerson's Sphinx.[10]

The truth-seeker of "Woodnotes I" affirms his faith, and the poem ends on a note of correspondence; much more characteristic of Emerson's later view is the situation in "Woodnotes II," where the poet is dumbstruck with wonder at the "rushing Metamorphosis." The pine as nature's surrogate is as fugitive as Brahma or the Sphinx—

> Hearken once more!
> I will tell thee the mundane lore.
> Older am I than thy numbers wot,
> Change I may, but I pass not.
>
> (IX, 57)

The lore is Pythagorean as well as Pentecostal, as several commentaries have shown, and I think Barbara Carson rightly identifies the pine tree's creation myth and the "eternal Pan" with the Orphic Pan as described by Taylor and Cudworth.[11] For this Pan was before all things, a personification of the universe and the creative Demiourgos, and Emerson's Pan is a syncretic deity who will grant his worshippers "dominion o'er the palm and vine," that is, over Christianity and Dionysian paganism. Only the initiates, however, those who have taken upon themselves the "formidable innocence" of the "wild-eyed boy" in the woods, will hear the harmony of the spheres. A brief illustration (IX, 55), similar to the classic Wordsworthian episodes, shows the uninitiated poet looking on a precipice or at the shore from his skiff, and his eye sees only "emptiness." Unlike Wordsworth's cliff, that rose up and "like a living thing, strode after me," nature here holds no drama, not even a moral nudge, for the man still unredeemed.[12] The fault is clearly a failing of imaginative vision—in Emerson's gnomic phrase, the predominance of "peacock wit" over "primal mind." So the American democratic hero is asked to renounce all the solid things that might be associated with the Understanding—the wealth and comforts of the city, the easy, explicit answers of established faiths, and even the parochialities of his own native speech—to return, not of course to the courtly languages of Europe, but to the Pentecostal and universal tongue of antiquity (IX, 53), which is the language of nature. In this he may read "the world's incessant plan," the ascending order announced at the end of the poem, and know the mind of God, not by any fixed name but in the law of the world's changes. Fugitive form the pine tree may be, but there are no painfully unanswerable questions in "Woodnotes"; the reiterative assurances of the negative theology are sufficient evidence of the deity:

> Thou seek'st in globe and galaxy,
> He hides in pure transparency;
> Thou askest in fountains and in fires,
> He is the essence that inquires.

He is the axis of the star;
He is the sparkle of the spar;
He is the heart of every creature;
He is the meaning of each feature;
And his mind is the sky.
Than all it holds more deep, more high.

(IX, 59)

Closure is undisturbed by the extreme variations in meter and rhyme found elsewhere in the poem, and an ease infused into this revelation by the final couplet that offers, rhythmically and contextually, one vast, cerulean resolution.

Taken as a whole, then, "Woodnotes" is Emerson's attempt to merge the relatively indigenous frontier myth and its Natty Bumppo figure with what he regarded as the oldest traditions of Europe. "Woodnotes II" marks a personal transition, in that it joins his later ideas, fully propounded, with his earlier attitude of serene confidence. And, it is fair to say, this attitude determines the overall structure of the poem: "Woodnotes II" is organized into four major movements, the first and third mainly concerned with the fate of man, the second and fourth giving the secret revelations of the mystic song. In each movement the imagery and details are developed in antitheses of the Reason-Understanding type—peasant valued over lord, forest over city, child over learned pedant, "primal mind" over "peacock wit." And the revelation in the poem moves from an exposition of the flux or the dissolving of solid things (beginning at IX, 51, bottom), apparently intended to shock the complacency of ordinary man, to the superior insight of the last movement (beginning on IX, 57), the law behind the flux. Confidence is restored when unity triumphs over diversity, another antithesis in the same parallel series. Thus, although "Woodnotes II" is a looser arrangement than any of Emerson's early poems, structurally it belongs to the earlier form observed in the prose of *Nature* and "The Over-Soul," and in it an Orphic inquirer solves, in his fashion, the riddle of Proteus.

When he published "Woodnotes," Emerson was already at work on a poem of similar design in which a mountain plays the role of the pine tree. "Monadnoc," however, was not completed until sometime between 1845 and its publication in the volume of 1847, so that it must represent a step further in Emerson's development of the encounter between the poet and nature. "Woodnotes" gave no hint of an observer set apart from the forester-poet, and there was nothing equivocal or complex about the pine tree's role as nature's spokesman. But in "Monadnoc," as in "The Sphinx," the "I" of the poem (with whom Emerson identifies) is separate: the protagonist of "Monadnoc" stands as an observer midway between the "spruce clerk" (IX, 71), type of the urban tourists who daily climb the mountain in summer, and the heroic "bard and sage" (IX, 70) whom the mountain awaits. The mountain itself is complex, a personification of nature in its encounter with man, but also a Titan, an imprisoned demigod and perhaps a friend of man, like the bound Prometheus awaiting a human intercessor. Moreover, the claims of the mountain are significantly more cautious than those of the pine: the order it hints of is the flux behind solid-seeming things, which is only the first stage of reality in "Woodnotes II." Monadnoc itself belongs to this order; it obeys the law expressed by the gnomic paradox "adamant is soft to wit," and therefore it will dissolve when the apocalyptic hero comes to solve the riddle of its being (IX, 69).

The secret of the mountain is essentially a scientific account of its nature and origin. Common sense and simple observation see only a solid pyramid, but the "bard and sage" probes deeper and "in large thoughts, like fair-pearl-seed, / Shall string Monadnoc like a bead" (IX, 70). Emerson's repeated image for the ordering of matter is a string of beads:

> . . . these gray crags
> Not on crags are hung,
> But beads are of a rosary
> On prayer and music strung.
>
> (IX, 68)

And he explicates the image in "Poetry and Imagination"—

> Thin or solid, everything is in flight. I believe this conviction makes the charm of chemistry,—that we have the same avoirdupois matter in an alembic, without a vestige of the old form; and in animal transformation not the less, as in grub and fly, in egg and bird, in embryo and man; everything undressing and stealing away from its old into new form, and nothing fast but those invisible cords which we call laws, on which all is strung.
>
> (VIII, 5)

The beads are bits of matter, not things-in-themselves, but impermanent, infinitely convertible cohesions; the material world is not built stone upon stone, it is hung upon a string, an organizing principle that corresponds to the divine Idea or Law and gives to the whole image the religious efficacy of a rosary. The string is also a fitting emblem for the concept of rhyme or musical order that Emerson found inherent in nature. The material universe is really an intellectual dance for which "rhyme [is] the pipe, and Time the warder" (IX, 69). All things begin and end in motion, the mountain itself having begun as "chemic eddies," finally rising "with inward fires and pain" like "a bubble from the plain" (IX, 70), in accord with the theory of upheavals that Emerson had set forth in his early lectures. At its end, the mountain "shall throb," and metaphorically it becomes the monster of primary myth, to be slain not by the sword but by the song of a "troubadour" who will "string" up the carcass on his rhyme. Then, Monadnoc prophesies, like a whale or volcano the mountain will shower the earth, and this rain—sacramental liquid called the true wine of remembering in "Bacchus"—will reclaim mankind.

125

There is the apocalyptic fable, but the curious thing
about "Monadnoc" is that the poet-observer who concludes the poem disregards what the mountain has
prophesied. This may be because he is not the heroic bard
of the future and has been, from the start, concerned with
the practical and immediate effect of Monadnoc upon the
people who live there, hoping that the mountain would be
"their life's ornament, / And mix itself with each event"
(IX, 61). For him the mountain already dislimns by "pour-
ing many a cheerful river," which in turn offer practical
gifts to the inhabitants. In the final apostrophe to Monadnoc the protagonist is still concerned with the immediately
practical, what he calls "pure use." The epithet, surely
paradoxical to the Romantic mind, is appropriate because
what the poet is trying to define is the fruit or harvest of
the "barren cone," the mountain's top above the timber-
line. The passage then floods in paradoxes—stones that
flower, the "sumptuous indigence" of man, the "plenties"
of the "barren mound," and the mountain described as an
"opaker star" and finally as a "Mute orator." The point
made by the poet-observer is that, notwithstanding the
mountain's own prediction that it will someday disinte-
grate, Monadnoc's rocky summit is for men a "type of
permanence." It is, too, a religious temple to comfort
men's "insect miseries," and no less a "complement" of
the erect human form with mind at its summit. Indeed, the
triangular shape leading to an apex is a symbol of all progress toward unity, hence of the One or Good which is now
introduced in terms similar to those of "Woodnotes II":

> Thou . . . imagest the stable good
> For which we all our lifetime grope,
> In shifting form the formless mind,
> And though the substance us elude,
> We in thee the shadow find.
>
> (IX, 74)

This statement, however, is much more limited: the pine

expressed confidence that despite the fleeting forms "substances survive," but here substance eludes us. The substance or reality of the Good, which is formless, we can never know; but it is shadowed forth in all the changing forms of nature, most clearly in the large, stable objects which seem to us to change least. The use of the mountain, then, is purely symbolical, but in a world where motion is ever faster and more frivolous, this symbolic role, recalling us in wayside moments and making us sane, is actually more practical than all its physical bounties. This is the thematic paradox at the center of a number of paradoxes evoked in the last section of the poem.

Thus "Monadnoc" is a more complicated poem than "Woodnotes," and more suited to Emerson's later thought. It is, of course, another version of the story of Orpheus, the poet who will move the earth by solving its riddle in song. But "Monadnoc" is resolved by the poet-observer as distinct from the Orphic bard, and as concerned about everyday life as about apocalyptic revelation. The apostrophe that ends the poem is an outburst of American poetry unparalleled, at least until Hart Crane wrote his similarly rugged and free, figuratively intricate and compressed paeans to Brooklyn Bridge. Emerson's passage clearly displaces the apocalypse from any millennial future event—whether an outward correspondent revolution or an inward telling of nature's secret—to a paradise within the present imagination. While the pine tree of "Woodnotes" was merely a spokesman for the doctrine of the poem, the mountain itself and not the doctrine becomes the center of interest in "Monadnoc," and the poet-observer recognizes it as a complex symbol, something that cannot be expressed by any other means, and a mediator between the eternal and the quotidian. Again, to use Emerson's own formula, philosophy becomes poetry, the fluid symbolism of art replaces a more rigid framework for ideas in the transition from the earlier to the later poem.

In more personal meditations as well as in the mythic encounters, the poet as central actor matures into the poet-observer, and a law of polarity governs the poetic changes. "Give All to Love," perhaps Emerson's finest poem on this theme, is a statement of his Platonic theory of love with the strong suggestion, in the last two stanzas, of his own parting from the pale and short-lived beauty of Ellen Tucker. Formally it is a true conjunction of opposites based on two maxims, "Give all to love" and "Keep . . . Free as an Arab / Of the beloved," both set in the dominant two-stress line. The production of such double advice is the paradox common to intellectual and erotic energy, that "one pulse more" generates its own antithesis. The poem leaves the paradox unresolved while a series of longer cadences describes a specific love affair that could represent Emerson's first marriage, and then, returning to the short line, the poem closes with a gnomic summary of the essay "Compensation" (especially the last paragraph on II, 126–127) and the lesson of the *Symposium*:

> Though thou loved her as thyself,
> As a self of purer clay,
> Though her parting dims the day,
> Stealing grace from all alive;
> Heartily know,
> When half-gods go,
> The gods arrive.
>
> (IX, 92)

The beloved person is the half-god, and the god is love itself directed toward impersonal ideals. Emerson's prose account is even more austere—

> . . . love, which is the deification of persons, must become more impersonal every day. . . . as life wears on, it proves a game of permutation and combination of all possible positions of the parties. . . . Thus are we put in training for a love which knows not sex, nor person, nor partiality, but which seeks virtue and wisdom everywhere. . . .
>
> ("Love," II, 184–188)

128

"Give All to Love" illustrates the kind of structure implied by Emerson's dialectical habit of mind—in the middle of the poem (the turn marked by the line, "Yet, hear me, yet") the thesis is suddenly confronted by its opposite, and we learn to ascend by "the staircase of surprise." So it is with form and technique: once meter is established or the tendency toward compression asserts itself, Emerson is apt to introduce a contrary pattern at a strategic moment, balancing long line against short or catalogue against gnome. To the poet of Orphic range all such extremes are possible, as "Merlin" says in his longest line:

Bird that from the nadir's floor
To the zenith's top can soar,—
The soaring orbit of the muse exceeds that journey's length.
(IX, 122)

In the "Ode, Inscribed to W. H. Channing," Emerson embodied these tendencies in a way that is exemplary for all of American poetry. The "Ode" offers both a structure for the meditative poem—what might be called a "dialectical meditation," based on the method of polarity—and guidelines for the position of "armed neutrality" or "strategic retreat" that has figured widely in our poetic tradition from Whitman to the present. Technically Pindaric and an expression of Emerson's "wildest freedom," the poem nevertheless shapes itself to the natural history of intellect, for, like the natural order it commends, it embraces the greatest possible variation in order to achieve its final progressive balance. Lines range in syllables from four to eleven, no one of the twelve stanzas is exactly like any other, and there is a profusion of off-rhyme and disguised or counterpointed rhymes. The discrepancy of a couplet like "Sex to sex, and even to odd;— / The overgod" reflects a world apparently unbalanced by the spirit of materialism and the cumulative mechanical energy it has harnessed; in the middle of the poem this power grinds and devours man's kingdom in regimented phrases, so that one can only throw up one's hands and say bluntly, "Things are of the snake." And yet out of this confusion, according to the last turn of thought, comes order and balance restored. The last stanza exemplifies just that movement, dramatizing a situation in which the cause of freedom appears hopeless:

> The Cossack eats Poland,
> Like stolen fruit;
> Her last noble is ruined,
> Her last poet mute:
> Straight, into double band
> The victors divide;
> Half for freedom strike and stand;—
> The astonished Muse finds thousands at her side.
>
> (IX, 79)

With a jerky inertia the short lines build to an abrupt suspension, and then the last moves as smoothly and breathlessly as Milton's "They also serve who only stand and wait": the reader is as astonished as the Muse to find that Emerson's most irregular poem ends in a graceful pentameter.

Like "The Problem," the "Ode" is an attempt to resolve a personal dilemma in poetic form; it too gives over the neatness of more formal meditation for a loose structure that approaches monologue, or more precisely, the dialogue with oneself so often found in Emerson's private writings. But it goes beyond "The Problem," which gave no evidence of struggle, by recreating the dilemma, the difficulties of coming to a decision, and the passions that animate conflict. Here is a mind aroused—sharing the fiery, Promethean indignation of Emerson's interlocutor, moving almost too rapidly for full, explicit statement, and yet skeptical of any conclusion that makes for easy, partisan action. The staccato lines, varied and irregularly rhyming, promote this sense of tough-minded vitality. Thus while the poem may have been a response to the actual roles of William Henry Channing and Daniel Webster,

130

"glowing friend" and "unwilling senator" respectively,[13] at its center is the psychomachia, the struggle within Emerson's own mind.

This struggle is shaped as an Hegelian triad, divided into thesis, antithesis, and synthesis by the conjunctions "but" in the third stanza and "yet" in the eleventh. At the beginning the poet states opposing courses: in the first two stanzas he refuses to join Channing, "the evil time's sole patriot," but in the third and fourth stanzas he turns on his own inactive stance, belittling the "prate" and "praise" of poetry that ignores the real conditions of life. An acknowledgement that the times demand action rises against the original thesis of not leaving "honied thought." This self-questioning once set in motion is not easily stopped, however, and the next development (in the fifth and sixth stanzas) reveals a crucial flaw in the activist party: they have not pierced to the center of the issue, which involves both North and South. In the summer of 1846 it seemed to Emerson more clearly than ever that "man is a dwarf of himself": "little men"—so contemptible that they are described as jackals, bats and wrens, crocodiles, and finally subsumed under "the snake"—have disturbed the balance of nature with their furious, materialistic drive. Emerson's distrust of activism is framed in his famous distinction between "two laws discrete, / Not reconciled,— / Law for man, and law for thing" (IX, 78). This is the popular expression of Kantian and Coleridgean ethics that gripped Transcendentalist New England, but perhaps more important for Emerson personally it is also the great gap of "Experience," "the irreconcilableness of the two spheres." He did not imagine a world recreated as a realm of ends, for "things have their laws, as well as men; and things refuse to be trifled with" ("Politics," III, 205). But a Promethean poet-hero hitching himself to things obviously upsets the polar balance, and he must pass his torch to an Orpheus, even a hesitant and husky-voiced one like Emerson who sings here, at a sufficient perspective on events, with "thrushes in the solitudes." Emerson's own poetic persona, in a journal passage written about the same time as the "Ode," refused to come "to the aid of disturbed institutions" because

> I can best help them by going on with the creation of my own. I am a sad bungler at laws, being afflicted with a certain inconsecutiveness of thought, impertinent associations, and extreme skepticism; but I recover my eyesight and spirits in solitude.
>
> (*J*, VII, 175)[14]

Poetic weakness—Emerson surely describes the attributes of his own poetry, as he saw them—is magically transformed into poetic strength. In the final section of the poem the poet-observer in his detached position is assured that compensatory nature redresses partial wrong even in the most ominous of her permutations. Thus a natural dialectic works on historical as well as personal levels, manifesting in the Polish resistance its "small balance" favorable to reason and freedom (I, 372).

The ending of the poem is accurately described as a synthesis because, although it apparently retreats to the inaction of the original thesis, Emerson has actually scaled the craggy steeps of truth to a new vantage point. The poem itself, the meditation that others might look on as mere inaction, has disclosed the limitations of mere action: elaborating the underlying causes of discontent and the two discrete laws is in fact the poet's active contribution to the political turmoil of his times. "Words are also actions," said "The Poet" (III, 8), and in the alchemy of imagination words become things. What Emerson may have calculated as the practical, public effect of his dialectical meditation is suggested in the larger argument against concerted action:

> Do you ask my aid? I also wish to be a benefactor. I wish more to be a benefactor and servant than you wish to be served by me; and surely the greatest good fortune that

could befall me is precisely to be so moved by you that I should say, 'Take me and all mine, and use me and mine freely to your ends!' . . . If therefore we start objections to your project, O friend of the slave, or friend of the poor or of the race, understand well that it is because we wish to drive you to drive us into your measures. We wish to hear ourselves confuted. We are haunted with a belief that you have a secret which it would highliest advantage us to learn, and we would force you to impart it to us, though it should bring us to prison or to worse extremity.

("New England Reformers," III, 277–278)

Up and up goes the spiral stair of Orphic riddle-solving, for in the fable everything outside the soul, both nature and other men, belongs to the NOT ME and must be constrained or subdued by song. Emerson was struck by Flaxman's drawing of *The Eumenides* of Aeschylus (III, 82), in which Apollo sits calm above the conflict; and in the motto for "Politics" he seemed to remember that the true god of poetry could not abide the violence of Amphion, the counterpart of Orpheus, who built Thebes with his lyre but was later punished for his vengeance.

> Fear, Craft, and Avarice
> Cannot rear a State.
> Out of dust to build
> What is more than dust—
> Walls Amphion piled
> Phoebus stablish must.
>
> (III, 197; IX, 271)

The ultimate harmony requires a unique mode, and in his meditative poetry, placed internally, in personal and historical time rather than in space, Emerson intoned the reconciling "middle measure" (III, 212) of his own Orpheus and came closest to a new form for the Romantic lyric. The "Ode, Inscribed to W.H. Channing" remains the best index of the "original polarity" in the *Poems* of 1847, and its poet-hero is that singular thing, the man of the middle who is also at the edge, the "balanced soul" of *Representative Men*.

VII

Toward the Titmouse Dimension

———

> But never yet the man was found
> Who could the mystery expound,
> Though Adam, born when oaks were
> young,
> Endured, the Bible says, as long;
> But when at last the patriarch died
> The Gordian noose was still untied.
> He left, though goodly centuries old,
> Meek Nature's secret still untold.
>
> —EMERSON, poetic fragment

> We have seen or heard of many extraordinary young men
> who never ripened, or whose performance in actual life was
> not extraordinary. . . . theirs is the tone of a youthful giant
> who is set to work revolutions. But they enter an active
> profession and the forming Colossus shrinks to the
> common size of man. The magic they used was the ideal
> tendencies, which always make the Actual ridiculous; but
> the tough world had its revenge the moment they put their
> horses of the sun to plough in its furrow.
>
> —EMERSON, "Heroism"

"HORSED ON THE PROTEUS," as Emerson wrote in the motto
for "Illusions," the poet rides to power and endurance.
Emerson's poet stayed up, first, by internalizing the revolution as a fable of naming or riddle-solving, and then,
when the riddle refused to be solved, by displacing the
solution itself from the poetic center and affirming ineffable beauty and ultimate order in the encounter. Inevitably
perhaps, the tough world revenges itself upon this concept
of the poet as noble rider, and in Emerson's poetry the

Colossus shrinks to "little man." If he intended such implications when in "Experience" he prophesied "the transformation of genius into practical power" he could not have been more accurate with respect to his own thinking. In *The Conduct of Life*, which represents his philosophy of the 1850s, the idea of power is insistently practical and associated with everything that Emerson in 1836 would have ranked under the heading of the Understanding. There the "minor skills and accomplishments," most especially riding (VI, 143) and the acrobatics that enable the equestrian of "Fate" to leap from horse to horse or ride two simultaneously (VI, 47; cf. IX, 331), are Emerson's metaphors for an attainable felicity in life and art.

Characteristically, these tendencies appear earlier in Emerson's poetry, in transformations of the Orphic poet and the primary fable before 1847. There the "original polarity" asserted itself, so that when the doctrine of flux began to erode the poet's visionary faith and heroic stature, Emerson's compressed style, first tailored for the hero, then took on a different color and tonality—less horses' hoofs or cannon strokes, more like the nimble leaps of the squirrel in "Fable." If it was "The Poet" that brought forth *Leaves of Grass*, then Emerson, always the even-handed oracle, also summoned a poet like Emily Dickinson. There was a need, he had already prophesied in 1840, for voices smaller than drumbeats:

> The philosophy of the day has long since broached a more liberal doctrine of the poetic faculty than our fathers held. . . . This new taste for a certain private and household poetry, for somewhat less pretending than festal and solemn verses which are written for the nations really indicates, we suppose, that a new style of poetry exists. . . . Is there not room for a new department in poetry, namely, *Verses of the Portfolio*? We have fancied that we drew greater pleasure from some manuscript verses than from printed ones of equal talent. For there was herein the charm of character; they were confessions; and the faults, the imper-

fect parts, the fragmentary verses, the halting rhymes, had
a worth beyond that of high finish.[1]

This might describe Emerson's own roughened verses (in
fact it is part of an introduction to poems by William Ellery
Channing printed in *The Dial*), but the tone here is consid-
erably less bardic, much more private and self-effacing,
and it suggests that Emerson's view of the world would be
better expressed in a little slant of wit than in Vatic pro-
nouncements. For the author of "Experience" Uriel or
Saadi is a better spokesman than Merlin the bard—
Emerson's Saadi, principally a "joygiver and enjoyer," sits
tranquilly in the sun and possesses "cheerfulness, without
which no man can be a poet" (IV, 215). This is not a shal-
low optimism, for it is precisely Emerson's awareness of an
incomprehensible NOT ME, and of the individual man's
shrinking before destiny, that makes cheerfulness the
paramount virtue. And so serenity in the face of flux and a
love for small things became salient aspects of Emerson's
later poetic program.

In the first of these tonal variations there is relatively
little diminution in the poet's power. Transvaluation of the
common and low had been Emerson's theme since *The
American Scholar*, and science, he thought, bore out the rule
of poetry that "the fairies largest in power were the least in
size" (VII, 176). Uriel is banished, it is true, but the gods
still shudder at the sound of his mischievously scornful
voice. His sentiments are gnomic hints whose purpose is to
shatter old decrees and formulas, not to create new ones,
and thus Emerson is not pressed in Uriel's poem for the
kind of answer he felt obliged to provide in others like
"Threnody" or "Woodnotes." An oblique counterpunch
often topples by virtue of its swiftness and surprise, rather
than its inherent strength. There is this kind of artfulness
in "Fable," a gem-like or microcosmic version of "Monadnoc" in which the squirrel plays the role of poet-hero. The

squirrel is spry in word and deed, and he turns the tables on the mountain with Emerson's doctrine of compensation disguised as New England wise-cracking.

> The mountain and the squirrel
> Had a quarrel,
> And the former called the latter 'Little Prig;'
> Bun replied,
> 'You are doubtless very big;
> But all sorts of things and weather
> Must be taken in together,
> To make up a year
> And a sphere.
> And I think it no disgrace
> To occupy my place.
> If I'm not so large as you,
> You are not so small as I,
> And not half so spry.
> I'll not deny you make
> A very pretty squirrel track;
> Talents differ; all is well and wisely put;
> If I cannot carry forests on my back,
> Neither can you crack a nut.'
>
> ("Fable," IX, 75)

The squirrel's incongruous victory is underlined by off-rhymes and counterpoint, and his finishing punch is a quick, colloquial jab after the characteristic suspension and pause just before it. Not the least of the charm in this poem is the squirrel's ability to speak like a real New Englander, with dragging Yankee cadences and a profusion of lengthened vowels and final r's. Similar effects are found in the best and most Dickinsonian of Emerson's quatrains—the cunning "Orator" (IX, 291) is exemplary in this respect—and in "Berrying," which has the distinctive two-part structure, a composition setting the question, and then as the answer a colloquy between the poet and the vines.

> 'May be true what I had heard,—
> Earth's a howling wilderness,

Truculent with fraud and force,'
Said I, strolling through the pastures,
And along the river-side.
Caught among the blackberry vines,
Feeding on the Ethiops sweet,
Pleasant fancies overtook me.
I said, 'What influence me preferred,
Elect, to dreams thus beautiful?'
The vines replied, 'And didst thou deem
No wisdom from our berries went?'

("Berrying," IX, 41)

Emerson's touch is sure: the insistent first-person and pre-cise balancing, "said I" against "I said," recall the landlord of "Hamatreya," and just enough emphasis on "elect" completes the sketch of a Calvinist Yankee farmer sur-prised into vision. Perhaps no god elected him, as he him-self wonders, but in the sensuous, inebriating "Ethiops sweet" there is an influx of wisdom freely given. The jour-nals seem to indicate that this captain of a berrying party has Eastern roots, as well, and is a version of Osman, the ideal poet tempering his promise of abstinence with this surreptitious indulgence (*J*, VI, 48–49). The ending of the poem points toward the displacement of riddle-solving, for the true vine of the imagination answers a question only with another question.

Nature, however, "is no Sentimentalist" (VI, 6), and the passage following that predication in "Fate" is evidence that pleasant fancies of apocalypse will not forestall another hard look at earth as a "howling wilderness." A succession of moments, not the moment, characterizes the day, and continuous daylight affords no such intensity as the visionary's flash-of-lightning faith. Thus time, which was the false reply in 1840, or so the Sphinx said, turns out to be the only reply in 1853, the only means to the "suffi-cient perspective" at which the tooth-and-claw circle of life pleases (VI, 36). The Orpheus who would reconcile the imagination with nature cannot expect, like the poet of

Nature, to conform things to his thoughts; rather, he must like Goethe (the "pivotal man" in 1851, *J*, VIII, 249) observe the minute gradations of nature and calculate their law, in effect conforming or adapting himself to things. Under the freedom of metamorphosis Emerson thought that the poet, by virtue of his imaginative analogies and generalizations, was the true scientist, but as he began to stress the invariability of natural law his conception seems to have limited poetry to the strictly scientific:

> Natural Science *is* the point of interest now, &, I think, is dimming & extinguishing a good deal that was called poetry. These sublime & all-reconciling revelations of nature will exact of poetry a correspondent height & scope, or put an end to it.
>
> (*L*, VI, 63: to Anna C. L. Botta, 16 March 1869)

Less than a decade after 1839, when he had demanded freedom and spontaneity, Emerson was asking the poet to write wildest odes with the hardest precision (*JMN*, X, 91). Noting in his 1850 journal that poetic symbols can always be explained by "snailish arithmetic," he then exclaimed, "Cause & Effect forever!" (*JMN*, XI, 235).

These new limits to poetry are indicated in the way Emerson's early belief that revelation has always been in the world is translated as the law of conservation of forces in the 1850s. And there is an important difference between the identity of morality and physics as interpreted by de Staël (I, 33) and Emerson's later admission, in 1857, that "if natural philosophy is faithfully written, moral philosophy need not be . . . we shall read off the commandments and gospels in chemistry—without need of translation" (*J*, IX, 107–108).[2] Similarly, the principles of adjustment and adaptation that are observed to keep balances in nature (VI, 36–37) are the final arbiters of beauty as well:

> Herein we have the explanation of the necessity that reigns in all the kingdom of Art. Arising out of eternal Reason, one and perfect, whatever is beautiful rests on the

foundation of the necessary. Nothing is arbitrary, nothing
is insulated in beauty. It depends forever on the necessary
and the useful. The plumage of the bird, the mimic plumage of the insect, has a reason for its rich colors in the
constitution of the animal. Fitness is so inseparable an ac-
companiment of beauty that it has been taken for it. The
most perfect form to answer an end is so far beautiful. We
feel, in seeing a noble building, which rhymes well, as we
do in hearing a perfect song, that it is spiritually organic;
that is, had a necessity, in Nature, for being; was one of the
possible forms in the Divine mind, and is now only discovered and executed by the artist, not arbitrarily composed by
him.

("Art," VII, 52–53)

Art follows nature, and the artist needs only to trace the
pattern of this wonderfully intricate web (VI, 46).

As a corollary of this view, nature replaces man as the
mythic giant form, and her "colossal ciphers" do most of
the talking in Emerson's later poetic encounters. The poet
as hero speaks in "Bacchus," and the squirrel in "Fable,"
but already in "The Sphinx" and in "Monadnoc" nature's
spokesman or the poet as observer monopolizes the
dialogue, while in "Woodnotes II" and "Song of Nature"
the NOT ME assumes the monologue. Emerson's primary
motifs are reversed in the manuscript poem that is said to
have ushered in his skeptical mood.[3] There divine intoxication is treated as real madness rather than ecstasy, and the
giant forms in this poem are not men but "the arch-
deceiver Hope" and "performance-hating Nemesis." The
men who aspire to flight do not flow but fix in stone:

> Madness, madness,
> Madness from the gods!
> To every brain a special vein
> Of madness from the gods!
> Their heads they toss each one aloft,
> They toss their heads with pride,
> Though to break free they struggle oft
> And shoulder each aside,

What boots it, though their arms stretch out,
And wings behind their shoulders sprout,
If as at first also at last,
Their planted feet like trees are fast,
Rooted in the Slime of Fate,
Sepulchre predestinate:
As if their feet were flint, & soon
All the trunk will grow to stone.

Common enough in Ovid, this dehumanizing metamorphosis is in particular the punishment dealt to the
Maenads in Book XI for mutilating Orpheus in their frenzy.
Here it is visited upon the line of prophetic heroes who
aspire beyond the middle flight of Emerson's later Orphic
figure, and they are pictured as proud seekers, would-be
liberating gods, who are in fact duped by Nemesis and the
baubles held out to animate their quest.[4]

In the same mood, Emerson wrote a short poem whose
appropriate context is in a journal of 1841, where it appears, and not next to the "Nahant" quatrain where it was
first published by his editors.

I saw Webster in the street,—but he was changed since I
saw him last,—black as a thunder cloud, & care worn: the
anxiety that withers this generation among the young &
thinking class had crept up also into the great lawyer's
chair, & too plainly, too plainly he was one of us. I did not
wonder that he depressed his eyes when he saw me, and
would not meet my face. The canker worms have crawled
to the topmost bough of the wild elm & swing down from
that. No wonder the elm is a little uneasy.

The water understands
Civilization well—
It wets my foot but prettily
It chills my life but wittily
It is not disconcerted
It is not broken hearted
Well used it decketh joy
Adorneth doubleth joy
Ill used it will destroy

141

> In perfect time & measure
> With a face of golden pleasure
> Elegantly destroy
> (*JMN*, VIII, 111–112)

Surveying the times in 1841 Emerson saw weighty men everywhere withered and paralyzed by an oozing, capillary disease, as undeviatingly steady in its attack as the force that set upon Judge Pyncheon in *The House of the Seven Gables*. In his lecture (I, 286) he described it much as Hawthorne would, as the despair of intellects unredeemed by "the Fountain of Love." In this state, according to Swedenborg, the waters which represent the influx of God will withdraw; or, to use the more natural imagery of the poem, water will work "prettily" and "wittily"— that is, by small but relentless effects—to destroy what it created, and since the destructive process is as elegantly beautiful as the creative, water takes the same pleasure in either. "Water" reverses the usual poetic connotations Emerson gave to dissolving and circulating, but in doing so it only demonstrates the converse of his observation about water in 1834, "the same power that destroys in different circumstances is made to reproduce" (*EL*, I, 55), as well as Frost's neatly balanced line, "Water came to rebuke the too clear water."

Thus, even before the death of Waldo, Emerson was uneasy about the fragility of nature's balance in favor of life, and these ominous overtones of fate's perfect indifference toward man return in the "subtle rhymes" of "Merlin II." Nor is there any relief in the later language of the sea as it spoke to Emerson in 1857. The water is strong and beautiful, chipping and dissolving the solid-seeming earth—

> I make your sculptured architecture vain,
> Vain beside mine. I drive my wedges home,
> And carve the coastwise mountains into caves.
> . . . .

> I with my hammer pounding evermore
> The rocky coast, smite Andes into dust
>
> (IX, 242–243)

—and it elevates a race of men, cunning enough to harness this power, yet the sea is no friend of imaginative man. The dominant tenor of the poem is that the process, and not necessarily progress, is eternal: only "my mathematical ebb and flow" gives "a hint of that which changes not," and the waves themselves give out endlessly alluring illusions that enfold men just as the songs of the sister Fates do:

> I too have arts and sorceries;
> Illusion dwells forever with the wave.
> I know what spells are laid. Leave me to deal
> With credulous and imaginative man;
> For, though he scoop my water in his palm,
> A few rods off he deems it gems and clouds.
> Planting strange fruits and sunshine on the shore,
> I make some coast alluring, some lone isle,
> To distant men, who must go there, or die.
>
> (IX, 243)

Their shimmer is the mid-century music of Tennyson's "Ulysses" and "The Lotus-Eaters."

Nature in the primary fable was supposed to welcome the poet-hero, for in both "The Sphinx" and "Song of Nature" she is distressed that man still crouches and that the "man-child glorious," "the summit of the whole," has not yet appeared. The poet of "Threnody" is rebuked for suggesting that nature is not yet ripe enough to sustain true genius. But Emerson's later personifications of nature seem to enjoy keeping secrets and cutting men down to their proper size. Perhaps the best expression of Emerson's Orphic compromise and the principle of balance is his fragment on "The patient Pan," which implies that nature favors life precisely by opposing bardic heroism. Pan

143

feigns sleep, but is alway alert to any disproportion in the system:

> 'Tis his manner,
> Well he knows his own affair,
> Piling mountain chains of phlegm
> On the nervous brain of man,
> As he holds down central fires
> Under Alps and Andes cold;
> Haply else we could not live,
> Life would be too wild an ode.
>
> (IX, 335)

So Emerson's odes of wildest freedom, stoked in fiery bardic brains, are damped by the method of nature.[5]

We must turn then to the history of Merlin as it is written in Emerson's poetry, for Merlin is the bard and heroic pulse personified, yet his woven sinews carry the practical genius of the British race (V, 74, 94, 97, 299) and he is a figure who bears out Emerson's favorite quotation from Charles Fourier, "*Nature aime les croissements*" (*JMN*, IX, 296, 365). The most proximate sources for the first Merlin poems are the histories Emerson drew upon in his lectures of 1835 and the eighteenth-century mystique represented by Thomas Gray's "Bard."[6] Gray's prophetic poet accosts Edward I from a rocky precipice at Snowden—

> "Ruin seize thee, ruthless king!
> Confusion on thy banners wait,
> Though fanned by conquest's crimson wing
> They mock the air with idle state."

—and after telling the future of England he plunges to a triumphant death, assured that the Welsh will regain their rule and that the orb of poetic vision will never be quenched by tyranny. In similar cadences Emerson's bard bereaves a tyrant of his will, and he also passes beyond, though in ecstasy rather than in death, at the conclusion of "Merlin I" (IX, 122). The Welsh Merlin or Myrddin is sup-

posed to have been maddened at the Battle of Arfelerydd
(573 A.D.) and to have lived thereafter in the forest except
for brief periods. He eventually recovered his reason after
drinking the waters of a mountain stream.[7] Thus Emerson
actually follows the original legend in assimilating to his
Merlin elements of the forester in "Woodnotes" and the
Orphic purification of "Bacchus." In other respects, however, Merlin is the magician and counsellor who instituted
the Round Table in the Arthurian legend. Emerson makes
him "a blameless master of the games" who dispenses joy
and peace and "modulates the king's affairs" (IX, 121, 123).
Apparently he is not bothered, as the poet (IX, 317) was, by
"unhappy times" when inspiration is lax; hence truth
seeks him ("the God's will sallies free"), and in the moment of revelation at the end of "Merlin I" finds him
effortless and "unawares."

Emerson's continuation of the Merlin story is more Arthurian than Welsh, and if "Merlin I" concentrates on the
free, heroic bard, "Merlin II" is primarily about the magic
of "balance-loving Nature" and the justice—as distinct
from visionary truth—that is achieved through the compensating actions of nature over a long period of time. The
wild notes of hammer or mace fall, for the most part, into
orderly rhyme, and the marriages of "Merlin II" are not
mystical unions but simply the "elementary opposites
of the universe" (IX, 442). Nemesis finishes this song, re-
dressing partial wrongs like the over-god of the Channing
"Ode," but the concluding stanza is eerie and uncom-
forting:

> Subtle rhymes, with ruin rife,
> Murmur in the house of life,
> Sung by the Sisters as they spin;
> In perfect time and measure they
> Build and unbuild our echoing clay,
> As the two twilights of the day
> Fold us music-drunken in.
>
> (IX, 124)

145

The poet fades to insignificance before the relentlessly perfect weaving of the three Fates. We are intoxicated by the music of their song, but it is not clear whether we have drunk the true wine of "Bacchus" or the drugged cup of "The Sphinx."

The later Merlin poems, "Merlin's Song" and "The Harp," are undoubtedly composites, but perhaps for that very reason they render a remarkably true account of the fragmented poet after "Experience." We are asked to "hear what British Merlin sung" (IX, 218), but the magnified bard seems to have disappeared forever. In the end an aeolian harp, perhaps Merlin's own, speaks in place of the poet-hero, and then only intermittently at best, for the string has fallen silent and the solitary poet-observer, in numbers less wild than elegiac, is not really sure that he has heard anything at all (IX, 240–241). "Genius too has bound and term," he generalizes, and cites a choir of great poets who have not measured up to the harp's song, which is clearly the song of nature. Wordsworth is among them, and Wordsworth certainly stands behind Emerson's poet-observer, who recollects the true notes once heard, "The sights and voices ravishing / The boy knew on the hills in spring." When he thinks that the harp has again prompted a vision of lost youth, he cries out in a rather perfunctory Wordsworthian strain,

> O joy, for what recoveries rare!
> Renewed, I breathe Elysian air,
> See youth's glad mates in earliest bloom,—
> Break not my dream, obtrusive tomb!
>
> (IX, 241)

There may be reason for dismissing this framing viewpoint in "The Harp" as an old man's dream, but "Merlin's Song" is supposed to restore health and youth. It recommends the temperance of Saadi, who, though he sits alone in the sun, is gentle and cheerful to his fellowmen, and a sense of appropriate limits is evident in the kind of activity or "Use" proposed—not the "pure Use" of "Monadnoc," but purely practical and commonplace, in the tradition of the wayside paradise. This restraint is clearest in the lines added to the "Song" when it became the motto for "Considerations By the Way" in *The Conduct of Life*:

> Cleave to thine acre; the round year
> Will fetch all fruits and virtues here:
> Fool and foe may harmless roam,
> Loved and lovers bide at home.
> A day for toil, an hour for sport,
> But for a friend is life too short.
>
> (VI, 244)

What the harp really speaks of, then, is not the rejuvenation an old man thinks about, but the weaving of the Parcae which is natural law—

> Speaks not of self that mystic tone,
> But of the Overgods alone:
> It trembles to the cosmic breath,—
> As it heareth, so it saith;
> Obeying meek the primal Cause,
> It is the tongue of mundane laws.
>
> (IX, 239)

The web of nature is complete: the poet listens passively, the harp meekly obeys the wind. And the surrender of self-reliant imagination to the mundane shell is accomplished.

Echoes of Wordsworth are heard in Emerson's older Merlin, but the story of Merlin's disappearance in the *Morte d'Arthur* was popularly revived by the new laureate who in 1859 published the first of the *Idylls of the King*, including the one finally titled *Merlin and Vivien*. Emerson was not enthusiastic about Tennyson's poetry, but he certainly listened to it, as is evident in "Seashore," and still hoping for a resurgence of epic or "the national poem," he wrote on the appearance of the *Idylls* that Tennyson had ripened to the task, adding,

> A collection there should be of those fables which are
> agreeable to the human mind. One is the orator or singer
> who can control all minds. The Perfect Poet again is de-
> scribed in Taliesin's *Songs*, in the *Mabinogion*. Tennyson has
> drawn Merlin.
>
> (*J*, IX, 207–208)

Emerson again places his orator or singer in the Orphic role
of civilizer; similarly, the theme of civility and control is
uppermost in Tennyson's treatment of the epic and the
bard. We can see that the work of Merlin and Arthur in the
Idylls is an Orphic creation, for Camelot is a "city built to
music, therefore never built at all, / And therefore built for
ever";[8] and Arthur's order insists upon the taming of
human energies—

> For every fiery prophet of old times,
> And all the sacred madness of the bard,
> When God made music thro' them, could but speak
> His music by the framework and the chord.
>
> (*The Holy Grail*)

—even of visionary powers and desires, as he explains to
the knights wasted from the high quest. In Emersonian
terms, Arthur takes over the restrained practicality of
Emerson's later hero and Merlin the circuitous wizardry
of his later prose art. Tennyson's old seer rebukes the
young truth-seeker Gareth, " 'Know ye not then the Riddling of the Bards? / Confusion, and illusion, and relation, / Elusion, and occasion, and evasion'?"[9] Thus the
disappearance of Merlin, and more precisely his capitula-
tion to Vivien, which is Tennyson's dramatic focus, is a
crucial turn in the history of the Round Table, indicative of
"the meanest having power upon the highest, / And the
high purpose broken by the worm." In Vivien's song the
fall of Merlin and the disintegration of Camelot are fore-
shadowed, first in an Orphic image and then in a disturbing analogy from nature:

"It is the little rift within the lute,
That by and by will make the music mute,
And ever widening slowly silence all.

"The little rift within the lover's lute
Or little pitted speck in garner'd fruit,
That rotting inward slowly moulders all."
                                    (*Merlin and Vivien*)

How profoundly this analogy struck at the heart of Emerson's happier developmental schemes is suggested by what he made of Merlin after 1860.

Emerson liked the story of Merlin's imprisonment well enough to quote at length from Malory in "Poetry and Imagination" (VIII, 60–63), but the poet who had lately warned Whitman against publishing the *Calamus* poems gives little hint, there or in his poetic version, of the theme of sexual enchantment that runs beneath Tennyson's *Idylls*. For Emerson inward rotting is the natural aging process, nothing more, and the function of poetry is to soothe the declining years of the bard:

Reporting what old minstrels told
Of Merlin locked the harp within,—
Merlin paying the pain of sin,
Pent in a dungeon made of air,—
And some attain his voice to hear,
Words of pain and cries of fear,
But pillowed all on melody,
As fits the griefs of bards to be.
                                    (IX, 239)

Vivien is not named here, and her siren song hums only in the wheel of the Parcae, a symbol of the natural process. The tower of air (in other versions the prison is a tree or bower) makes the imprisonment an emblem for the power of a primeval energy, whether spiritual or libidinous, over the solid world; but it also stands for the power of nature over the poet, since in Emerson's poem Merlin is locked

149

inside his harp, and the harp is a natural object like the pine tree of "Woodnotes," not a man-made instrument. Merlin, the tempered bard, goes gentle into the night, his grief assuaged by song, and Emerson's prose quotation (VIII, 62–63) ends with the departure of Gawain, who, after listening to Merlin's last prophetic testament, leaves in a mood both joyful and sorrowful, the "intermixture" of emotions that is the inevitable complement of life in the balanced tradition of Emerson and Hawthorne.

Two laureates contributed to Emerson's portrait of the native British bard; and the Wordsworthian frame for "The Harp," Tennyson's Merlin *Vinctus*, and even Merlin's brief role in *Jerusalem* may argue for reading Emerson's history of Merlin as part of the English Romantic myth of the Imagination Impaired. And yet his Merlin reaches beyond this national tradition; for the great riddle-solvers of mythology—Oedipus, Samson, and even Orpheus himself, with the Maenads—nemesis lies in their encounter with the Eternal Feminine. According to legend, when the flowing locks of the virile poet are woven or shorn, and even when he is dismembered and his body scattered, his song will still be heard in the winds. But Merlin tells Gawain that he will speak no more to men, and he does not say, with Walt Whitman, "If you want me again look for me under your boot-soles." The poet of "Experience" is finally bested in his encounter with nature or the Mother-Goddess. All of the poetic encounters point this way: the bard who wove efficacious rhymes discovers that the grand weaver-god, seemingly so friendly and garrulous, is really deaf and mute to human entreaties, and so the speech of the bard "becomes less, and finally ceases in a nobler silence," as Emerson wrote prophetically in his journal of 1842 (*JMN*, VIII, 286–287).

I emphasize that early date because what occurs is not simply the effects of aging, as Emerson later wanted to believe; it is an upshot of the profound confrontation of the

150

Romantic artist with his art, as readily documented in Hawthorne and Melville as in Emerson. How does the pen speak without a hand to guide it? Hawthorne saw this Orphic query obscurely mirrored in the North Adams amputee, who lacked a hand to "make the pen go fast," and Melville provided the touchstone for the natural enchantment that silences the artist in "A Bower in the Arsacides":

> Oh, busy weaver! unseen weaver!—pause!—one word!—whither flows the fabric? what palace may it deck? wherefore all these ceaseless toilings? Speak, weaver!—stay thy hand!—but one single word with thee! Nay—the shuttle flies—the figures float from forth the loom; the freshet-rushing carpet for ever slides away. The weaver-god, he weaves; and by that weaving is he deafened, that he hears no mortal voice; and by that humming, we, too, who look on the loom are deafened; and only when we escape it shall we hear the thousand voices that speak through it. For even so it is in all material factories. The spoken words that are inaudible among the flying spindles; those same words are plainly heard without the walls, bursting from the opened casements.[10]

After *Moby-Dick* Melville wrote savagely ironic indictments of nature's demand for production and reproduction, most pointedly in "The Tartarus of Maids." During the same years Emerson studied Beautiful Necessity in nature's golden net—"Wonderful intricacy in the web, wonderful constancy in the design this vagabond life admits" (VI, 46). All the apparent ills of "Fate" can be worked out of the fabric by a right perspective, a major part of which is the adjustment and specialization of the individual as a part in the whole. Evidently that is what Emerson came to mean by "yielding to the perfect whole" when he wrote *The Conduct of Life*. Even to one versed in Emerson's metamorphoses of meaning, the conclusion to the essay "Power" must be astonishing:

> A man hardly knows how much he is a machine until he begins to make telegraph, loom, press and locomotive, in

his own image. But in these he is forced to leave out his follies and hindrances so that when we go to the mill, the machine is more moral than we. Let a man dare go to a loom and see if he be equal to it. Let machine confront machine, and see how they come out. The world-mill is more complex than the calico-mill, and the architect stooped less. . . . A day is a more magnificent cloth than any muslin, the mechanism that makes it is infinitely cunninger, and you shall not conceal the sleezy, fraudulent, rotten hours you have slipped into the piece; nor fear that any honest thread, or straighter steel, or more inflexible shaft, will not testify in the web.

(VI, 81–82)

Shamed like a child by the precision of its beautiful mother, the tiny poet will humbly take a few herbs and apples from his acre and let go the Orphic task.

Merlin's history is Emerson's also, for it traces the decline of visionary power and the substitution of natural and rhetorical magic, like the structures of surprise and polarity, for the insight of the seer. This craft served Emerson well, for there are major artistic triumphs among his later works. But the silencing of Merlin remains a symbol for the loss of Orpheus, not only to Emerson, but to later poets like E. A. Robinson or Richard Wilbur who have taken up this theme. Jung in his autobiography tells of his Walden, the round tower he built on the lake at Bollingen and the philosopher's stone he set in front of it. For him the stone was *"le cri de Merlin,"* the cry of Merlin in the forest, heard by men but never rightly interpreted or understood, and Jung fancied that the secret of Merlin was passed on, through the alchemical Mercurius, to his own psychology of the unconscious.[11] In Emerson's Merlin, not only banished, like Uriel, but no longer making ripples in nature's smooth and glassy order, the poet as "liberating god" passes into a *deus absconditus*.

The silencing of Merlin is symbolic, of course, and Emerson continued to write poems through the 1860s; but this larger symbol hangs over them all, holding within it the full implications of Emerson's remark that natural science was "dimming & extinguishing a good deal that was called poetry." Moreover, in the 1860s, as the late Merlin poems indicate, the symbol was explicitly associated with aging and death. "Terminus," which probably reached its completed form in 1866, begins, "It is time to be old, / To take in sail," but its gnomic economy—"Contract thy firmament / To compass of a tent"—is essentially the advice of Saadi, given more than twenty years before.[12] E. W. Emerson was right in suggesting (*J*, V, 226) that one of the ways his father took in sail poetically was to trim his poetic line to the metrical orthodoxies of couplet or quatrain. His concern for poetic surfaces seems to have narrowed just as his notions of power and propriety were restricted to the most practical affairs of life. In "Behavior" Emerson accepts the surfaces we live amid by arguing that "the core will come to the surface" (VI, 187). But the standard of manners in this essay would undoubtedly have muzzled Uriel, and Emerson's judgments here, which begin with the surface and merely assume that it represents a core, are decidedly behaviorist in perspective.

Again the change of perspective can be illustrated by earlier work, especially in the spatial motifs of the 1840s. "Circles," the transitional essay of 1840, develops its key figure from the center or core outward, the soul generating concentric circles around it like a pebble thrown into a pond. There are, however, disturbing undercurrents of anxiety in "Circles," and perhaps with them in mind Emerson changed his angle of vision when he wrote the poetic motto for the essay some six or seven years later:

> Nature centres into balls,
> And her proud ephemerals,
> Fast to surface and outside,
> Scan the profile of the sphere;
> Knew they what that signified,
> A new genesis were here.
>
> (II, 299)

Bound to surfaces, and looking on from the outside, these men are perplexed and peripheral creatures who cannot tell the central secret; theirs is not so much the optative mood as the subjunctive contrary-to-fact, which Emerson uses with full import in these verses.

"Blight," one of three blank-verse poems grouped with "Xenophanes" in *Poems* (1847), writhes with this sense of displacement from the center:

> Give me truths;
> For I am weary of the surfaces,
> And die of inanition. If I knew
> Only the herbs and simples of the wood,
> . . . which in these woods
> Draw untold juices from the common earth,
> Untold, unknown, and I could surely spell
> Their fragrance, and their chemistry apply
> By sweet affinities to human flesh,
> Driving the foe and stablishing the friend,—
> O, that were much, and I could be a part
> Of the round day, related to the sun
> And planted world, and full executor
> Of their imperfect functions.
>
> (IX, 139–140)

But Emerson's speaker, like Stevens' in "The Ultimate Poem Is Abstract," stays helplessly at the edge, "shut out / Daily to a more thin and outward rind." His alienated eye makes the world itself appear stunted, and the three poems taken together represent an attempt at accommodation that will relieve this condition. The poet in "A Day's Ration" accepts the role of a diminished thing symbolized by the "little cup" that Fate offers him (IX, 138). In "Blight" and "Musketaquid" he would practice subordinate arts as a kind of compensation for the loss of larger things. He asks to be an apothecary, a man of minor healings distantly (but only distantly) linked to his great Renaissance predecessors, and to follow "in small copy in my acre" the Concord farmers who have transmuted the landscape into fruitful use. Emerson himself seems to speak when in

tones of a reproved and earth-bound Uriel the protagonist
of "Musketaquid" turns to the salve of gardening:

> And, chiefest prize, found I true liberty
> In the glad home plain-dealing Nature gave.
> The polite found me impolite; the great
> Would mortify me, but in vain; for still
> I am a willow of the wilderness,
> Loving the wind that bent me. All my hurts
> My garden spade can heal.
>
> (IX, 144)

Recognition of our brief and tiny appearance on the great
circles of nature will spare us the pain of failed apocalypse,
and we can recognize the desire for an unbuffeted equilibrium and the renunciation of Wilhelm Meister, early
themes of Emerson's journal (1838–1840), now returning
full force in poems of these later decades.

This early accommodation to the edge, so to speak, and
practice in the minor arts of balance braced Emerson for his
encounters with the last of the edges men face. Expert
sailors and swimmers are the ones to venture out beyond
the dip of bell in the essay "Fate" and the poem "Terminus," for they are most likely to stay up. "Terminus"
ends in an even, hymn-like quatrain,

> As the bird trims her to the gale,
> I trim myself to the storm of time,
> I man the rudder, reef the sail,
> Obey the voice at eve obeyed at prime:
> 'Lowly faithful, banish fear,
> Right onward drive unharmed;
> The port, well worth the cruise, is near,
> And every wave is charmed.'
>
> (IX, 252)

An Ishmael comes home, auguring again of Orpheus-
Christ charming the opposing elements; but the Orphic
work is left undone, for the voice obeyed seems to have
counselled only low tasks, and Emerson portrays himself
as a poet who failed to inherit the poetic gift, hence was left

155

"amid the Muses . . . deaf and dumb" (IX, 252; IX, 490). Although "Threnody," the elegy for Waldo, was written well before Emerson's sense of his own aging and dying had grown acute, he wrote that "this losing is true dying" (IX, 153), and set out in this poem a strategy he later repeated. In 1844, two years after Waldo died, the journal (*J*, VI, 488) shows that this wound was still so painful that small compensations like gardening were not enough, and only a full resolution to the poet's query could console the grieving father. Thus the poem parades the metaphysics of Emerson's bardic faith, treating death as simply an extension of visionary ecstasy, and of the metaphor of dissolution that makes the annihilation of particular things part of the work of the whole:

> My servant Death, with solving rite,
> Pours finite into infinite,
> Wilt thou freeze love's tidal flow,
> Whose streams through Nature circling go?
> Nail the wild star to its track
> On the half-climbed zodiac?
> Light is light which radiates,
> Blood is blood which circulates,
> Life is life which generates,
> And many-seeming life is one,—
> Wilt thou transfix and make it none?
> Its onward force too starkly pent
> In figure, bone and lineament?
> Wilt thou, uncalled, interrogate,
> Talker! the unreplying Fate?

(IX, 156–157)

As God spoke to Job, this chemist or alchemist Lord of "Threnody" rebukes his "proud ephemeral" and fulfills the prophecy of Uriel by building greater systems out of the ruins of smaller ones.

> Silent rushes the swift Lord
> Through ruined systems still restored,
> Broadsowing, bleak and void to bless,
> Plants with worlds the wilderness.

(IX, 158)

156

The last line of the poem, "Lost in God, in Godhead found," foreshadows "Brahma" and the destruction of all finite boundaries in infinity: not in creeds or formulas, but in this wider and natural faith are the dead restored.

"The Nun's Aspiration," published in the *May-Day* volume of 1867, faces death squarely, though admittedly Emerson, in basing the poem upon a diary entry of his sternly Calvinist aunt, drew upon someone else's inner life rather than his own. Unlike Waldo, who died before his time, Mary Moody Emerson, the nun of the poem, feels she has outlived hers; this life is drudgery for her, and she aspires to a fuller existence—"On earth I dream;—I die to be." Like Merlin she wishes to be free by passing beyond:

> I tire of shams, I rush to be:
> I pass with yonder comet free,—
> Pass with the comet into space
> Which mocks thy æons to embrace;
> Æons which tardily unfold
> Realm beyond realm,—extent untold.
>
> (IX, 254)

But Merlin's unfolding doors were the poet's figure for visionary insight; for the nun the passage beyond is a literal death, an annihilation of the self and consigning of her name, unspoken by any tragic bard, to oblivion. There, in the same rushing metamorphosis as in "Threnody," is her comfort.

The best of the late poems that deal with death does not borrow inspiration or trade upon earlier ecstasies. Instead, it works ingeniously with the established resources of Emerson's major poetry—displacement of metaphysics and apocalypse in the fabled encounter and its oblique wit. At the same time, "The Titmouse," which was written and published in 1862, is Emerson's indirect tribute to Thoreau, expressing a fundamental agreement in their ideas that had been obscured by the essentially temperamental rift evident in Thoreau's journal of the 1850s.[13] Thoreau, dying in the spring of 1862, heard Emerson's account of the incident that sparked the poem, and may have repeated to him then the anecdote about the woodchopper, Alex Therien, that appears in *Walden*:

> In the winter he had a fire by which at noon he warmed his coffee in a kettle; and as he sat on a log to eat his dinner the chickadees would sometimes come round and alight on his arm and peck at the potato in his fingers; and he said that he "liked to have the little *fellers* about him."
> In him the animal man chiefly was developed.
>
> ("Visitors"; cf. Emerson, J, IX, 405 and IX, 482)

Here is another version of the taming of beasts, and the point of it for Thoreau (as clarified in his next paragraph) was that this Orpheus is also Antaeus—his power derives from the earth: the woodchopper is able to tame animals because he lives like them, "simply and naturally humble," satisfied with nature exactly as it is and adapting himself to his surroundings with a primitive wisdom.

Emerson's titmouse is the exemplum and symbolic expounder of this wisdom. The opening admonishment of the poem reminds us of the poet's late discovery—the lesson of the poem "Water"—about his relation to nature:

> You shall not be overbold
> When you deal with arctic cold,
> As late I found my lukewarm blood
> Chilled wading in the snow-choked wood.
> How should I fight? my foeman fine
> Has million arms to one of mine.
>
> (IX, 233)

Myriad-handed nature, once friend and tutor, can also appear as foe. Lost in a storm, the aging poet gives in, more casually than in "The Nun's Aspiration," to a crescent death-wish—"Well, in this broad bed lie and sleep." The great symbols of nature's eternal verities now speak only of death: stars and winds, moon and cloud will be his mourners, the snow his shroud. Suddenly, breaking both rhythm and mood, a new and tiny voice sounds in the forest, though to us it should be by now familiar, for the titmouse echoes the tones of Saadi and the squirrel of Emerson's "Fable," and it behaves like the popinjay in "Montaigne." The bird is another surrogate for the poet, and more than Monadnoc a kin to tiny man, standing with him, "head downward," "hurling defiance at vast death" with whom nature now appears to be in league. This is animal endurance, and from it the defeated poet takes his major pitch:

> 'I think no virtue goes with size;
> The reason of all cowardice
> Is, that men are overgrown,
> And, to be valiant, must come down
> To the titmouse dimension.'
>
> (IX, 235)

Man is no Colossus: his strength lies in wisdom, but wisdom of the special kind cited by Goethe's Arabian poet who was sunshine to the cold day and shade in the dogstar (*JMN*, VII, 384). The titmouse, too, is a "wee San Salvador" in his acre of Labrador, by virtue of the balance or compensation in nature's larger and longer process. And so he stands big as a whale.

Hyatt Waggoner, who is to be thanked for bringing this poem to prominence, reads the soul's transcendence into this mechanism,[14] but I see only Emerson's conception of the perfect whole that, despite its real threat to and final destruction of individuals, works ultimately in favor of life. The trick of Uriel, to make evil bless and ice burn, the titmouse as species has learned only over aeons of evolution, during which its feathery exterior and hollow bone structure developed so that "polar frost my frame defied, / Made of the air that blows outside" (IX, 236). This is the bird's way of maintaining an equilibrium or the constant *milieu interieur* that is the condition of life. Thoreau acknowledged in *Walden* that the "grand necessity" of our bodies is preserving the vital heat in us, and, alluding to

Darwin's report of naked savages perspiring while clothed Europeans shivered in Tierra del Fuego, he wondered if intellectual, civilized man might not have strayed too far from the appropriate mean heat. The great natural thermometer of *Walden* is the pond itself, a "classic" instance of self-regulating organization, as Thoreau's account of its life painstakingly demonstrates: "The largest pond is as sensitive to atmospheric changes as the globule of mercury in its tube," and therefore Walden Pond is not only alive but an adequate measure of all other life. Emerson's own concern for vital heat is a matter of calculating the fixed points that represent the laws or systematic self-regulation of nature. He took a special interest in the thermometer, which he made the speaker of a late unpublished riddle:[15]

> Mine to watch the sun at work
> Or if he hide in clouds & shirk
> I test the force of wood & bark
> And keep the pitcoal to the mark
> On my white enamelled Scale
> The warning numbers never fail
> From sixty up to seventy-one
> The grades of household comfort run
> If they climb a hairsbreadth higher
> Fling wide the doors, put out the fire.
> Each year will have its holidays
> Which I report nor blame nor praise
> Twice I dive twenty below zero
> Twice climb to heat would blacken Nero
> But health & heart will prosper more
> At the mean point of 54

The thermometer dives and soars like Merlin (Thoreau's name for the hawk) and the traditional Orphic poet, but these extremities are holidays from the balance that serves life best and they will trigger compensating reactions in the whole system.

If there is a kind of transcendence in "The Titmouse," it comes in the final stanza where Emerson writes his paean to the small bird. The passage recalls the grand apostrophe to Monadnoc, for the titmouse is enshrined and the poet will return as a pilgrim bringing offerings to it. But the bird is not an alien idol like the mountain: the remote Platonic promontory symbolized the Idea or "stable good"; the titmouse is, within the natural order, all that it symbolizes. It is the law within the flux, and like the prayer and music in "Monadnoc" (IX, 68), the bird with its "cheerful song" is the wire or invisible cord on which all matter is strung. Thus Emerson makes a special play upon the bird's frame and song—"Henceforth I prize thy wiry chant / O'er all that mass and minster vaunt" (IX, 236)—which, he seems to think, presages a new religion of nature. For the present, however, the poem turns downward to its simple and cheerful conclusion, an "antidote to fear." In keeping with Emerson's view of the world as metamorphosis, the transcendence of fear is no apocalypse nor even a riddle-solution but only a matter of playing on words—flashing off into a wild connection, leaping to the great conceit that ends the poem, where the bird's song *"Chic-a-dee-dee"* is recast as Caesar's *"Veni, Vidi, Vici."* That's it, Emerson might have mused, and someday they may get it straight in our hallowed institutions:[16] the essential transformations in life are merely poetic, nothing more or less, and we can make them if only we heed the moral of the poem and "come down / To the titmouse dimension."

Head down and minding mainly his own cheerful song, Emerson's titmouse is probably the most fitting response of a Saadi to the riddle-wrangles of life and death: he does not solve them, he simply gets around them, hopping about and yet staying in one place. The price of this poetic peace may well be the abdication, not simply the internalization, of Promethean and Orphic quest. By 1860, however, Emerson was clearly content to live with the "unanswered question." If pressed he sometimes sounded as confident as he had in 1836, but the difference that time makes is everything—

> Why should I hasten to solve every riddle which life of-
> fers me? I am well assured that the Questioner who brings
> me so many problems will bring the answers also *in due
> time*. Very rich, very potent, very cheerful Giver that he is,
> he shall have it all his own way, for me. Why should I give
> up my thought, because I cannot answer an objection to it?
> ("Worship," VI, 230; my italics)

What would have been a clarion to artistic battle for the
younger man is dutifully, patiently ignored.

Thus in "Days" and "Brahma," the two celebrated
poems of Emerson's later years, we see only the ghostlier
demarcations of his primary form and fable. They are, respectively, the ultimate though faded dramatizations of the
poet's encounter with nature and the answer nature returns, but in both cases the answer is effectively silence.
There are no words, only things, in "Days," and without
language nothing in Emerson's world can be transformed
into meaning. This poem has been read as a variant on the
parable of talents, and since the motif can be traced in
Emerson's notebooks as far back as the 1830s, it may owe
something to the close-muffled stranger who brings the
infant Teufelsdröckh in a Persian basket and then vanishes
from the Futterals' garden.[17] The Days come dumb and in
"an endless file," like Succession in "Experience"; the
poet, obviously confused and unsettled by this procession,
impulsively chooses a ration that will merely suffice, and
the Day departs, silent and scornful as the Sphinx. The gap
has not been bridged: nature and the poet have not really
met in this encounter, and the details that remain in the
poem—the intricate maze of the poet's "pleachèd garden"
and the Day's "solemn fillet"—are evanescent symbols of
man's bewilderment and the restraint that prevents full
communication. So the stress in suspended cadences falls
on a lonely, solipsistic "I," much as it did in the concluding
paragraph of "Experience."

"Brahma" has been Emerson's most successful, unanswerable riddle. It has led scholars to India, and Emer-

son certainly intended to tap wisdom at its ancient source in this poem; but Emerson's spirit was always eclectic, and, according to his own comments on "Brahma" (IX, 466–467), nothing is lost on the reader who chooses to stay at home. Frost, in this respect, said what needed to be said about Emerson's "dark saying."[18] For "Brahma" is pure Emerson in that whatever is taken from the *Katha-Upanishad* or the *Bhagavad-Gita* corroborates what he had already drawn from a long line of Western prophets, especially Heraclitus, Nicholas Cusanus, Coleridge, and Goethe (though Emerson did not necessarily reach them in that order). If Emerson has changed in "Brahma," the crucial change is to the tonality and perspective which have been the primary theme of this chapter.

Emerson's first title for the poem was "Song of the Soul," but neither the poem nor its Hindu sources suggest anything of an individual or personal soul; it is the universe speaking to us, in a voice sonorously regular and loaded with every kind of aural repetition, so that its effect is hauntingly impersonal. Frederic Carpenter was right to identify the speaker as "the impersonal creative force of the world," and to think of "Brahma" as an expression of the conservation of energy, for Emerson's drafts of the poem date from the late 1840s when he took a renewed interest in the physical sciences. There he hoped to find the key to metamorphosis, as after reading Robert Chambers' *Vestiges of the Natural History of Creation* he had written, "The Avatars of Brahma will presently be textbooks of natural history."[19] The new theories of Robert Mayer and Hermann von Helmholtz and Michael Faraday, then popularly referred to as the conservation and correlation of forces, seemed to explain the universe as Emerson understood it in "Song of Nature," a poem that also grew out of this same period:

> No ray is dimmed, no atom worn,
> My oldest force is good as new,

And the fresh rose on yonder thorn
Gives back the bending heaven in dew.
                    (IX, 247)

Like that other great mother the Sphinx, nature in this poem still waits upon the messianic hero. Her cup has never been filled, yet her consolation is that no energy is ever lost from the whole system, and for Emerson the rose is symbolic assurance that the great circle of nature is divinely beneficent.[20] Brahma, too, stands for the great mysterious circle of nature whose primal force or energy is indescribable, except by its effects, and its effects are inexhaustibly various. Thus at the center of the poem are paradoxes that make it literally unsolvable, a modern, naturalistic version of the *coincidentia oppositorum* in the negative theology. Brahma is the unfathomable reconciliation of all differences, and Emerson might have glossed his poem with a Melvillian sentence from "Illusions"—"All is riddle, and the key to a riddle is another riddle" (VI, 313). We have seen variations on phrases of "Brahma" in earlier poems such as "Woodnotes" and "Threnody," and indeed before 1840 Emerson had written the Western complement to the Hindu "Brahma" in his "Bohemian Hymn" (IX, 359). Brahma likewise transcends language and the laws of thought, and can be found only by those who seek through the moral sentiment and acknowledge the goodness of the whole. The problematic last line of the poem is in fact an Emersonian commonplace and can be glossed with a number of earlier passages;[21] but for Emerson in the 1850s the full significance of "turn thy back on heaven" would have gone beyond apostasy from the church or theological systems to the realization that nature itself, without a metaphysical overlay, is sufficient.

Little of Emerson's original encounter is left in "Brahma," since it is neither drama nor dialogue, but the poem does give a compressed version of nature's later answers to the poet, spoken not by a personified object but by a wholly disembodied voice. It is the formulaic speech of the riddle, one of the oldest of poetic forms predating Western culture, though Emerson probably knew it best from the early English versions he had collected from George Ellis's *Specimens of the Early English Poets*, Turner's *History*, and William Owens' *Heroic Elegies*. Thematically and formally Emerson's poetry drifted toward this unanswered question, a single, elaborate metaphor, often composed of paradoxes and in itself a kind of *mundi figura* or cosmic symbol (though most riddles allow specific answers from ordinary life, like a thermometer).[22] The subject usually speaks for itself in the riddle, with a tag-line challenge to "find me" (as in "Brahma") or "guess what I am," and if the poet speaks at all it is to express wonder and astonishment toward the unknown subject. And that is in fact an outline of Emerson's final encounters. His riddles of nature exhibit what Emerson and later Holmes called the "algebra" of poetry, using symbols of "undetermined amounts and indefinite possibilities."[23] If there are no answers in these poems it is because for the poet answers matter less than the evocative power by which poetry works upon and transforms the things of earth. After all, any subject or any answer will do, as Emerson wrote: "The Metamorphosis of Nature shows itself in nothing more than this, that there is no word that cannot become typical to us of Nature by giving it emphasis" (*JMN*, VIII, 23). Thus the Romantic returns to the Renaissance mind, where poetry is the dark way of knowing, and the Romantic riddle, in Carlyle and Melville and Dickinson, continually posits by negation.

So long ago the wind defied limitation in Taliessin's "Invocation," which Emerson quoted (from D. W. Nash's recent 1858 translation) in "Poetry and Imagination":

Discover thou what it is,—
The strong creature from before the flood,
Without flesh, without bone, without head, without feet,

It will neither be younger nor older than at the beginning;
It has no fear, nor the rude wants of created things.
Great God! how the sea whitens when it comes!
It is in the field, it is in the wood,
Without hand, without foot,
Without age, without season,
It is always of the same age with the age of ages,
And of equal breadth with the surface of the earth.
It was not born, it sees not,
And is not seen; it does not come when desired;
It has no form, it bears no burden,
For it is void of sin.
It makes no perturbation in the place where God wills it,
On the sea, on the land.

(VIII, 57–58)

As a young man Emerson had written, "The wind is the great poet of the world" (*JMN*, III, 14). In earlier poems like "The Problem" or "Woodnotes" we can feel the wind as a constant and unifying influx or *spiritus*, as Coleridge's "one intellectual breeze" animating all the wind-harps of nature. To the pine tree the wind revives the miracle of Pentecost:

'Heed the old oracles,
Ponder my spells;
Song wakes in my pinnacles
When the wind swells.
Soundeth the prophetic wind,
The shadows shake on the rock behind,
And the countless leaves of the pine are strings
Tuned to the lay the wood-god sings.'

(IX, 51–52)

But the wind in Emerson's later prose and poetry is chiefly a negative symbol of the ineffable plenitude of nature.

A thousand tunes the variable wind plays, a thousand spectacles it brings, and each is the frame or dwelling of a new spirit. . . . the treasures which Nature spent itself to amass,—the secular, refined, composite anatomy of man, which all strata go to form, which the prior races, from infusory and saurian, existed to ripen; the surrounding

166

plastic natures; the earth with its foods; the intellectual, temperamenting air; the sea with its invitations; the heaven deep with worlds; and the answering brain and nervous structure replying to these; the eye that looketh into the deeps, which again look back to the eye, abyss to abyss;— these, not like a glass bead, or the coins or carpets, are given immeasurably to all.

("Works and Days," VII, 169–171)

Emerson's prose yearns toward Whitman, but the poetry more often tells the inevitable other side of the coin. The wind as world-poet offers infinite variety, and we, like the poet of "Days," must choose, though we have really no basis for choosing. "We cannot write the order of the variable winds" (VI, 321), and for all its volume, the profuse, roaring wind, like the one Wallace Stevens named "Vocalissimus," speaks not one syllable intelligible to man. Loving the wind that bends it, the willow knows not how or why it is bent (IX, 144). Only the long process of nature tests truth, just as "time and tide" will judge the myriad verses Emerson hangs in the wind, and only the Muse who is co-eternal with nature can tell which will survive (IX, 220). Thus in the riddling form of the wind—variable, limitless, extensive and elusive as Brahma or God or eternally persisting energy or nature herself—Emerson found an ultimate way to make nature speak (*J*, IX, 472).

Yet this is not all that Emerson wanted: he had hoped to "constrain" nature to speak "*his* thoughts," and all that nature says now is in her own language of negations and silence. That, I think, is the price of the poet's diminution, and it involves the modern world in another loss of Orpheus. Orpheus or the ideal poet had become Emerson's symbol for the method and work of mediation between all the "two's" he encountered. This Orpheus is lost when we no longer sense the need and the possibility of mediation, as when man stands on the outside edge of a perfectly woven sphere and contemplates a whole which he may be a part of but which he did not participate in creating.

167

"Brahma" is a unity from which soul in the personal sense—what is unmistakably felt in "Gnothi Seauton," or even in the dialectical meditation of the Channing "Ode" that neutralizes the poet—is fully detached. The soul of the titmouse is the form of his body, which is also the frame or lyre of his song, but writing odes with the body conceived as an abstract mechanism is not exactly writing them with men. This poetry is a biology in which the concept of the personal is transformed into the principle of development and equated with the final or progressive form the body takes. It is impossible, then, to write true odes of Orpheus, because men living as well as men fabled have become such diminished things; the "incalculable energy" of poetry resides entirely with nature.

Perhaps we should not insist too much on these more general or philosophical implications of Emerson's poetry, for, as he said, he had no system. He did, however, acknowledge "tendency," indeed he depended on it, and sorting out tendencies or implications is a way of expressing an important and felt distinction: that is, the vast difference between the Whole Man represented by the original Orphic poet and the work he assumes before 1840, and, on the other hand, man as an analogue of the titmouse. Emerson's major phase as a poet coincided with a period of growing doubts and detachment, so that these poems, in form as in substance, show increasing signs of man's limitation, his perplexity in the face of incomprehensible nature, serenity despite his inability to comprehend, and, finally, an acquiescent faith in the grand mechanism of nature and history. This may be why Emerson's poetry appealed so much to Robert Frost—indeed, much of "Hamatreya" and a poem like "The Titmouse" are the essence of Frost—and why it is increasingly meaningful to some who are put off by his prose. Often the rhetoric of Emerson's essays is too assured, too conscious of the audience it manipulates with sleight-of-hand magic, and Emerson seems to look down at us from his podium, himself a genteel Sphinx. His poetry was not this kind of performance, but is more natural, more like Frost's "sleight of wing"; in it Emerson is more commonly on our side, a less pretentious yet representative man, trying with us to fathom the mystery of existence.

From its beginnings Emerson's poetry followed, and can be said to have completed, the arc established by his prose. Its tendency is away from revelation and transcendence and toward solution by immanent equilibriums. It is compressed in both form and consciousness, concentrating finally on ordinary, wayside experiences, relaxing its original heroic energy and the grander claims of the formulating imagination as it comes down to ordinary size. So Emerson the poet points away from high Romantic vision, and it is Frost rather than Whitman who read the poetry clearly and as a whole. Despite the link between them, Whitman and Emerson are dissimilar poets, Whitman's cosmic consciousness and expansive verse standing almost at the extreme from Emerson's compressed poetics. Thus Emerson's place in our native tradition is not, with Whitman, at the head of a "Dionysian strain of American poetry,"[24] for his poems must register a very different influence from Whitman's, and in fact did, upon poets like Emily Dickinson, Stephen Crane, Robinson and Frost, who are his direct descendants, and upon Stevens, a new Emerson aspiring to converse with "Central Man." In them and in others less direct can be seen the line of Orpheus still descending, the fragmented poet making his way through the silence and the dark.

PART THREE:
Legacy

—

Who, then, will read and enjoy these volumes of the prose and verse of Emerson? Not he who is still looking for a system of philosophy, woven out of the cob-webs of logic, that shall pretend to expound "the riddle of the painful earth"; nor he who cares only for the processes of brute nature; but rather those fewer persons who are already disposed to believe that we shall never get wisdom from gazing up into the fog, or down into the sand, but from looking around us on human life, trying with cheerful courage to see what is the precise fact of our condition, and what is the nearest duty to be done.

—EDWARD ROWLAND SILL,
in *The Overland Monthly* (1884)

. . . a discussion of all our Emersonian poets soon would become very nearly a discussion of all our poets. There are six or seven Emersons in Emerson's prose, and three or four more in his verse, and he would have been delighted at our total inability to reconcile all of them, for more than Whitman he was large; he did contain multitudes of his descendants. He was indeed the American Orpheus. . . . Emerson denounced all influence as pernicious, and his involuntary disciples have fought so bitterly against influence that they have all become one version or another of their brilliantly scattered, ever metamorphic father, whose oracular Yankee skull goes on chanting in their repudiations of Transcendental influx.

—HAROLD BLOOM, *Figures
of Capable Imagination* (1976)

VIII

Orpheus Descending

———

> . . . all
> flight, of imaginative hope or
> fact, takes accuracy from stone:
> . . . .
> that you needed
> to get up and I down
> leaves us both still
> sharing stone and flight.
>
> —A. R. AMMONS, "Emerson"

W HY HAS EMERSON BEEN NAMED the father of so many subsequent poets? I think we can say, in retrospect, and with
one of those nineteenth-century admirers who were wiser
about Emerson than many modern critics, that "the secret
of the land was in the poet."[1] Because America has always
had great expectations of a sublime and philosophical literature, its poets have accepted the tradition that Orpheus,
the first poet, was the Whole or Universal Man, and they
have tried to live up to Emerson's magnificent fable of the
Orphic poet that promises freedom, revolution, and transcendence. But fable meets fact, and in that meeting prog-
eny discover the severer limitations of their kind. The
key to Emerson's prolific fatherhood is that, having made
impossible demands upon poets, he does not abandon
them when they cannot do what he asks; his own example
offers the ideal of a lesser Orpheus, who understands "the
precise fact of our condition," whose promises are of civility, longevity, and reconciliation.

Emerson's last word on Orpheus came significantly
early, in 1849, and with his full poetic career now before us
we should recognize that this is indeed the culmination of
his Orphic inquiry:

> Chladni's experiment seems to me central. He strewed
> sand on glass, and then struck the glass with tuneful ac-
> cords, and the sand assumed symmetrical figures. With
> discords the sand was thrown about amorphously. It
> seems, then, that Orpheus is no fable: you have only to
> sing, and the rocks will crystallize; sing, and the plant will
> organize; sing, and the animal will be born.
>
> (*JMN*, XI, 203)[2]

Nailing the fable to reality on the authority of a half-
fabulous experiment, Emerson pronounced an alliance between poetry and natural history more radical than most
interpreters have realized. He had moved away from Blake
relatively early in his career, and tended to discount artifices of eternity, the antitheses to natural order symbolized by Jerusalem and Xanadu and Byzantium in the
tradition of the English Romantics. And in rallying on nature he went well beyond the metamorphic and biological
assumptions of the Orphic voice that Elizabeth Sewell describes in Wordsworth, Goethe, and Emerson himself.[3] To
take Orpheus as a fact and poetry as an expression of
natural law diminished the poet, leaving him only a
peripheral part in the whole cosmic process; Emerson's
compensation lay in assurances of order and systematic
progress that he thought could be drawn from facts, even
when nature as the Sphinx refused to speak.

Typical of Emerson's inclusiveness is his relation to the
two great and polar poets of nineteenth-century America.
He stands behind their divergence, Whitman heeding his
call to explore the nation as a poem, and Dickinson focusing inward upon the poetics of the soul.[4] But Emerson is
also a source of convergence, for both Whitman and Dickinson borrowed his structure for poetic experience. Both
poets repeated Emerson's primary fable, beginning with
the recognition of ME and NOT ME and the hope of Orphic
apocalypse, and then discovering the predicament of the
late Emersonian poet unable to pierce an inch into the cen-

tral truth of nature. Both struggled with problems of vision and wholeness that their contemporaries, being genteel or resigned or both, more easily put by.

Emerson of course recognized Whitman as one of his own in the famous letter of 1855; he was perhaps nearer the mark in his journal where he linked Whitman to the authentic bard Taliessin (*J*, X, 147), for Whitman, too, riddled in song about the giant forms of self and nature. Whitman tried consciously to be the poet Emerson imagined, and whatever else awakened him, the "Walt Whitman" of the first *Leaves of Grass* is a rough, lusty version of Emerson's original Orphic poet. He is "complete" and "equable," a Universal Man, an "answerer" for all the world's riddles.

Formally, Whitman's poetry is nearly the antithesis of Emerson's. Emerson's shorter line and gnomic device suited the prudence that checked his spiralling flights, but at the beginning of his career Whitman unwound an expansive style to express the unstopped spirit he created in his poem. The style remained, but the singer did not stay so spontaneously Me. For Whitman was a poet of "En-Masse" as well as "One's-Self." Better than any other he spoke the "antinomian, Adamic impulse" that Roy Harvey Pearce identified as a continuous thread in American poetry; but, perhaps from his personal experience in the dark year before 1860 and certainly from what he saw during the Civil War, Whitman learned the other strand in his lesson, the need to affirm an order existing apart from and before the self.[5] Even in 1855, when the vital "I" dominated, it was possible to explain oneself only because there was more, there was "form and union and plan," "the pattern is systematic," it is "the exquisite scheme." In *Children of Adam* "all is a procession, / The universe is a procession with measured and perfect motion," as in Emerson's "Merlin II." Over the next three decades the system gradually outgrew the bard. The "I" that had always been representative became part of a great "literatus order," a tradition like Emerson's band of grandees, descending (in "The Base of All Metaphysics") from Socrates and Christ to makers of "germanic systems." The messianic poet in "Passage to India" comes as the fulfillment of a long line of scientists and technicians, all of whom have contributed practical works of fusion; his work is to be the metaphysical fusion of man and nature. And the last of Whitman's poet-figures, at the very end of *Leaves of Grass*, is defined exactly as Emerson's mature Orphic poet, a reconciler of two extremes:

When the full-grown poet came,
Out spake pleased Nature (the round impassive globe, with
    all its shows of day and night,) saying, *He is mine;*
But out spake too the Soul of man, proud, jealous and
    unreconciled, *Nay, he is mine alone;*
—Then the full-grown poet stood between the two, and
    took each by the hand;
And to-day and ever so stands, as blender, uniter,
    tightly holding hands,
Which he will never release until he reconciles the two,
And wholly and joyously blends them.

("Second Annex": 1891)

If Whitman began a new tradition of native poetry in rebellion against the British, as Edwin Fussell has argued, Whitman came to understand his independence from England as an alliance with philosophical Germany.[6]

In the prophetic literature of these States . . . Nature, true Nature, and the true idea of Nature, long absent, must, above all, become fully restored, enlarged, and must furnish the pervading atmosphere to poems, and the test of all high literary and aesthetic compositions. I do not mean the smooth walks, trimm'd hedges, poseys and nightingales of the English poets, but the whole orb, with its geologic history, the kosmos, carrying fire and snow, that rolls through the illimitable areas, light as a feather, though weighing billions of tons.

(*Democratic Vistas*: 1871)

The "true Nature" he sought was neither animal nor spiritual merely, but a whole, paradoxical system of the sort presided over by the "Sancta Spirita" of "Chanting the Square Deific," Whitman's version of Emerson's "Brahma." The United States, too, was such a system of reconciled contraries, in which individualism worked as "the compensating balance-wheel of the successful working machinery of aggregate America." In *Democratic Vistas,* as in *The Conduct of Life,* the idea of the machine displaced that of the garden.

Whitman's history as a poet is like Emerson's. As the orbic system swelled in grandeur, the figure of the poet declined, lost the splendid human lineaments Whitman had given him, and stood before the Sphinx or "mighty labyrinth" without the powers of Orpheus. Whitman's version of the eternal fugitive is the late "Riddle Song" (1881), whose subject is "that which eludes this verse and any verse," a something unnamed "hiding yet lingering" in all things—

> Haply God's riddle it, so vague and yet so certain,
> The soul for it, and all the visible universe for it,
> And heaven at last for it.

Confident of an order and reconciliation already implied in the whole, this poet accepts the late Emersonian role, not to build but to admire and imitate an existing, superior design. He is a mediator at best, and in less propitious times a capricious, fragmented figure, "a trail of drift and debris" walking aimlessly at the edge of life in Whitman's "As I Ebb'd," or Emerson's "Blight," or Thoreau's "Sic Vita." Literally paralyzed in 1874, Whitman described the analogous state of the poetic imagination in "Prayer of Columbus": feeling his terminus near, he clung helplessly to his shadowy vision. Earlier and much more easily the mainstream of nineteenth-century poets had abdicated the role of seer or riddle-solver, leaving unknown or oblique

followers of Emerson to struggle with the darker implications of his encounter between the self and nature in an era
when the poet and poetry were destined to become "minor
Things."

Emily Dickinson understood the motive for metaphor in
terms of Emerson's metamorphosis, where there is joy
precisely because everything is in flight and nature never
answers us tediously with "yesterday's surprise." But because her poetry is also nourished on the pain beyond
understanding, the cosmic riddle in her verse often turns
into grim humor.[7] Dickinson may have written in solitude,
with little thought given to her poetic contemporaries, but
her dark, gnomic manner and her vision of the world as
an incomprehensible puzzle, personified as "a Juggler"
(like Melville's "Juggularius"), are not at all unique. Indeed, the notion of a secret in the center and the poet
helplessly lost on the edge are common recurrences in
major poets after Emerson and Dickinson. Some of Melville's short poems—"Buddha," for example—and many
of the stark encounters of Stephen Crane are demonic riddles, inversions or serious parodies of a poem like
"Brahma." The connection between Emerson and Dickinson that begins with Ben Newton's gift of the *Poems* in 1850
is now well known.[8] The case is not so clear with Crane,
however, who may never have looked at Emerson's poems
and was not particularly impressed when Howells read to
him from Emily Dickinson's in 1893. Yet Howells criticized
Crane's prose-poems as "too Orphic," not "solid and real"
enough, and Hamlin Garland correctly saw in them "the
sting and compression of Emily Dickinson's verse."[9] Crane
had listened to the darker voice of Orpheus, the eerier
sounds that issue from confessions like "if I am the Devil's
child, I will live then from the Devil" and its Dickinsonian
counterpart, "if he does not know me—there is a darker
spirit, will not disown its child."[10]

Black Riders is a litany on this theme. The Emerson closest to Crane was the motto chalked on his studio wall and carried in his pocket at the time he was writing *Maggie*: "Congratulate yourselves if you have done something strange and extravagant and broken the monotony of a decorous age."[11] Crane did this in his poems, though Emerson stands behind these lean encounters of "the small man confronting the bleak and lonely world."[12] Emerson was not as detached from the squirrel of "Fable" as Crane is from the little man who stands against the mountain (*Black Riders*, XXII), but there are anecdotes in Emerson's prose that match Crane's in both form and spirit:

> The man finishes his story,—how good! how final! how it puts a new face on all things! He fills the sky. Lo! on the other side rises also a man and draws a circle around the circle we had just pronounced the outline of the sphere. Then already is our first speaker not man, but only a first speaker. His only redress is forthwith to draw a circle outside of his antagonist. And so men do by themselves.
>
> (II, 304–305)

> I seemed in the height of a tempest to see men overboard struggling in the waves, and driven about here and there. They glanced intelligently at each other, but 'twas little they could do for one another; 'twas much if each could keep afloat alone. Well, they had a right to their eye-beams, and all the rest was Fate.
>
> (VI, 19)

These are ideal sources for man pursuing the horizon or adrift on a slim spar. And Emerson's description of our struggle with nature is the essence of Crane's poetic proto-drama of the man against the mountain:

> . . . this unequal conflict, with powers so vast and unwea-riable ranged on one side, and this little conceited vulnerable popinjay that a man is, bobbing up and down into every danger, on the other.
>
> (IV, 160)

Like Emerson in his late phase, Crane believed in law that was, ultimately, a law of inertia or mass and motion. It is reflected in the circling antiphonies of *Black Riders* as well as in the primary oscillating patterns of his greatest fiction, in *The Open Boat* or *The Red Badge of Courage*. Immersing himself in the flux of battle, Henry Fleming finally wins the "sobering balance" of manhood and a "large sympathy for the machinery of the universe."[13] Crane's hero, like Emerson, came to respect the morality of the world-loom.

Crane's most explicit riddle is the epigraph for a tale called "The Clan of No-Name":

> Unwind my riddle.
> Cruel as hawks the hours fly;
> Wounded men seldom come home to die;
> The hard waves see an arm flung high;
> Scorn hits strong because of a lie;
> Yet there exists a mystic tie.
> Unwind my riddle.

It is answered in the story when a young lieutenant moves consciously and "inexorably" into a death-trap because he is one of the clan who acknowledge the law. Crane's balance between choice and necessity reiterates the order of Emerson in "Fate" or of Melville in "DuPont's Round Fight": victory, or consolation, lies in the fact of ultimate, if inexpressible, LAW.

At about the same time as Crane, Robinson and Frost were reading Emerson in a similar spirit. That is, they were plagued by what Robinson called the "diabolical system" of a materialism they could not deny, they sought answers in the idealism of the sage, and they ended by discovering the serious, relieving qualification of that idealism in Emerson's poems and later prose. The young Robinson found no relief in Emerson's early essays, but seeking to reconcile spirit and science he discovered the value of "Compensation" and *The Conduct of Life*, which, he was ashamed to admit, he read for the first time in 1899. Exactly what that

value was becomes clearer when Robinson quotes approv-
ingly the great metaphor of the loom at the end of "Power"
(VI, 81–82), or when in an earlier letter he recalls lines from
"Monadnoc" that helped him to accept the universe as
Herbert Spencer or Robinson's friend Lawrence Hender-
son explained it. If "the world was made in order, and the
atoms march in time," and if a stringent morality always
testifies in the web of existence, then the most scarred men
and strangest humorists that Robinson could imagine
would all demonstrate the truths of Orpheus.[14] Robinson's
Captain Craig offers no solution to the riddle of the world
and its Unknown God, but the poem does assure us that
nothing is lost in all its transmutations and its hero confronts the Cosmic Joke by putting himself in the place of
Brahma, quoting a line from Emerson's poem. Craig is a
diminished and eccentric version of Emerson's messianic
poet-figure, whom his own monologue continually alludes
to; his "mystic cheerfulness" sustains him even to his very
last word—" 'Trombones,' he said," and the spirit will
leap to his trope because every word can stand for the
whole. For Frost as well as for Robinson the sagacity of
Emerson and the greatness of his poetry, to which they
both attested,[15] were bound up with the *persona* of Uriel
(the squirrel, the titmouse, and Saadi, too, though they do
not mention them), the little figure who survives the assault of bigger things, the small one who exemplifies an
answer to the question all the birds seem to frame for the
poet: "what to make of a diminished thing."

Strange indeed that poets beginning to see through to
the poetic dimensions of Emerson did not see that this
question had already been answered by a diminutive poet
in Emerson's line. In 1862, the year Emerson was greeted
by the titmouse, Emily Dickinson found a small bird in her
garden whom she asked, "Wherefore sing, since nobody
hears?"—"*My* business is to *sing*," the bird replied. Having
learned the lesson, the poet went about her business, even

though her "size felt small" and her "little Force" kept
exploding outside the orderly limits her mentor set. Her
business, she also said, was "circumference"; she was the
first of our poets to work fully and consciously from the
edge. She knew that as American poet and "Scholar" she
would have to be "a supposed person," but whether she
consciously modeled that self after Emerson's poetic *per-
sonae* is not certain; surely what she did find in his *Poems*
was justification for a style at the antipodes from Whitman,
an assurance that she could write as she did and take herself seriously as a poet. If she began as an ingenuous practitioner of sub-literary household poetry, reading "Good-
Bye" or Emerson's quatrains would have persuaded her
that private verses and public poetry are not mutually exclusive. His poems offered sufficient precedent for
roughened meters and playful rhymes, and she probably
borrowed elements for her own poetic dramas from the
antics of the humble-bee, the squirrel talking back to the
mountain, and Uriel upsetting the old gods. Years later
when Thomas Wentworth Higginson introduced her
poems to the world, he first recalled Emerson's remarks in
The Dial about a new "poetry of the Portfolio," of "fragmentary verses" and "halting rhymes" quite apart from
poetry that was eloquently public. If Higginson was desperately seeking a literary propriety his own taste did not
permit him to pronounce, he made the right connection:
the line between Emerson and Dickinson is indelible in
the way only poetry and not "Dear Master" letters can
make it.[16]

Dickinson's poetic protagonist resembles Uriel or Merlin
or Saadi, in part because she intuitively grasped the ideas
of indirection and artistic enchantment that Emerson had
discovered in 1839, and also because she profoundly understood the pathways of "Experience." She seems to have
internalized Emerson's binary form, in love poems as well
as poems about nature, and to have imagined as an ultimate poetic consummation the union of One and Other.[17]

"Tell all the Truth but tell it slant" (J1129) and "I only said the Syntax— / And left the Verb and the pronoun out" (J494) are the principles of her magic, and although her "Truth" sometimes implies full revelation, there are as many instances in her poems where the surprise is "Bald, and Cold" (J281) or doubt nibbles at the soul (J501). Then the staircase of surprise is like the staircase of "Experience," spiralling upward without end, and the eccentric or oblique angle of vision is as necessary when truth is obscure as when it is bright. In "Experience" self-consciousness, awareness of our own existence, is called the "Fall of Man" (III, 75); in Dickinson consciousness condemns the self to being eternally Two (J642). Confronting this "discrepance" in the world, Emily Dickinson might have said with Emerson, "I am *defeated* all the time; yet to Victory I am born," for she sometimes managed, with titmouse skill, to transform defeat into victory by sleight-of-word, and her popular triumph in this vein, "Success is counted Sweetest" (J67), was attributed to Emerson when it was published anonymously in 1876.[18]

Yet her greatest achievements are encounters with a nature that "affects to be sedate" but is really the riddle or "Juggler" of incomprehensible metamorphosis (J228, J1170). What cannot be explained calls out for a poetry unfinished and indirect, "Without Design / Or Order," as in the superbly blended sound and sense of "Four Trees—upon a solitary Acre" (J742). When the relation of things or their correspondence is not known, then accordingly the syntax should be missing. In such a world microscopes are prudent (J185), and although Dickinson had no great idea of a relation between science and poetry, her deliberate, detached perception was that of a naturalist like Thoreau. She wrote a credo for the modern, scientific figure of the poet:

> The missing All—prevented Me
> From missing minor Things.
> If nothing larger than a World's

> Departure from a Hinge—
> Or Sun's extinction, be observed—
> 'Twas not so large that I
> Could lift my Forehead from my work
> For Curiosity.
>
> (J985)

She obviously did not believe that minor things matter only because of the way they connect to make a whole; yet there is a sense that, like a patient spider, she was building, and that the minute research she could not interrupt would amount in the end to a treatise on the phenomenology of "Crumbling"—"Dilapidation's processes / Are organized Decays" (J997, part of which is quoted by Pynchon in *Gravity's Rainbow*, a book that completes her project). She carefully examined both the gradations and the crisis in a subject that was her lifelong study. What she found seemed to confirm her art: the little obliquities of her craft, dashes and off-rhymes, gained significance as the slight adjustments of a hair (J889) that keep us, despite our ignorance and the apparent lack of design in things, "nicely balanced" just this side of eternity. Thus, in Emerson's sense of evolutionary survival—"every jet of chaos which threatens to exterminate us is convertible by intellect into wholesome force" (VI, 32)—she learned to skate at the edge.

In her encounter with the Intruder or the "Force illegible" (J820) behind all things, the Dickinsonian poet-figure gains no certainties, but she does uncover compensations that approach winning. That a rat can live rent-free is the reaction of nature, "Lawful as Equilibrium," against human artifices (J1356); similarly, light cannot be bought, but is available "To Squirrel in the Himmaleh / Precisely, as to you" (J862). If there was dark, Dickinson did not call for a beacon bright, as the early Robinson did in tremulous grievings, but she went out in it because "we grow accustomed to the Dark—"

The Bravest—grope a little—
And sometimes hit a Tree
Directly in the Forehead—
But as they learn to see—

Either the Darkness alters—
Or something in the sight
Adjusts itself to Midnight—
And Life steps almost straight.
(J419)

Beyond this adjustment, the last defense of her intellect against cosmic "Ambush" was irony, the same insect's sting that was available to Stephen Crane. Her poem beginning with the affirmation, "I know that He exists" (J338), moves immediately toward the piercing queries of this *Black Rider*:

If I should cast off this tattered coat,
And go free into the mighty sky;
If I should find nothing there
But a vast blue,
Echoless, ignorant—
What then?
(*Black Riders*, LXVI)

—why, then "the jest— / Have crawled too far!" is Emily Dickinson's pungent conclusion.

Frost, who certainly follows in this line, rarely resorts to the same sharp irony. His is usually gentler and directed against doubters, as in the oblique last line of "Design." Frost like Dickinson had to go out in the dark, but he kept a sufficient distance from the trees and knew better than to stop; he survives "Stopping by Woods" or "Come In" because he once bumped his forehead indoors and thenceforth understood that correspondence is not all it might seem.

A slim door got in past my guard,
And hit me a blow in the head so hard
I had my native simile jarred.

185

> So people and things don't pair anymore
> With what they used to pair with before.
> ("The Door in the Dark")

Thus even the worst mismatchings that Frost can imagine—even the gratuitous malignity, worthy of Crane, in "The Draft Horse"—are simply turned aside, without irony, in effortless subordination to the metrical order of things as they are. Birds and most men in Frost's poetry know enough to say, "let what will be, be" ("Acceptance"). There is also, at the other extreme, a Platonic or Puritan strain in Frost that urges him toward interpretation. Meserve, the tiny, tough preacher in "Snow," like a young Emerson or a troubled Ishmael, has inherited the Pentecostal gift of words with an eye for likenesses, and so he sees miracles in every slight adjustment of a leaf. Something more than necessity drives him out into the storm, and there is always a measure of admiration in Frost's dramas for man's stubborn, if pointless, challenge to fate. Meserve, groping for a reason, stumbles upon the titmouse dimension:

> "Our snowstorms as a rule
> Aren't looked on as man-killers, and although
> I'd rather be the beast that sleeps the sleep
> Under it all, his door sealed up and lost,
> Than the man fighting it to keep above it,
> Yet think of the small birds at roost and not
> In nests. Shall I be counted less than they are?
> Their bulk in water would be frozen rock
> In no time out tonight. And yet tomorrow
> They will come budding boughs from tree to tree,
> Flirting their wings and saying Chickadee,
> As if not knowing what you meant by the word storm."

Emerson might have added that knowing is being, and the titmouse as a product of evolutionary adaptation has pragmatic knowledge of what the storm is; moreover, Emerson's tiny bird evoked what Meserve's poetry seems to miss, the fun in how things are said. In this sense, a truer analogue of "The Titmouse" in Frost is the wood-chuck famous for his strategic retreat. This small animal is fully aware of emergencies, and what is more, he has fun with them: he makes them time off to meditate, and we learn (only in the penultimate stanza) that his poetic brag-gadocio is part of a larger whole, a dialogue of love. The woodchuck will survive—

> If I can with confidence say
> That still for another day,
> Or even another year,
> I will be there for you, my dear,
>
> It will be because, though small
> As measured against the All,
> I have been so instinctively thorough
> About my crevice and burrow.
> ("A Drumlin Woodchuck")

That is pure *Thoreau*—"My instinct tells me that my head is an organ for burrowing"—as was Emerson's wintry anecdote.

Early in the twentieth century the colossal poet of America had shrunk beneath the common size of man to the dimensions of smaller animals. This the poets them-selves affirmed: in Edgar Lee Masters' *Spoon River* "Petit, the Poet" could not match the music of the pine tree; like an earlier village aesthete, Mr. Churchill in Longfellow's *Kavanagh*, Petit's chief failure was not to have used the materials nature made readily available, "All in the loom, and oh what patterns." The contrasting vignette of "Theo-dore the Poet" suggests that Dreiser showed Masters where the artist ought to go for his yarn. As a boy Theo-dore stared at the crawfish by its burrow much as young Frank Cowperwood studied a lobster in Dreiser's *The Financeer*. Masters did not notice that Thoreau and later Frost were watching burrows, too, nor would he link Petit with Emerson's vulnerable popinjay fretting against the impossible odds of life. And yet the fact is that the Chicago School in 1915 simply confirmed what New England had long suspected—old Orpheus, the figure of the poet as prophet, was only whistling in the dark. Even the daylight symbol of infinity, the "one cerulean blue" in which Wordsworth found his ecstatic sense of union with God, had turned to a vast azure that oppressed poetic man in Crane (*Black Riders*, LXVI) or Frost ("An Encounter"). It hangs over us yet in Richard Wilbur's "Merlin Enthralled," the "still and woven blue" above the questing knights who are impotent without the old Merlin.

When the unfathomable design of the universe is stitched shut and its weaving presents only a mystery of totality, then the Central Man is not even possible to the imagination, and poets move inevitably toward the edges into detritus and driftwood. After Emerson's "Circles" and "Blight," Emily Dickinson wrote a definitive statement for these poets out on the thin rind:

> I saw no Way—The Heavens were stitched—
> I felt the Columns close—
> The Earth reversed her Hemispheres—
> I touched the Universe—
>
> And back it slid—and I alone—
> A speck upon a Ball—
> Went out upon Circumference—
> Beyond the Dip of Bell—
>
> (J378)

This is the sad self-knowledge of the outcast Uriel which has fostered a lasting poetry of the edge, sometimes seeking to give barrows the "grace and glimmer of romance" (Emerson's "Art"), as in Hart Crane's "Chaplinesque," Stevens' "The Man on the Dump," or Wilbur's "Junk," sometimes concentrating on the "Minimal" in nature, as in Theodore Roethke, Wilbur's "Marginalia," or in the

periphery poems of A. R. Ammons. Ammons knows as
well as Uriel that the truth is not perpendicular, but at the
same time he says, "Overall is beyond me: is the sum of
these events / I cannot draw . . ." ("Corson's Inlet"). So
like Dickinson he is drawn to the edge, or like Frost at the
well or in the March woods, thinking he sees the central
"Paradise-in-Bloom" ("A Boundless Moment"), Ammons
hesitates an instant, takes a closer look, and then names
the things of the thicket as they are (in "Periphery").

> The unassimilable fact leads us on:
> round the edges
>   where broken shapes make poor masonry
> the synthesis
> fails . . .
>
> .   .   .   .
>
>   we are led on
>
> to the boundaries
> where relations loosen into chaos
>   or where the nucleus fails to control,
> fragments in odd shapes
> expressing more and more the interstitial sea
>
> ("The Misfit")

For this tradition, a poetry of minor things, Stevens and
not Eliot asked the overwhelming question and wrote the
appropriate apostrophe (the one of failed vision, that
Emerson had not written to Monadnoc, is in "This Solitude of Cataracts"): how to recover centrality at the edge.
The learned astronomer, the sage who lectured so brilliantly (*Black Riders*, LVIII), in fact the whole Chautauqua
circuit could hem and haw the planet as they liked, but
they could not satisfy the mischievous pupil, the deprived
poet:

> If the day writhes, it is not with revelations.
> One goes on asking questions. That, then, is one
> Of the categories. So said, this placid space

Is changed. It is not so blue as we thought. To be blue,
There must be no questions. It is an intellect
Of windings round and dodges to and fro,

Writhings in wrong obliques and distances,
Not an intellect in which we are fleet: present
Everywhere in space at once, cloud-pole

Of communication. It would be enough
If we were ever, just once, at the middle, fixed
In This Beautiful World of Ours and not as now,

Helplessly at the edge, enough to be
Complete, because at the middle, if only in sense,
And in that enormous sense, merely enjoy.

("The Ultimate Poem is Abstract")

Stevens winds and writhes toward completion, but at every "now" we find ourselves still ephemerals at the edge. Emerson said the question and the answer are one; for the child's consciousness "Questions are Remarks," complete in themselves, and after his rounds of "never-ending meditation" Stevens left us not the giant orb, but the final dwarf of ourselves ("The Dwarf"), its amplification in "The Aurora of Autumns," and at last this unnamed brooder, "A Child Asleep in Its Own Life."

Tell me not in joyful numbers
We can make our lives sublime
By—well, at least, not by
Dabbling much in rhyme.

Stephen Crane's acidic parody speaks for the low state of American poetry in 1900. In terms of the Emersonian fable, tiny man had lost so much ground to the mountain that there was little left for him to say. In 1846, even when he had been turned toward silence by his great loss, Emerson still looked for the Central Man. So, too, poets of the twentieth century would try, in their own desperation, to revive the precedent myth. Consciously in the shadow of *The Waste Land*, accepting it as description but not remedy, they set themselves the poetic task of delineating the giants, new versions of the Cosmic Man or "King-self."

This has been the task of the modern American epic, as it is defined by Roy Harvey Pearce, and clearly if the myth was passed from Emerson the poetic method and the "proto-epic" must be acknowledged as Whitman's.[19] Ezra Pound, William Carlos Williams, and Hart Crane were all lyricists, but their great goal was to set the quest for a humanized order into epic form. And like Whitman they became inclusive and architectonic poets, building huge mosaics or tapestries, defining cumulatively rather than by reduction and so continually expanding their poems. Broadly speaking, their manner of poetic making was experiential, drawing together the widest assortment of historical and personal reference, rather than quintessential; spatial rather than temporal (for they intentionally fragmented narrative and chronology, just as they insisted on breaking down the traditional sequences of English metrics); urban rather than pastoral—the city and its artifacts supplied them with materials and ultimately with an organized vision. In summary, they found Orpheus and the poetic work in artifact, not mere fact, in the cordage of Brooklyn Bridge or in chiselled stone. Pound's own cult, from Malatesta through Jefferson-Adams to the more nearly mythic figures of Amphion, Apollonius, and the Pythagorean seers in *Rock-Drill*, are all heroes by virtue of imposing order on chaos; and despite the strain of humility in *The Pisan Cantos* or the "minimum" vision of the poet in "The Tunnel" section of *The Bridge*, the epic desire of these poets was to invoke again the kingdom of man over nature. Thus their roots in an American tradition go back to Whitman in 1855, perhaps as well to Emerson's original Orphic poet and Central Man, but not to the Orphic protagonist that emerges from his poetry.

There is a sense in which all our poets are Emersonian, even some who have never gone to Emerson. But I would distinguish between an Emerson-Whitman line invoking the myth of the whole, cosmic man and a second, more restrictive Emersonian line—in this century represented chiefly by Frost, Stevens, and Ammons—attentive to Emerson's poems and later essays and thus followers of a lesser Orpheus. These latter poets have continued the tradition of a dramatic or situational lyric characteristically shaped by the Emersonian encounter between the self and nature. In so limiting their poetic scope they have acknowledged the limited stature of man and his small part in an immense natural order, and they have centered the Orphic aspirations of the poet on ordinary human needs. Since they have not claimed to solve the Orphic riddle, they have been wary of esoteric solutions, citing, with Richard Wilbur, Emerson's own rejection of Swedenborgian "Mathematic hell."

Harold Bloom has spoken of Emerson and Stevens together as "failed Orphics who refuse to accept defeat."[20] In fact, the strategy of these poets from Emerson and Dickinson onward has been the conversion of defeat into victory. The American poet as failed Orphic is to that extent a happy failure, like Melville's fiddler Hautboy who was also "something of an Orpheus." Hautboy charmed the ambitious poet Helmstone into acquiescence. Likewise Emily Dickinson's Orpheus, who follows directly in Emerson's line:

> The Bible is an antique Volume—
> Written by faded Men
> At the suggestion of Holy Spectres—
>
> . . . .
>
> Had but the tale a warbling Teller—
> All the boys would come—
> Orpheus' sermon captivated—
> It did not condemn—
>
> (J1545)

Orpheus as founder of the ancient theology and revealer of sacred truth risks the oblivion of other "faded Men"; but Orpheus as Merlin or Saadi, artfully soothing and persuasive, unifies the company of poetic believers and has an enviable staying power. These are casual uses of Orpheus by Melville and Dickinson, certainly not memorable ones for their contemporaries, but they do suggest, as Ishmael did in *Moby-Dick*, lowering one's "conceit of attainable felicity." Poetry, having failed to make our lives sublime at the end of the nineteenth century, might succeed in making them at least satisfactory in the twentieth.

It was Stevens, of course, who defined poetry most precisely as failed sublimity and the finding of satisfaction.

> . . . The actor is
> A metaphysician in the dark, twanging
> An instrument, twanging a wiry string that gives
> Sounds passing through sudden rightnesses, wholly
> Containing the mind, below which it cannot descend,
> Beyond which it has no will to rise.
>
> It must
> Be the finding of a satisfaction, and may
> Be of a man skating, a woman dancing, a woman
> Combing. The poem of the act of the mind.
> ("Of Modern Poetry")

The modern Orphic mind cannot dive and soar as it traditionally did, but is contained within the limits Stevens set. Merely to describe the motions of this mid-world, with all the rightness words afford, was prophecy enough for Stevens. His poems move incessantly toward fragile, tentative equilibriums that dramatize the kind of reconciliation held out in "The Titmouse" or "Experience." Emerson, as we have seen, came to admire adroitness on the surface of life, and he praised the heroism of a mind that can describe it:

> How much self-reliance it implies to write a true description of anything, for example, Wordsworth's picture of skating;

that leaning back on your heels and stopping in mid-career.
So simple a fact no common man would have trusted himself to detach as a thought.[21]

As the focal act of skating suggests, Wordsworth, Emerson, and Stevens are Romantic poets of a common climate.
Stevens, knowing that "his soil is man's intelligence,"
found his poetic forbears in his symbolic return to the wintry regions of New England.

Stevens' definition of modern poetry fits surprisingly
well into the context of his predecessors, those nineteenth-century New England poets who used the Emersonian encounter as a stage for the "metaphysician in the
dark." The new stage Stevens insisted upon was not a
change in dramatic setting but in the terms of the encounter. And this change was already apparent near the
turn of the century; one of its earliest indicators is the difference between Robinson's and Frost's reading of William
James in 1897. For Robinson there was nothing in James
that could rescue the metaphysician; but Frost immediately
set out to study under James, and though he never did, he
was deeply affected by the help James offered to the man
in darkness.[22] James' version of the encounter between the
poet and nature made the artist inseparable from the
metamorphosis, so that terms like "defeat" or even "metaphysician," in its strict sense, no longer applied. In the
turbulence of Jamesian reality truth was redefined as satisfaction, a state of relative equilibrium or constancy, and
goodness as that which "makes for the best *whole*, in the
sense of awakening the least sum of dissatisfactions." Thus
poetry could be seen as part of the larger human search for
a richer, more inclusive order—as James put it, the moral
philosopher seeks "the good which seems most organiza-
ble, most fit to enter into complex combinations, most apt
to be a member of a more inclusive whole"; his statements
are never final, but rather akin to "a literature which is

confessedly tentative and suggestive rather than dogmatic."[23]

Nearly all that Frost said about metaphor and the nature of poetry follows in this Jamesian and Emersonian line. As a Swedenborgian apostate Frost also knew the interstices of analogy and believed in "both symbols and change," hence in "changing symbols." He found metaphor not true in the old sense but in the Jamesian sense of being vital, useful, satisfying:

> All metaphor breaks down somewhere. That is the beauty of it. It is touch and go with metaphor, and until you have lived with it long enough you don't know when it is going. You don't know how much you can get out of it and when it will cease to yield. It is a very living thing. It is as life itself.[24]

Toward the end of his life there is a kind of liberation in poetic departures, the freedom an artist feels when he is alone with his material and he can "flash off into wild connections" ("How Hard It Is To Keep From Being King").

An aesthetic privacy, like that of "The Poet" or "Experience," distinguishes the moment when the ideal becomes real. The world is what you will—with Frost's pragmatic proviso—so long as you learn "how much you can get out of it." Frost as poet is not deceived by his own pretenses and holds to delicate balances between imagination and fact as in "A Boundless Moment" or "For Once, Then, Something." The moment when "water comes to rebuke the too clear water" gives the feeling of James' phrase "something there,"[25] an ecstasy or overplus beyond the exact levelling that water in nature makes. Taking into consideration what we put into it, the universe is turning out as we desire; there is the "small balance in brute facts always favorable to the side of reason" (I, 372), and so aided by James and Emerson, Frost could dismiss apparent designs of darkness and claim that the balance of nature as a whole makes for a continuous string of slim victories:

> We may doubt the just proportion of good to ill.
> There is much in nature against us. But we forget:
> Take nature altogether since time began,
> Including human nature, in peace and war,
> And it must be a little more in favor of man,
> Say a fraction of one percent at the very least,
> Or our number living wouldn't be steadily more,
> Our hold on the planet wouldn't have so increased.
>
> ("Our Hold On The Planet")

The margin here implies the value of craftsmanship and what Emerson called "minor skills and accomplishments" (VI, 143). Frost thought of men as riders mounted bareback on a seemingly untamed earth, and said they must think of themselves as "guiders," staying on by using all the wit that they have. If evil tendencies do cancel, then the Chaplinesque strategy of ducking may assist in the collision of the two. Frost's poetic strategies are acts of this kind, the sleight-of-mind we have seen in the woodchuck or the squirrel, the slight deviation in language that makes all the difference. It is just the right effort to win any single encounter by a hair and still have strength "for yet another blow" (the last line of verse Frost published).

Through James, too, descends Emerson's primary figure of Orphic consummation, the marriage of opposites. When Emerson's poet could not solve the riddle of the Sphinx, he discovered the reconciliation of mind and nature in the local equilibriums that words, acting like organic clusters of matter, can achieve. James developed the concept of dynamic equilibrium as a principle of his psychology, and later he used the metaphor of marriage to explain his pragmatic notion of truth as organically evolved, mediating between old and new, between visionary and scientific:

> New truth is always a go-between, a smoother-over of
> transitions. It marries old opinion to new fact so as ever to

show a minimum of jolt, a maximum of continuity. . . . It makes itself true, gets itself classed as true, by the way it works; grafting itself then upon the ancient body of truth, which thus grows by the activity of a new layer of cambium. . . . Purely objective truth, truth in whose establishment the function of giving human satisfaction in marrying previous parts of experience with newer parts played no role whatever, is nowhere to be found. The reasons [*sic*] why we call things true is the reason why they *are* true, for "to be true" *means* only to perform this marriage-function.[26]

The most significant of modern Emersonian poems have been, quite consciously, performances of this marriage-function.

In "West-Running Brook" Frost measured man's achievement against the larger material universe that is slowly running down. Man and nature make a marriage of disparities that holds because the last white tip of that stream, the mind, throws itself back against the cataract, counter to the flow. Our momentary stay is the dance of Pirouot and Pirouette; it is our ability to balance, and it is also the vital quality of the mind that envelops skeptics and believers. Rich in sources and in its own contrariety, Frost's "backward force" suggests on the one hand a Bergsonian desire that seeks to "climb / Back up a stream of radiance to the sky" ("The Master Speed"), and on the other, the skeptical resistance of the mind to vast over-simplifications that would make it run with the current. Both are in Frost; his metaphor implies spur and bridle, and the accomplished rider can use them both. Taken as a whole, the poem is a uniquely human act and a dramatization of balance achieved. The truth of "West-Running Brook" is worked out in dialogue and thus subtly contained within this over-riding or constituting metaphor, in which it begins and ends.

The marriage-function is a sign of poetic affinity between Frost and Stevens, and of a legacy shared by otherwise dissimilar poets.[27] Stevens' exploration of Emersonian

ground began with *Ideas of Order*, a fitting centenary for
Nature in 1936, and continued as the search for Central Man
in key poems like "Asides on the Oboe," "Chocorua to Its
Neighbor" (a version of "Monadnoc"), and "A Primitive
Like an Orb." It climaxed in *Notes Toward a Supreme Fiction*,
a poem that is a fleshing out of the poetic theory offered in
"The Noble Rider and the Sound of Words." There Stevens
had expounded on the charioteer of the *Phaedrus* and
proposed his own version of the noble rider who, like the
equestrian of "Fate," rides only so long as he maintains a
perfect balance between his two horses of imagination and
reality. *Notes* is the preliminary elaboration of a supreme
fiction that, in the words of Stevens' essay, "will help
people live their lives."[28] It is shaped around climaxes of
insight or mythy narratives, each an approximation of the
union of opposites or the incalculable, perfect balance that
the poet seeks. That balance cannot be achieved by "romantic intoning" or "declaimed clairvoyance"; naming the
unnameable sun begets only sterile decrees and statues that
are finally rubbish, as Emerson had implied in his hymns of
the negative theology. A supreme fiction must be vital and
organic:

> Two things of opposite natures seem to depend
> On one another, as a man depends
> On a woman, day on night, the imagined
>
> On the real. This is the origin of change.
> Winter and spring, cold copulars, embrace
> And forth the particulars of rapture come.
>
> Music falls on the silence like a sense,
> A passion that we feel, not understand.
> Morning and afternoon are clasped together
>
> And North and South are an intrinsic couple
> And sun and rain a plural, like two lovers
> That walk away as one in the greenest body.
>
> (II, iv)

This is Stevens' sensuous version of the "one body grooms and brides" in "Merlin II."

In the final section of *Notes* the pageantry of Catawba joins the Captain of order to the maiden Bawda in a marriage place that is "neither heaven nor hell." This marriage belongs in the middle region, the place of the modern mind, but it is not yet the supreme fiction. For Canon Aspirin, so aptly named, has performed only a conjunction of convenience, a momentary balking of the elements. His dream is the last doomed effort of a noble rider to place reality within his own imagination:

> Forth then with huge pathetic force
> Straight to the utmost crown of night he flew.
> The nothingness was a nakedness, a point
>
> Beyond which thought could not progress as thought.
> He had to choose. But it was not a choice
> Between excluding things. It was not a choice
>
> Between, but of. He chose to include the things
> That in each other are included, the whole,
> The complicate, the amassing harmony.
>
> (III, vi)

But the Canon's great conception is too overreaching an effort of the imagination, too much an imposition on the real. Helen Vendler rightly says that Stevens himself enters the poem at this point: his own diminished "I" rejects the tremendous chords promised in the ritual of the dead shepherd, the mythic Orpheus, and finds satisfaction in the mere song of robins and wrens.[29] Stevens has come down to the titmouse dimension, and the Orphic truth is contained within the repetitions of nature. The only marriage that can possibly be supreme, then, is the last one of the poem, which is not formalized but rather an irregular alliance between the poet and his unnamed interior paramour. Stevens returns, with the aging Whitman of "The Terrible Doubt of Appearances," to a state where just being there together will suffice. The hope of a crystal, central poem in which the woman will be named still flickers before the poet, but the drift of Stevens' last phase, toward windswept beaches and empty rooms where the scholar huddles before his one candle, is also darkly implied.

Notes helped to make Stevens a prince among secondary men because the poem and the theory associated with it suggest a way for poetry and science to meet. Stevens flourished in the critical context of I. A. Richards and the merger of two Jamesian strands, neo-Kantian aesthetics and empirical psychology, that Richards continued.[30] In this context some of the formalist poets most disapproving of Emersonian idealism embraced the crucial, countervailing elements of Emerson's poetics, though they still identified with Coleridge and not Emerson. The contemporary poet closest to Emerson is not formalist in this sense, and seems to have approached Emerson through poetry rather than theory. A. R. Ammons wrote early poems in the form of an abbreviated encounter, perhaps without reference to Emersonian predecessors, though many such as "High & Low" or "Close-up" sound like a more genial Stephen Crane. But Emerson is apparent in "What This Mode of Motion Said":

> You will someday
> try to prove me wrong
> (I am the wings when you me fly)
> to replace me with some mode
>   you made
> and think is right:

> I am the way by
> which you prove me
>   wrong,
> the reason you
> reason against me:

> I change shape,
> turn easily into the shapes you make

and even you
in moving
I leave, betray:

what has not yet been imagined has been
imagined by me
whom you honor, reach for—
change unending though
slowed into nearly limited modes:

The parenthetical allusion to "Brahma" shows that Ammons had already grasped the riddle of Orpheus and its translation from the old theology to modern physics. The wind is Ammons' favorite antagonist in the encounter, because wind is the ageless riddler from Taliessin through Emerson and Stevens, and Ammons knows that "the shapes nearest shapelessness awe us most." His poetic *persona* "old Ezra" also knows that mountains tired of lying down are moved only by liars, not by the lyre that would have dissolved Monadnoc or the Sphinx by telling its secret. For Ammons the poet's place is on the edge, accepting his smallness but actively participating, Jamesian fashion, in the motions of the whole:

the proud ephemerals play discretely in their energizing
laws and play out, transformations taking their ways, bending
their boundaries, giving and losing: the outface of the

sphere, the skinny seat on infinity, this holding, this
gentle stay in the bosom of reconciling but progressing
motions:

(Sphere)

In longer poems Ammons fulfills Emerson's late prophecy that science would dominate modern poetry. Quoting from texts on ecological and botanical structure in his "Essay on Poetics," Ammons explains,

so my point is that the poem
is the symbolical representation of the ideal organization,

whether
the cell, the body politic, the business, the religious

group, the university, computer, or whatever: I used to
wonder
why, when they are so little met and understood, poems are
taught
in schools: they are taught because they are convenient
examples

of the supreme functioning of one and many in an
organization of
cooperation and subordination; young minds, if they are to
"take
their place in society" need to learn patience—

Verging on irony, Ammons turns his patient, Dickinsonian
analysis to the "transcendental vegetative analogy," bringing into focus the statistically minute and marginal adjustments on which the evolution of species depends. His own
illumination is both terrifying and pleasing to the poet, and
in the strange sublimity of this passage he goes beyond
Emerson and the first law of thermodynamics translated
into "Song of Nature" to confront the "bottomless entropy"
implied by the second law.

Sphere, Ammons' most ambitious poem to date, opens
with the marriage metaphor, an explicitly sexual reconciliation of opposites. The figure quickly dissolves, a "total
diminishment" of oneness to its infinite, irreducible elements; but it is immediately reconstituted as Ammons'
inevitable subject, the abstract, primal opposition of the one
and the many. Later in the poem he engagingly defends his
preoccupation, citing *"E pluribus unum"* and Whitman;
Ammons' delight in all eddies and ragged peripheries and
his assimilation of them as poetic method are truly in
Whitman's vein. But on the problem of the one and the
many Ammons is critically speculative, not merely rhap-

sodic; in this he is heir to Emerson, who named unity and variety the cardinal facts, and to James, whose "long brooding" over this ancient question made it for him the "most central of all philosophical problems." James' treatment of this subject sometimes reads like an Ammons poem: it can be summarized in his statement, "What our intellect really aims at is neither variety nor unity taken singly, but *totality*."[31] Ammons' response can be taken from the little poem "At Once" (within the "Essay on Poetics")— "maximum / diversity with maximum unity / prevents hollow easiness"—and from "One:Many," the first and last lines—

To maintain balance
between one and many by
    keeping in operation both one and many:

    fear a too great consistency, an arbitrary
imposition
    from the abstract *one*
    downwardly into the realities of manyness:
  this makes unity
not deriving from the balance of manyness
but by destruction of diversity:
  it is unity
    unavailable to change,
cut off from the reordering possibilities of
    variety:
 . . . .

out of many, one:
from variety an over-riding unity, the expression of
variety:

no book of laws, short of unattainable reality itself,
can anticipate every event,
control every event: only the book of laws founded
    against itself,
founded on freedom of each event to occur as itself,
lasts into the inevitable balances events will take.

The order of nature, taken in its totality, contains in its mathematical precision all the freedom poetry needs. The middle of "One:Many" ranges over the whole United States, and in Whitman's cadences, but its power rises from the closing, in echoes of Frost's contrariety and Stevens' ease, a reiteration of the late Orphic stance.

This has not been a demonstration of poetic influence, but a selective view, an essay intent upon direction rather than detail. For it is in directions, in schemata of argument and structure, that Emerson's mark upon modern poetry is clearest. He had something for nearly every follower, and no one can summarily deny other connections—to the poets of the long view, to a tradition of Dionysus or other visionary strains in American poetry. That, after all, is the secret and hope of the land—something for everyone, bridging contradictions, seeking reconciliation, getting maximum diversity and maximum unity. My point is that Emerson made this secret, in its abstract nakedness, the subject of his poetry. As the first American poet to do so he used the only poetic and mythic tradition that would serve, one that he inherited through the English Romantics. When he began to see what science offered and what it refused to poetry, Emerson bent his mythic matter accordingly, naturalizing the aspirations of his Orphic poet and converting a once sacred marriage into a series of pragmatic reconciliations. There can be no doubt that, whatever theories he popularized, Emerson as a poet was cautious and accommodating in his relation to the NOT ME, to whatever formlessness he sensed beyond himself.

The modern poets I find most Emersonian are those who share his ideals and his restraint. They assume the value of imagination, and they sense, too, the need to be trued in flight, to have the pressure of reality counter to the imagination keeping them on their way. Stevens spoke for all of them when he wrote that poetry "seems, in the last analysis, to have something to do with our self-preservation." Seeing poetry in this light, they are new Romantics returning to the source: the principle of equilibrium, as Coleridge and Emerson first defined it, has been their germinal concept, and in figures like Goethe's Arabian poet, Melville's whale, or Emerson's titmouse—all systems delicately adjusted for survival—they have precursory symbols from the nineteenth century for what Stevens said poetry seems to be about. For them Emerson's great legacy has been Orphic in its broadest sense—a concept of poetry that could eventually make peace with science, and a figure of the poet as reconciler, comforter, and balanced soul.

Notes

———

Introduction

1. *Blake and Tradition* (Princeton, 1968), II, 189ff.

2. The Renaissance has been the basis for our revisionary understanding of Romanticism. Geoffrey Hartman, *Wordsworth's Poetry 1787–1814* (New Haven, 1964), p. 191, writes that English Romanticism returned to the spirit of Spenser and Milton. Hartman refers to Northrop Frye, *Fearful Symmetry* (Princeton, 1947), who discussed the tradition of Renaissance magic and the Elizabethan heritage of poetry as prophecy epitomized by the Ovidian line "*Est deus in nobis; agitante calescimus illo*" (p. 157), which is a crucial line for Emerson. Emerson called the Renaissance the "richest period of the English mind" (VII, 207), and he apparently linked this richness to its Platonic heritage. See William M. Wynkoop, *Three Children of the Universe: Emerson's View of Shakespeare, Bacon, and Milton* (The Hague, 1966), pp. 15ff.

3. Most notably Harold Bloom has established a trans-Atlantic visionary company, and perhaps the most important context we now have for Emerson's poetry is Bloom's dialectic of Romantic poetry called Prometheus and "Man, the Imagination" in England, and in Emersonian terms Bacchus and Merlin in America. See especially Bloom's essays, "The Internalization of Quest-Romance" (*Yale Review*, 1969), "The Central Man" (*Massachusetts Review*, 1966), and "Bacchus and Merlin" (*Southern Review*, 1971), collected in *The Ringers in the Tower: Studies in Romantic Tradition* (Chicago, 1971); "*Emerson*: The Self-Reliance of American Romanticism" (*Virginia Quarterly Review*, 1971), and "*The Native Strain*: American Orphism," both in Bloom's *Figures of Capable Imagination* (New York, 1976). See also the discussion of Emerson in R. W. B. Lewis, *The Poetry of Hart Crane* (Princeton, 1967), especially Chapter 8, and the delineations of "internalized apocalypse" by M. H. Abrams, "English Romanticism: The Spirit of the Age," in Northrop Frye, ed., *Romanticism Reconsidered* (New York, 1963), pp. 26–72, and in Abrams, *Natural Supernaturalism: Tradition and Revolution in Romantic Literature* (New York, 1971).

4. *Natural Supernaturalism*, p. 260. An organized or balanced unity is a crucial motif for the Romantic and American line of poetry descending from Emerson. For Abrams' references to Emerson and modern American writers, see Chapter 8, pp. 412–413ff.

5. *The Orphic Voice: Poetry and Natural History* (New Haven, 1960). For Sewell, Emerson is most Orphic when he seems to anticipate the modern attempt to resolve Cartesian dualism by a theory of symbolic form, a view of Emerson expounded by Charles Feidelson, Jr., in *Symbolism and American Literature* (Chicago, 1953). She also shows Emerson attuned to the Ovidian strains of Orpheus, which, primarily through Goethe, brought poetry into an intimate relation with biology at the beginning of the nineteenth century. See especially pp. 186–190, 219–222.

6. *Freedom and Fate: An Inner Life of RWE* (Philadelphia, 1953). In this line are Jonathan Bishop, *Emerson on the Soul* (Cambridge, 1964), especially Part III, and two treatments of other poets, Reuben Brower, *The Poetry of Robert Frost* (Oxford, 1963) and David Ferry, *The Limits of Mortality: An Essay on Wordsworth's Major Poems* (Middletown, Conn., 1959). Taken together, these works suggest a Wordsworth–Emerson–Frost line of poetry, hinged on the idea of a "double consciousness," and opposed to the more apocalyptic line envisioned by Lewis. Hyatt Waggoner's claim for Emerson's greatness as a poet in *American Poets: From the Puritans to the Present* (Boston, 1968) and *Emerson as Poet* (Princeton, 1974) is a broad one that seems to rest on a more orthodox interpretation of Emerson's poetry and does not emphasize the changes in his thought. Albert Gelpi, *The Tenth Muse: The Psyche of the American Poet* (Cambridge, 1975), pp. 57–111, also neglects Emerson's development and therefore does not explain what he does observe, namely, the discrepancy between Emerson's "Dionysian" theory and his poetic practice. Gelpi's stress on Jungian paradigms and the quest for wholeness does represent a valuable approach to Emerson and nineteenth-century American poetry.

7. *The American Renaissance* (Oxford, 1941), pp. 47, 55.

Chapter I. The Growth of an Orphic Mind

1. Orestes Brownson's review of Cousin (*Christian Examiner*, 1836), in Perry Miller, ed., *The Transcendentalists* (Cambridge, 1950), pp. 108, 114. For background see George Mills Harper's introductory essay in *Thomas Taylor The Platonist: Selected*

Writings, ed. Kathleen Raine and George Mills Harper (Princeton, 1969), pp. 49–102, and Barbara Harrell Carson, "Orpheus in New England: Alcott, Emerson, and Thoreau" (Ph.D. diss., Johns Hopkins, 1968).

2. *The Writings of Margaret Fuller*, ed. Mason Wade (New York, 1941), pp. 111–115.

3. See D. P. Walker, "Orpheus the Theologian and the Renaissance Platonists," *Journal of the Warburg and Courtauld Institutes* (1953) 16: 100–120.

4. The Quattrocento Platonists are so characterized by Ernst Cassirer, *The Individual and the Cosmos in Renaissance Philosophy*, trans. Mario Domandi (New York, 1963), p. 3.

5. Emerson described both the mind and history as alternating or polar processes. See "the mind now thinks, now acts" (I, 99), and the "alternating of expansions and contractions" (XII, 58), which should be compared with Arnold's theory of epochs in "The Function of Criticism at the Present Time." Though they differ about Emerson on England, both Philip Nicoloff, *Emerson on Race and History* (New York, 1961), and Michael Cowan, *City of the West: Emerson, America, and Urban Metaphor* (New Haven, 1967), show Emerson struggling to combine cyclical and progressive views of history. Nicoloff, pp. 54, 64–65, 81, cites Empedocles, Coleridge, and Goethe (through Carlyle) as Emerson's sources for the theory of alternating epochs.

6. *The Mystical Initiations; or, Hymns of Orpheus* (London, 1787), p. iii. (This preface was not reprinted in the 1824 edition which Emerson owned.) Cf. "Advertisement," *A Dissertation on the Eleusinian and Bacchic Mysteries* (1790), in Raine and Harper, p. 345.

7. *Hymns of Orpheus*, pp. 14–15. By somewhat tortuous arguments the Renaissance commentators had made Orphism monotheistic. See Walker, p. 110, and later English examples in Cudworth's *True Intellectual System of the Universe* (London, 1845) I, 500–506, and Coleridge's *The Friend* (Burlington, 1931), pp. 441–442 (II, x).

8. D. P. Walker, *Spiritual and Demonic Magic from Ficino to Campanella* (London, 1958), pp. 7–8.

9. See Sewell, especially pp. 21–51, and Michael Polanyi, *The Study of Man* (Chicago, 1958), for a summary of his larger work *Personal Knowledge*.

10. Emerson's Sermon 134 (1831), Houghton Library MS, Harvard University, Cambridge, Mass.

11. Reed, *Observations* (Boston, 1826), pp. 25–26, reprinted in Kenneth W. Cameron, *Young Emerson's Transcendental Vision* (Hartford, 1971), an abridged revision of Cameron's *Emerson the Essayist*.

12. *JMN*, IV, 368, 370–372, fully discussed by Merton M. Sealts, "Emerson on the Scholar, 1833–1837," *PMLA* 85 (March 1970): 186–188.

13. *The Origins of American Critical Thought* (New York, 1961), pp. 86–110.

14. *The Works of William E. Channing* (Boston, 1880), pp. 497–498. See Lawrence Buell, "Unitarian Aesthetics and Emerson's Poet-Priest," *American Quarterly* 20 (Spring 1968): 3–18, and *Literary Transcendentalism* (Ithaca, 1973), pp. 21–54.

15. See, e.g., *JMN*, III, 80–81. The line from Ovid's *Fasti* is quoted in Hugh Blair, *Lectures on Rhetoric and Belles Lettres* (London, 1853), p. 43, and also by Victor Cousin in his *Introduction to the History of Philosophy* (Boston, 1832), p. 165, which Emerson read in this translation. See also *JMN*, III, 139, and the verses, *JMN*, III, 290, for this idea.

16. Reed, p. 25.

17. Lines 1270–1271. Cf. *The Prelude*, Book V, and Sewell's interpretation of the Arab's shell and stone as the two books of myth and mathematics, respectively. In *The Excursion* IV, 1132–1146, the shell is a symbol for mythic or imaginative visitings.

18. See Abrams, *Natural Supernaturalism*, pp. 32–65, especially p. 47. For Emerson's view, see "History."

19. *Freedom and Fate*, pp. 17–24.

20. See Bishop, p. 170. Emerson also opened his son Waldo's coffin, July 8, 1857 (*J*, IX, 102).

21. Elizabeth Peabody, *Reminiscences of Rev. William Ellery Channing* (Boston, 1880), pp. 75, 279, 364.

22. "Coleridge and his American Disciples," *Biblioteca Sacra* (1847), 164–165. See also E. P. Whipple, "Coleridge as Philosophical Critic" (*American Review*, June 1846), in his *Essays and Reviews* (Boston, 1878) I, 405–421.

23. See Cameron, *Transcendental Vision*, p. 170, and the full discussion there of Coleridge. Emerson's references to Coleridge in letters and journals are only the barest indication of Coleridge's enormous influence. It is significant, however, that the earliest references are to Coleridge and Reed in support of the argument against miracles as evidence of divinity. Emerson eyed miracles suspiciously as transgressions of the perfect order of nature. By

1834, certainly, he found the Reason-Understanding distinction most valuable, and wrote of Reason in the imagery of miraculous intervention.

24. See Coleridge, *On the Constitution of Church and State*, in *Complete Works*, ed. W. H. Shedd (New York, 1853) VI, 61. Emerson wrote, "Reason . . . is vision" (*L*, I, 412–413).

25. See Cameron's discussion of the "First Philosophy" in *Transcendental Vision*, pp. 162–199, and the journals, especially *JMN*, III, 360–362 and *JMN*, V, 270–276.

26. Frye, *Fearful Symmetry*, pp. 138–139 and *passim*, discusses the opposition between water-chaos and the imagination in the Bible and mythology. For the alchemical tradition see Carl Jung, *Psychology and Alchemy* (Princeton, 1968), especially pp. 233–234, and the excellent summaries by Ronald Gray, *Goethe the Alchemist* (Cambridge, England, 1952), pp. 1–37.

27. See Nina Baym, "From Metaphysics to Metaphor: The Image of Water in Emerson and Thoreau," *Studies in Romanticism* 5 (Summer 1966): 231–243. The confluence of waters and "rivulet" imagery figure significantly in American poetry from Anne Bradstreet to Whitman in "Passage to India" and Frost in "A Hillside Thaw."

28. Whicher, *Freedom and Fate*, p. 57, offers a "rude scaffolding," a major axis ranging between Reason and Understanding bisected by a minor axis of temperament running between assertiveness and acquiescence. Sherman Paul, *Emerson's Angle of Vision* (Cambridge, 1952), pp. 21–26, raises an axis of Reason and spiritual ascent above a horizontal field of "linear logic." Emerson's use of light and the sun in the passages describing Reason suggests that this vertical axis is polarized on the true East. However, my own scheme would have the vertical axis crossed by an equally important horizontal one, representing the laws of nature that Emerson later summarized as "gravity" (*JMN*, XI, 76–77). The geography of Emerson's thought is then like Coleridge's, reflecting a world of two organizing counter-powers, Light and Gravitation. See M. H. Abrams, "Coleridge's 'A Light in Sound': Science, Metascience, and Poetic Imagination," *Proceedings of the American Philosophical Society* 116 (December 1972): 461–466. And this world holds together only when true East (which is, in one sense, a point outside, toward which the world aspires) is also a spherical center—Emerson may have realized this when he wrote, "Blessed is the day when the youth discovers that Within and Above are synonyms" (Paul, p. 35; *J*, III, 399).

211

Chapter II. High Arguments in the Negative Way

1. Joseph Slater, ed., *The Correspondence of Emerson and Carlyle* (New York, 1964), pp. 149, 156–157.

2. My view of *Nature* is somewhat at odds with two valuable recent studies—Richard Lee Francis, "The Architectonics of Emerson's *Nature*," *American Quarterly* 19 (Spring 1967): 39–52; and Kenneth Burke, "I, Eye, Aye—Emerson's Early Essay on 'Nature,'" which first appeared in the *Sewanee Review* 74 (1966): 875–893. Both are reprinted in Merton M. Sealts, Jr., and Alfred R. Ferguson, eds., *Emerson's 'Nature'* (New York, 1969). The baroque analysis by Francis underplays the "break-through" of apocalypse, and Burke focuses on "Discipline" rather than "Idealism" as the turning point of the essay. Moreover, Emerson's use of "Negativity" is more Renaissance than Existential.

3. Vivian Hopkins, quoting Emerson, in *Spires of Form* (Cambridge, 1951), p. 23. Cf. imagery in Emerson's "Water" (*EL*, I, 53–55).

4. See Alexander Gilchrist, *Life of William Blake* (London, 1863), II, 133, 176. E. W. Emerson quotes a related passage from *Songs of Innocence* (VIII, 365).

5. See Milton's *De Doctrina Christiana*, I, xii (first published and translated in 1825), and Coleridge's *Literary Remains* (London, 1836), II, 336, together with the commentary by Owen Barfield, *What Coleridge Thought* (Middletown, Conn., 1971), pp. 114–122.

6. For the *via negativa* and negative theology in Renaissance NeoPlatonism and Orphism, see Frances Yates, *Giordano Bruno and the Hermetic Tradition* (New York, 1969) especially pp. 124–126; Edgar Wind, *Pagan Mysteries of the Renaissance* (London, 1958); Rosalie Colie, *Paradoxia Epidemica* (Princeton, 1966), especially pp. 23–33. Hyatt Waggoner, *Emerson as Poet*, pp. 71–72, 110–120, 160, makes brief but pregnant comparisons between Emerson and the NeoPlatonic negative theology. I would put more emphasis than Waggoner does on the difference between Emerson's early reference to the "sturdy negative" (*EL*, III, 99), resisting the worldly demands of the Understanding in a way that suggests the post-Hegelian left, and a late example like "Brahma," in which the negative theology is tailored to physical determinism.

7. There are an increasing number of journal references to Heraclitus during this period (see especially *JMN*, VII, 13, 37, 413, 457), issuing in the discussion of God and fixed meaning in

relation to Heraclitus in "The Method of Nature" (I, 194–195, 204, 210, 214). At Nantasket Beach in the summer of 1841, when he was writing that oration, Emerson also began to reread Plato (*L*, II, 429–430). His modern sources for the negative theology included Taylor's *Hymns of Orpheus* and NeoPlatonic translations and the line of commentators from Plato to Schelling traced by Coleridge in Chapter IX of the *Biographia Literaria*.

    8. Wade, ed., *Writings of Margaret Fuller*, p. 391 (New York *Daily Tribune*, December 7, 1844). Paul, pp. 109–119, suggests that an "anti-method" was needed because Emerson realized at this point that "nature falsified all methods of classification." Emerson conceived of dialectical method as grandly synthetic, in Platonic and Coleridgean terms, but as a structural device in his prose it is much more limited; the anti-method as evidenced in the changing structure of his essays is traced in my article, "Emerson's Dialectic," *Criticism* 11 (Fall 1969): 313–328.

    9. Emerson's darker side, personal and artistic, has been expounded by Whicher in *Freedom and Fate*; Carl Strauch, "The Importance of Emerson's Skeptical Mood," *Harvard Library Bulletin* 11 (Winter 1957): 117–139; Newton Arvin, "The House of Pain: Emerson and the Tragic Sense," *Hudson Review* 12 (Spring 1959): 37–53; John Lydenberg, "Emerson and the Dark Tradition," *Critical Quarterly* 4 (1962): 352–358; Bishop, *Emerson on the Soul*, pp. 187–215; H. H. Clark, "Conservative and Mediatory Emphases in Emerson's Thought," in Myron Simon and Thorton H. Parsons, eds., *Transcendentalism and Its Legacy* (Ann Arbor, 1966), pp. 25–62.

    10. See II, 318; III, 194–195; IV, 183; VI, 14–15, 22–23, 43. Clifford Pyncheon's theory of human progress is ironically expounded in Chapter XVII of Hawthorne's *House of the Seven Gables*. For the relation between circular or spiral forms and regenerative knowledge in Emerson and Hawthorne, see Hyatt Waggoner, *Hawthorne: A Critical Study* (Cambridge, 1963), pp. 15–16, 29–30, 160–187, and my "Transcendental Conservatism and *The House of the Seven Gables*," *Georgia Review* 28 (Spring 1974): 33–51. The importance of self-conscious, historical understanding as part of the Romantic spiral is stressed in Abrams' treatment of Hegel, *Natural Supernaturalism*, pp. 225–237. Ishmael's discourse on the balance of wisdom and woe is in "The Try-Works," Chapter XCVI of *Moby-Dick*. Cf. Abrams' treatment of Wordsworthian dialectic, *Natural Supernaturalism*, p. 282 and n. 51.

    11. Cf. Poe, "A Descent into the Maelstrom" and Dickin-

son, "I Saw No Way" (J378). Emerson's free and paradoxical elaboration of circle-circumference imagery invites the charge of "a fine Pyrrhonism" that surfaces late in "Circles." Wind, pp. 183–185, ingeniously relates the negative logic of Cusanus and Bruno to Halifax's *Character of a Trimmer* and the traditional view that England is central in the European balance of power precisely because it is on the margin or circumference. Emerson perpetuates this view in *English Traits* (V, 41).

12. Emerson himself, in writing "I dare not give their order" of the lords of life (III, 83), calls in question W. T. Harris, "The Dialectical Unity of Emerson's Prose," *Journal of Speculative Philosophy* 18 (April 1884): 195–202. Harris argues that the procession from illusion to subjectiveness is a series of logical steps or *stadia* leading to greatest insight and toward absolute unity.

13. *City of the West* (New Haven, 1967), pp. 112–123.

14. Cowan, pp. 121–122, rightly reads hope of the City of God into Emerson's conclusion. However, this hope is based on fleeting moments of "sanity and revelations" (III, 85), and for Emerson personally as well as in the full context of his essay these moments no longer outweigh the quotidian.

15. See Lydenberg, p. 355, and Bishop on the "mid-world," pp. 195–201.

Chapter III. Orpheus in the Mid-World

1. The major division of Elizabeth Sewell's *Orphic Voice* is between a Renaissance and a modern Orpheus, the latter more closely associated with Ovid and the Eleusinian Mysteries by Erasmus Darwin, his English predecessors Warburton and Thomas Taylor, and finally by Goethe. See especially pp. 171–178 and 219–236. See also the excellent introductory chapter, "The Metamorphosis of Orpheus," in Walter Strauss, *Descent and Return: The Orphic Theme in Modern Literature* (Cambridge, 1971), pp. 1–19.

2. References to Coleridge in this paragraph are as follows: *The Friend*, pp. 431–432 (II, ix) and p. 77 (I, xiii); *Biographia Literaria*, ed. J. Shawcross (Oxford, 1907), I, 93–107, 178; "Theory of Life," in *Miscellanies, Aesthetic and Literary*, ed. T. Ashe (London, 1892), pp. 392–393. On Coleridge's method, see Barry Wood, "The Growth of the Soul: Coleridge's Dialectical Method and the Strategy of Emerson's *Nature*," *PMLA* 91 (May 1976): 385–397; Paul, pp. 38–48, 108–116; and Abrams, "Coleridge's 'A Light in Sound,' " p. 465.

3. See Slater, ed., *Correspondence*, p. 269.

4. For Goethe's method see Rudolf Magnus, *Goethe as a Scientist*, trans. Heinz Norden (New York, 1949), pp. 223–231; Agnes Arber, *Goethe's Botany* (Waltham, 1946), an introductory essay and translation of Goethe's *Versuch die Metamorphose der Planzen zu Erklaren*; and Gray, *Goethe the Alchemist*, pp. 49–67.

5. Cf. "Thinking and doing, doing and thinking—that is the sum of all wisdom, recognized and practiced from of old, yet not understood by everyone. Like breathing in and out, both should occupy life in a ceaseless alternating flux; like question and answer, neither should occur without the support of the other. The genius of the human understanding whispers this maxim into the ears of every new-born babe. He who abides by it, checking thinking against doing, doing against thinking, cannot go astray. . . ." (*Wilhelm Meister's Travels*, Bk. II, Ch. IX).

6. See the Centenary editor's note (VIII, 359–361) on Moncure Conway's attempt to find the phrase in Hunter and to date Emerson's reference; also H. H. Clark, "Emerson and Science," *Philological Quarterly* 10 (1931): 246; F. W. Conner, *Cosmic Optimism* (Gainesville, Fla., 1949), pp. 64–65, n. 131; Nicoloff, pp. 111–114, n. 37. Clark, following the Centenary editor (I, xxix), suggests that Richard Owen told Emerson he found the phrase in Hunter's manuscripts. Both Conner and Nicoloff trace it to *Vestiges*, where Chambers acknowledged that the ground was first broken by Hunter. See *Vestiges of the Natural History of Creation* (New York, 1856), pp. 103–106. Emerson appears to have applied the theory to the development of species, as Hunter and Owen did. Like Darwin (in the third edition of *The Origin of Species*), Emerson acknowledges the line of nineteenth-century evolutionary theorists, including Erasmus Darwin, Saint-Hilaire, and Goethe, and like the Darwinists, Emerson underlined what he considered the moral implications of change, hybridization, and conflict. See V, 48–50; *J*, IX, 313; XII, 59–60.

7. For Coleridge, following Schelling, the emergence of man is a "radical break-through" in the evolutionary scheme because his consciousness is reflexive, re-engendering the natural world within itself. See Abrams, "Coleridge's 'A Light in Sound,' " p. 466, and for Schelling's messianic poet, *Natural Supernaturalism*, pp. 223–224.

8. *Biographia Literaria*, II, 12 (Ch. xiv).

9. *Ibid*. Cf. Emerson, VII, 43.

10. The direct line of this motif seems to be from the Earth-Spirit in *Faust*, Part I, through *Sartor Resartus*, ed. C. F.

Harrold (New York, 1937), pp. 55–57 (I, viii). But the imagery pervades *Faust*, and Mephistopheles' advice to the student in this vein is an account of Goethe's distinction between *Darstellung* and *Erklarung*, in effect a denial of causal mechanism (see Arber, p. 85). Emerson similarly distinguished between Nature "distributive" and "linear" (*J*, IX, 114). See also Goethe's poem "Antepirrhema."

11. Cf. Coleridge: ". . . not the thing represented but that which is re-presented by the thing, shall be the source of pleasure. In this sense nature itself is to a religious observer the art of God; and for the same cause art itself might be defined as of a middle quality between a thought and a thing, or, as I said before, the union and reconciliation of that which is nature with that which is exclusively human" ("On Poesy or Art," *Biographia Literaria*, II, 254, originally printed in Coleridge's *Literary Remains*). See also the note to Schelling, p. 318.

12. Yates, pp. 64–65; Cassirer, *Individual and Cosmos*, pp. 39, 63–65.

13. For Orpheus and the worship of Apollo, Dionysus, and Christ, see W. K. C. Guthrie, *Orpheus and Greek Religion* (New York, 1966), pp. 41–48, 216–221, and 249–271; and John Block Friedman, *Orpheus in the Middle Ages* (Cambridge, 1970). The Unitarians began the reinterpretation of Jesus, but Orestes Brownson is perhaps the best example of the way the new religion blended with the philosophical spirit of the age. See his letter to William Ellery Channing of June 1842, published as "The Mediatorial Life of Jesus" in *The Works of Orestes A. Brownson* (AMS Reprint, New York, 1966), IV, 147–165. For Orphic symbolism in *Walden* see Carson, pp. 152–194, and Charles Anderson, *The Magic Circle of Walden* (New York, 1968), especially pp. 151–189 and 247–257.

14. Like others, I have discovered no source for the name "Osman." Oliver Wendell Holmes is cited (II, 407) as suggesting Herbert's poem "The Elixir" (quoted by Emerson in *EL*, I, 351–352) as a source for "Art." Similar images of servants or dwarfs transfigured occur in the poem "May-Day" (IX, 174–175) and "Voluntaries" (IX, 209).

15. For Emerson's reading of the *Divan*, see *JMN*, V, 188, and for his most characteristic use of East and West, Asia and Europe, "Plato," IV, 47–54. Frederic Carpenter, *Emerson and Asia* (Cambridge, 1930), p. 166, says that although Emerson classified Hafiz and Saadi as fatalists, he admired their expression of joy and lightness. In his essay on "Persian Poetry" Emerson puts

greatest stress on the contingency of life in the Orient (VIII, 237–238). See also the more detailed studies of J. D. Yohannan, "Emerson's Translations of Persian Poetry from German Sources," *American Literature* 14 (January 1943): 405–420, and "The Influence of Persian Poetry upon Emerson's Work," *American Literature* 15 (March 1943): 25–41.

16. This is the view of Theodore L. Gross, "Emerson and the Heroic Ideal," *Bucknell Review* 17 (March 1969): 22–34. But Nicoloff, pp. 83–90, sees Emerson's hero as merely representative of the forces of his time.

17. *Descent and Return*, pp. 10–11.

18. Mumford, *The Transformations of Man* (New York, 1972), pp. 25, 49; *The Conduct of Life* (New York, 1951), pp. 27–36. Emerson, I, 203–204 and VI, 55–59.

19. *The Golden Day* (1957 edition, New York, 1968), p. xxi.

20. See in Mumford's *Conduct of Life* the analysis of types, pp. 196–215, and 240–243, 252, 257. Cf. Jung on the role of the poet in "Psychology and Literature," *Modern Man in Search of a Soul* (New York, 1933), pp. 152–172; Jung interprets the poet as the archetypal wise man, savior, or redeemer, and the poet's vision as an instinctively triggered "compensatory adjustment" that aims to restore the "psychic equilibrium" of his times.

21. See Harold Bloom, ed., *Romanticism and Consciousness* (New York, 1970), pp. 11–12, and the development of this approach in Bloom's study of the Romantic heritage in *Yeats* (Oxford, 1970) and *The Visionary Company* (Garden City, 1963).

22. "Home at Grasmere," lines 575–580, 142–151. See Geoffrey Hartman, *Wordsworth's Poetry 1787–1814* (New Haven, 1964), pp. 171–179, for discussion of centroversion and blending imagery relevant to this and related passages of "Home at Grasmere." Wind on the paradox of center and periphery (*Pagan Mysteries*, pp. 183–185) should be read in relation to Edwin Fussell's study of the metaphorical West in American literature, *Frontier* (Princeton, 1965), especially pp. 15–25.

23. *Descent and Return*, p. 9 and n. 15, p. 276.

24. *The English Notebooks* (Boston, 1891), p. 25.

25. *Moby-Dick*, lxxxv ("equal eye"), lxviii (for the whale as Goethean model); cf. Emerson on Plato (IV, 54) with *Moby-Dick*, lxxiv.

26. Blake's letter to Cumberland, 12 April 1827, and marginalia on Wordsworth and Reynolds, in *Poetry and Prose of William Blake*, ed. Geoffrey Keynes (London, 1956), pp. 927, 821, 809.

Chapter IV. First Poetic Fruits

1. *Selections from RWE*, ed. Stephen E. Whicher (Cambridge, 1957), pp. 407–411.

2. Carl Strauch established this focal point in one of his many fine studies of Emerson's poems, "The Year of Emerson's Poetic Maturity: 1834," *Philological Quarterly* 34 (October 1955): 353–377.

3. See Louis Martz, *The Poetry of Meditation* (New Haven, 1962), pp. 267–268. "Symmetry" is Emerson's term for Correspondence in the 1833–34 lectures.

4. J. C. Broderick, "The Date and Source of Emerson's 'Grace,' " *Modern Language Notes* 73 (January 1958): 91–95; E. W. Emerson's note, IX, 510; and Coleridge's *Aids to Reflection* (London, 1913), p. 10, where Herbert's poem is quoted as a note to Aphorism XV. Whicher, *Selections*, p. 500, follows Carl Strauch in dating the poem 1833.

5. This discussion is directly indebted to Louis Martz, *The Paradise Within* (New Haven, 1964), especially pp. 17–31 where the passage quoted from Vaughan appears; *The Poetry of Meditation*, pp. 1–39, 56–61, and the later chapters where Martz shows how Herbert qualifies and relaxes the more rigorous form of meditation, and how he departs from the practice of Donne. The suggestion that the triadic formula of the Jesuits is generally a "natural, fundamental tendency of the human mind" and that later poets like Hopkins, Eliot, Wordsworth, and Emily Dickinson practiced a similar poetry (*Poetry of Meditation*, pp. 39, 324–330) is carried into Martz' essays on American poets in *The Poem of the Mind* (Oxford, 1966), especially with reference to Stevens, pp. 214–215. In contrast, Rosalie Colie argues that, despite his ideal of neatness or fitness, Herbert paradoxically reminds us of the failure to fit, of God's creation outrunning man's sense of logical order. See *Paradoxia Epidemica*, pp. 207–211.

6. This point seems to have been overlooked by Walter Blair and Clarence Faust, in "Emerson's Literary Method," *Modern Philology* 42 (November 1944): 89–91; they used the poem as an example of the Platonic movement from sensuous to spiritual. Goerge Arms, "The Dramatic Movement in Emerson's 'Each and All,' " *English Language Notes* 1 (March 1964): 207–209, stresses an opposite movement from didactic generalization to concrete experience.

7. See Abrams, "Structure and Style in the Greater Romantic Lyric," reprinted in *Romanticism and Consciousness*,

pp. 201–229, and see also *The Mirror and the Lamp* (New York, 1958), pp. 290–297.

Chapter V. Fables of Apocalypse

1. See IX, 403–404 and Oliver Wendell Holmes, *RWE* (Boston, 1884), pp. 129–131.

2. See Abrams, *Natural Supernaturalism*, pp. 51–56, 335–347; Frye, *Anatomy of Criticism* (New York, 1966), pp. 139–150; Hartman, *Wordsworth's Poetry*, pp. x, 16–18, 49–69.

3. See Frederick Tupper, ed., "Introduction," *The Riddles of the Exeter Book* (Boston, 1910), especially pp. xix–xxii; and Emerson's quotations from early English poetry in the 1835 lecture "Traits of the National Genius," *EL*, I, 233–252.

4. *True Intellectual System*, I, 500–517; *Hymns of Orpheus* (Chiswick, 1824), p. 78. In the *Hymns* "Night" explains the creation of the world by inverting the ordinary sense of up and down, a common motif in Renaissance paradoxy according to Colie, p. 13.

5. Cf. Kenneth W. Cameron, "The Potent Song in Emerson's Merlin Poems," *Philological Quarterly* 32 (1953): 22–28, and Nelson Adkins, "Emerson and the Bardic Tradition," *PMLA* 63 (1948): 662–667.

6. Cameron, "Potent Song," p. 24. Cameron says this formula is found in Emerson's early notebooks; I have seen it only in Houghton MS 92 (Emerson's "NP"), which contains drafts of poems written in the 1850s. See also Carl Strauch, " 'The Mind's Voice': Emerson's Poetic Styles," *Emerson Society Quarterly* 60 (1970): 43–59, citing William Owen's *Heroic Elegies and Other Pieces of Llywarc-Hen* (London, 1792) for the bard as neutralist and sacred herald of peace.

7. See Walker, *Spiritual and Demonic Magic*, pp. 1–24, and Yates, pp. 62–83.

8. See Guthrie, pp. 69–130, for the full account.

9. See Taylor, *Dissertation on the Eleusinian and Bacchic Mysteries*, in Raine and Harper, pp. 408–413; also Carson, pp. 40–44.

10. Carson, p. 117, identifies this wine more specifically as that of the celestial Dionysus which reputedly gives insight into the One. Emerson's wines in "Bacchus" and "Monadnoc" are both unearthly, but the fruit of the mountain is a characteristic Emersonian melange of virtues drawn from past cultures (IX, 71); perhaps, then, this is the "miscellaneous potion" that enables

Ceres, or the Intellect, to enter material nature in Taylor's *Eleusinian Mysteries*, Raine and Harper, pp. 402ff.

11. See Carson, pp. 120–130, for an account of the Orphic concept of inspiration in "Bacchus" and for the relation of Demiourgos (IX, 445) to the Orphic creator-god who pours himself into the world.

12. Bernard Paris, "Emerson's 'Bacchus,' " *Modern Language Quarterly* 23 (June 1962): 158.

13. Jung, *Psychology and Alchemy*, pp. 188, 293.

Chapter VI. Metamorphoses; or, The Beautiful Changes

1. Kenneth W. Cameron, "Early Background for Emerson's 'The Problem,' " *Emerson Society Quarterly* 27 (1962): 37–45, makes this point.

2. For verses written by Emerson's family see Ralph Rusk, *The Life of RWE* (New York, 1949), pp. 137, 148–149. Emerson's natural interest in hymns is indicated by the article he wrote for the *Christian Examiner* in 1831, reprinted by K. W. Cameron, "An Early Prose Work of Emerson," *American Literature* 22 (November 1950): 332–338. See the discussion of devotional forms in David T. Porter, *The Art of Emily Dickinson's Early Poetry* (Cambridge, 1966), pp. 55–64.

3. (Philadelphia, 1841), pp. 339, 341–343, 346 (Bk. IX, Ch. i). Emerson read earlier editions of Turner in 1822 and 1835 (*JMN*, II, 77; *JMN*, V, 104–105).

4. *The Poets and Poetry of Europe* (Philadelphia, 1845), p. 4.

5. Emerson's verse-book "EL." Brackets indicate words crossed out. These lines are published by permission of the RWE Memorial Association, literary executor of RWE, and of the Harvard College Library. Cf. *J*, VIII, 66–68.

6. See Bryant's "On the Use of Trisyllabic Feet in Iambic Verse," *North American Review* 9 (1819): 426–431.

7. See Andrew Schiller, "Gnomic Structure in Emerson's Poetry," *Papers of the Michigan Academy of Science, Arts, and Letters* 40 (1955): 313–320.

8. "The Riddle of Emerson's 'Sphinx,' " *American Literature* 27 (1955): 179–195.

9. "Preface" to *Christabel*.

10. Gay Wilson Allen, *American Prosody* (New York, 1935), p. 91. The anecdote is Lowell's in *The Letters of James Russell Lowell*, ed. C. E. Norton (New York, 1894), II, 275. Emerson said he

lacked musical ability (*JMN*, II, 404; *J*, III, 486; *J*, V, 138), but see Charmenz Lenhart, *Musical Influence on American Poetry* (Atlanta, 1956), pp. 110–112 to the contrary.

11. Carson, pp. 113–115; Mentor L. Williams, " 'Why Nature Loves the Number Five': Emerson Toys with the Occult," *Papers of the Michigan Academy* 30 (1944): 639–649; Douglas Bush, *Mythology and the Romantic Tradition in English Poetry* (New York, 1963), pp. 486–488.

12. See Wordsworth, *The Prelude* (1850), I, lines 357–424 and V, lines 364–388, the latter first published in 1800 as "There Was a Boy," and the discussion linking this motif to Frost in Brower, *Poetry of Frost*, pp. 130–136.

13. C. F. Strauch, "Emerson's 'Unwilling Senator,' " *Emerson Society Quarterly* 42 (1966): 4–14. The views of Webster scattered through the journals of these years are generally uncomplimentary, until Emerson paid him a final compliment on his death in 1852:

> Nature had not in our days, or not since Napoleon, cut out such a masterpiece. He brought the strength of a savage into the height of culture. He was a man *in equilibrio*; a man within and without, the strong and perfect body of the first ages, with the civility and thought of the last.
>
> (*J*, VIII, 335)

14. Cf. the following, quoted by Strauch, "Unwilling Senator," p. 8: "To know the virtue of the soil, we do not taste the loam, but we eat the berries and apples; and to mend the bad world, we do not impeach Polk and Webster, but we supersede them by the Muse" (*J*, VII, 149).

Chapter VII. Toward the Titmouse Dimension

1. *The Dial 1840–1844* (New York, 1962) I, 220–221.

2. Emerson's sentence in *Nature*, "The axioms of physics translate the laws of ethics," is found in nearly the same form in Madame de Staël's *Germany* (New York, 1814), II, 183, 195; there are numerous other contemporary sources for that commonplace of the age.

3. See Strauch, "The Importance of Emerson's Skeptical Mood." Quotation from the poem is from Strauch's transcription; another version is given in *JMN*, VIII, 244.

4. Emerson varied his figure. Strauch (*ibid.*, p. 136) compares the vignette of Nemesis with a journal entry of 1845: "The

universe is like an infinite series of planes, each of which is a false bottom, and when we think our feet are planted now at last on the Adamant, the slide is drawn out from under us" (*J*, VIII, 112). For Emerson the flux loosened what Thoreau called his *point d'appui*, the hard bottom where a man can say, "This is, and no mistake," in *Walden*, and Emerson's Central Man is all at sea. Emerson accepted the naturalistic image of life cheerfully in "Montaigne" with the tag borrowed from a poem of William Ellery Channing—"If my bark sink, 'tis to another sea" (IV, 186).

5. Gelpi, *Tenth Muse*, pp. 84–85, quotes this passage to illustrate his point that Emerson's poems were "not nearly so wild" as his theory, which Gelpi says "ushered the Dionysian ideal into American literature."

6. These and other sources are discussed by Cameron, "The Potent Song" and Adkins, "Emerson and the Bardic Tradition."

7. A. O. H. Jarman's *The Legend of Merlin* (Cardiff, 1960) is a brief outline of the mixing of two traditions, the Arthurian legend or *matière Bretagne* and the Welsh tradition, by Geoffrey of Monmouth in the *Historica Regum Brittainae* (1136).

8. See Jerome H. Buckley, *Tennyson: The Growth of a Poet* (Cambridge, 1967), Ch. IX, especially pp. 173–176. The bard described by Tennyson's Merlin in the anecdote he tells Vivien is reminiscent of Emerson's Osman, a vegetarian recluse.

9. These lines from *Gareth and Lynette* were not published until 1872, but they may have been favorites of the aging Emerson, for they are quoted by his son as a gloss on "Song of Nature" (IX, 485).

10. *Moby-Dick*, CII. Hawthorne's encounter is related in *The American Notebooks*, ed. Randall Stewart (New Haven, 1932), pp. 36–37. The query is Orphic, in the Emersonian sense, because without the man's life the pen writes only syllables, not men.

11. *Memories, Dreams, Reflections* (New York, 1961), pp. 227–228.

12. Carl Strauch, "The Date of Emerson's 'Terminus,' " *PMLA* 65 (June 1950): 360–370, has shown that drafts of this poem existed in the early 1850s. Whicher's notes on the later poems, *Selections*, pp. 507–510, show others rooted in journal passages of the 1840s.

13. See Joel Porte, *Emerson and Thoreau: Transcendentalists in Conflict* (Middletown, Conn., 1966), pp. 93–130. Of the many journal comments perhaps the most telling is Thoreau's report for May 24, 1853, when he tried to talk with Emerson and "lost my

time, almost my identity" (*Journals*, V, 188). Emerson's journals do show an impatience with Thoreau (e.g., *J*, VIII, 228, 375; *J*, IX, 15–16), but at the same time an increasing respect for the naturalist's knowledge of detail in Thoreau, which Emerson at that time emulated. "Thoreau gives me, in flesh and blood and pertinacious Saxon belief, my own ethics. He is far more real, and daily practically obeying them, than I; and fortifies my memory at all times with an affirmative experience which refuses to be set aside" (*J*, VIII, 303).

14. *American Poets*, pp. 296–299.

15. Emerson's verse-book "NP." See also W. B. Barton, "Emerson's Method as a Philosopher," in Eric W. Carlson and J. Lasley Dameron, eds., *Emerson's Relevance Today* (Hartford, 1971), p. 26, quoting Houghton MS "Powers and Laws of Thought" (1848):

> [As the thermometer] has average points to which it often returns, so that the maker finds it necessary to fix these as determinate marks such as the freezing and boiling points of water, the blood heat, and the zero, so language has, amid hourly and monthly variations, fixed averages which in years and ages are self-same and secular.

Barton suggests that Emerson anticipated Walter Cannon's theories of homeostasis.

16. "Freedom to flash off into wild connections" is Frost's one-line definition of metaphor in "How Hard It Is To Keep From Being King," and what Emerson might have mused is a paraphrase of Stevens at the end of *Notes Toward a Supreme Fiction*, but Emersonian nonetheless:

> *Waftbrudnir.* The horse taught me something, the titmouse whispered a secret in my ear, and the Lespedeza looked at me, as I passed. Will the Academicians, in their "Annual Report," please tell me what they said?
>
> (*J*, IX, 32)

17. *Sartor Resartus*, pp. 83–84 (II, i). Matthiessen, *American Renaissance*, pp. 59–60, traces the genesis of "Days."

18. "I don't like obscurity and obfuscation, but I do like dark sayings I must leave the clearing of to time. And I don't want to be robbed of the pleasure of fathoming depths for myself." Frost's 1959 address to the American Academy of Arts and Sciences, in *Selected Prose of Robert Frost*, ed. Hyde Cox and Edward Connery Lathem (New York, 1966), p. 114.

19. Carpenter, *Emerson and Asia* (Cambridge, 1930), p. 113; Conner, *Cosmic Optimism*, p. 50, quoting *J*, VII, 53. For drafts of

"Brahma," see IX, 465, and Emerson's verse-book "EF," Houghton Library MS 127.

20. Emerson apparently learned of the conservation of energy through Faraday in England. See *JMN*, X, 225, 237; *J*, VIII, 57–58; *J*, IX, 106–107. For the genesis of the poem, see Strauch, "The Sources of Emerson's 'Song of Nature,' " *Harvard Library Bulletin* 9 (1955): 300–334.

21. See the Centenary editor's comment, IX, 465–467, and also *J*, VI, 161; XII, 6; II, 93–96 (on the theology of heavenly reward); IX, 135 (the apotheosis unveiled to the meek lover Saadi).

22. See Yates, pp. 73–78, and the chapter titled "The Cosmic Image" in Angus Fletcher, *Allegory: The Theory of a Symbolic Mode* (Ithaca, 1964), pp. 70–146.

23. Holmes, *RWE*, pp. 321–322. Cf. III, 34–35 and *J*, V, 81–82. See also Tupper, p. xciii, and for the poet's attitude and cosmic dimensions as illustrated by the Old English riddles, see W. S. Mackie, ed., *The Exeter Book, Part II* (London, 1934), riddles numbered 39, 40, 41, 66, and 93.

24. See Gelpi, *Emily Dickinson: The Mind of the Poet* (Cambridge, 1965), p. 146, and *The Tenth Muse*, pp. 72–85, 150–151, 163. Gelpi separates the Dionysian from the Apollonian strain, the latter including Eliot, Stevens, and Frost, the former Emerson, Whitman, Pound, Olson, Duncan, Ginsberg. Leslie Fiedler, *Waiting for the End* (New York, 1964), pp. 195–196, proposes four lines descending from Poe, Longfellow, Emerson, and Whitman. Waggoner, *American Poets*, pp. 91–92, revised this to distinct lines from Emerson and Whitman, and a third Emerson–cum–Whitman line leading to Hart Crane, Theodore Roethke, Denise Levertov, and others.

Chapter VIII. Orpheus Descending

1. E. C. Stedman, *Poets of America* (Cambridge, 1885), pp. 158–159, quoted by Waggoner, *Emerson as Poet*, p. 25.

2. See also *EL*, II, 29. Although this lecture was first given in 1836, the text is a heavily revised version probably prepared for the lecture Emerson delivered in January 1848. An outline for the later version appears in *JMN*, X, 163–165 (1847).

3. Emerson's late sense of physical necessity prevented him from spelling out the "postlogical" synthesis that Sewell attributes to her modern Orphic poets. When she comments on the "substitution of mathematics for poetry as a gauge of exactitude

and reliability" by scientists and poets in the second half of the nineteenth century, she is thinking of the French Symbolists, not Emerson (p. 288). Sewell regards the purely formal exactitude of the Symbolists as an impasse for poetry; she does not consider the physical exactitude that Emerson assumed in the nature of things.

4. Gelpi, *Tenth Muse*, pp. 221–222.

5. *The Continuity of American Poetry* (Princeton, 1961), pp. 5, 41–42, 168, 174 (n. 17). Pearce condemns the revisions of *Leaves of Grass* because they incorporate "formal clarity" and "intellectual systematization." On the poetic implications of Whitman's dark years, see Stephen Whicher, "Whitman's Awakening to Death," *Studies in Romanticism* 1 (1961): 9–28.

6. *Lucifer in Harness* (Princeton, 1973), pp. 3–17, 39–45. Whitman studied the Germans secondhand, much as Emerson had from George Ripley's *Specimens*, Baron de Penhoen's *Histoire de la Philosophie Allemande*, and J. B. Stallo's *Philosophy of Nature*. See F. W. Conner, p. 104.

7. On use of the riddle see Charles R. Anderson, *Emily Dickinson's Poetry: Staircase of Surprise* (New York, 1960), pp. xiii, 70; Dolores Dyer Lucas, *Emily Dickinson and Riddle* (De Kalb, Ill., 1969).

8. See Gelpi, *Emily Dickinson*, pp. 55–93; Jack Capps, *Emily Dickinson's Reading 1836–1886* (Cambridge, 1966), pp. 113–118; George F. Whicher, *This Was a Poet* (Ann Arbor, 1957), pp. 194–221; Waggoner, *American Poets*, pp. 181–222; Richard B. Sewall, *The Life of Emily Dickinson* (New York, 1974), pp. 402–403, 420–421, 676–677, 713–715. Dickinson appears to have associated Newton with Emerson all her life; see her comment on Emerson's death to Otis Lord, 30 April 1882, *The Letters of Emily Dickinson*, ed. Thomas H. Johnson (Cambridge, 1958), III, 727. Perhaps J360 refers to the *Poems* Newton gave her.

9. *The Poems of Stephen Crane*, ed. Joseph Katz (New York, 1966), pp. xxiii–xxiv.

10. *Letters of Emily Dickinson*, I, 306 (to Sue Gilbert, 1854).

11. R. W. Stallman, *Stephen Crane: A Biography* (New York, 1968), p. 81.

12. This is Ruth Miller's description of the encounter in "Regions of Snow: The Poetic Style of Stephen Crane," *Bulletin of the New York Public Library* 72 (1968): 335.

13. *The Red Badge of Courage and Selected Stories*, ed. R. W. Stallman (New York, 1960), pp. 133–134, passages from the manuscript version of Chapter XXIV.

14. Robinson to Daniel Gregory Mason, 27 August 1899, and to Harry De Forest Smith, 15 March 1897 (slightly misquoting "Monadnoc"). Emerson's essays are also mentioned in letters to Smith, 5 February 1893 and 7 December 1896. See *E. A. Robinson: Selected Early Poems and Letters*, ed. Charles T. Davis (New York, 1960), pp. 192, 213, 215–219, and Waggoner, *American Poets*, pp. 268–271.

15. Frost's praise of Emerson as a poet and his reference to "Uriel" as "the greatest Western poem yet" in *A Masque of Reason* are well known. See Waggoner, *American Poets*, pp. 293–327; Brower, *The Poetry of Robert Frost*, pp. 40–151; Alvan Ryan, "Frost and Emerson: Voice and Vision," *Massachusetts Review* 1 (October 1959): 5–28. Edwin Fussell, *Edwin Arlington Robinson* (Berkeley, 1954), pp. 25–35, assesses Robinson's relation to Emerson, quoting the 1916 interview in which Robinson is supposed to have said that "Emerson is the greatest poet who ever wrote in America."

16. Higginson's essay "An Open Portfolio" (*The Christian Union*, 25 September 1890) is reprinted in Daniel Hoffman, ed., *American Poetry and Poetics* (New York, 1964), pp. 417–426. Quotations from Dickinson are in the *Letters*, II, 413, 405, 414, 412, all written in the spring and summer of 1862.

17. Gelpi, *Tenth Muse*, pp. 261, 278. Gelpi interprets the problem of Dickinson's lover as a projected inner drama (pp. 247–248), suggesting that mythic otherness is finally absorbed in the fact of her own existence (p. 286).

18. *Letters of Emily Dickinson*, II, 626–627.

19. *Continuity of American Poetry*, Ch. II, "The Long View," especially pp. 61, 83.

20. *Figures of Capable Imagination*, p. 85.

21. Emerson in the journals, quoted by Hartman, *Wordsworth's Poetry*, p. 164.

22. Robinson dismissed the attack on the materialism of Herbert Spencer in James' *The Will to Believe*. See his letter to John Hays Gardiner, 2 November 1898, in *Selected Letters of Edwin Arlington Robinson*, ed. Ridgely Torrence (New York, 1940), pp. 15–16. For Frost on James, see Lawrence Thompson, *Robert Frost, The Early Years* (New York, 1966), pp. 231, 294–295, 383–388, and *The Years of Triumph* (New York, 1970), pp. 643, 661.

23. "The Moral Philosopher and the Moral Life," *Essays in Pragmatism*, ed. Albury Castell (New York, 1948), pp. 80–84.

24. *Interviews with Robert Frost*, ed. Edward Connery Lathem (New York, 1966), p. 49, and *Selected Prose of Robert Frost*,

ed. Edward Connery Lathem and Hyde Cox (New York, 1966), p. 41.

25. *The Varieties of Religious Experience* (New York, 1958), p. 61.

26. *Pragmatism* (London, 1921), pp. 61–64.

27. For James as an important common source, see Frank Lentricchia, "The Romanticism of William James," *Salmagundi* 25 (Winter 1974): 81–108. Todd M. Lieber suggests similarities between the two poets in "Robert Frost and Wallace Stevens: 'What to Make of a Diminished Thing,' " *American Literature* 47 (March 1975): 64–83.

28. *The Necessary Angel* (New York, 1951), p. 29. Cf. "Adagia," in *Opus Posthumous*, ed. S. F. Morse (New York, 1969), p. 159, on the relation of art to life.

29. *On Extended Wings* (Cambridge, 1969), pp. 197–201. Cf. Frank Doggett, "The Transition from *Harmonium*: Factors in the Development of Stevens' Later Poetry," *PMLA* 88 (January 1973): 125–126.

30. See Lentricchia, especially pp. 82–98, on James and Kant, and John Crowe Ransom, "The Planetary Poet," *Kenyon Review* 26 (Winter 1964): 233–264, on Kant and Stevens. Stevens drew heavily on Richards in "The Noble Rider" (*Necessary Angel*, pp. 9–10, 18–19), and Ransom suggests his own debt to Richards in "The Concrete Universal," *Poems and Essays* (New York, 1955), p. 181. The romanticism of Richards and New Critics like Ransom, Tate, and Brooks is treated by Murray Krieger, *The New Apologists for Poetry* (Minneapolis, 1956) and Richard Foster, *The New Romantics* (Bloomington, Ind., 1962); see also Richard Ohmann, "Teaching and Studying Literature at the End of Ideology," *The Politics of Literature*, ed. Louis Kampf and Paul Lauter (New York, 1973), especially pp. 134–142. Lentricchia himself challenges such a connection between Romantics and modernists in "Coleridge and Emerson: Prophets of Silence, Prophets of Language," *Journal of Aesthetics and Art Criticism* 32 (Fall 1973): 37–46, but his argument there depends on his interpretation of Emerson as a strict "idealistic monist."

31. *Pragmatism*, pp. 129–130.

Index

229

Index

235

Index